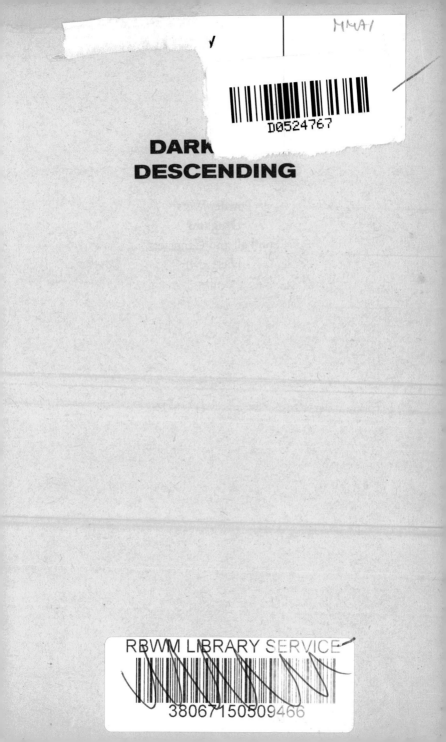

DARK
DESCENDING

Other books by Graham Johnson:

Powder Wars
Druglord
Football and Gangsters
The Devil
Soljas

DARKNESS DESCENDING

The Murder of Meredith Kercher

Paul Russell,
Graham Johnson

and Luciano Garofano

POCKET
BOOKS

LONDON • SYDNEY • NEW YORK • TORONTO

First published in Great Britain by Pocket Books, 2010
An imprint of Simon & Schuster UK Ltd
A CBS COMPANY

1 3 5 7 9 10 8 6 4 2

Simon & Schuster UK Ltd
1st Floor
222 Gray's Inn Road
London WC1X 8HB

www.simonandschuster.co.uk

Simon & Schuster Australia
Sydney

A CIP catalogue record for this book is available
from the British Library.

ISBN: 978-1-84739-862-8

Typeset in Garamond by M Rules
Printed by CPI Cox & Wyman, Reading, Berkshire RG1 8EX

To patient spouses

Contents

PART THREE – JUSTICE

PART ONE

The Murder

1–6 November 2007

1

Crime Scene

1 November, midnight

In death, her body is still beautiful – dark and lithe. She looks as though she has been aroused from a deep sleep. Though brown, her eyes appear green – more Indian silk than emerald. Bright, striking even. And rimmed with long, pointy lashes that curve gently towards her ears. Striking, even in death.

The whites of her eyes are unblemished and healthy. There is no sign of cannabis red-eye. No capillaries bloated by alcohol. No cracking micro-fissures across the smooth sclerotic coat. Just gleamy emulsion-white.

Dark-brown hair, youthful and shiny, tumbles down across her shoulders. But the ends are matted with blood. Caked with pints of congealed matter almost as dark as the strands. Blood that has run down her neck under gravity from an untidy rip wound under her chin. A hole that is the size of her mouth. Someone has carved another mouth – *gouged* a second mouth – on the left side of her neck. A flap of flesh, which should cover the gape like a lid, protrudes from her neck like a tongue. The subcutaneous fat is silvery-grey. The hole is pulled wide by the weight of her head, which is tilted backwards and resting on the tiled floor. Perfectly white inside, the elastic tissue on the opposite side of the hole has rolled itself up until it looks like a top lip, rising over the wound. Fibres hang down from it. The bloodstain on the loose skin around the hole is criss-crossed by wrinkle lines.

Her head is turned to the left. And her left hand, heavily blooded, is raised and pointing towards the wound. *This is why I am dead.* The gesture is subtle. The first finger is arched like a hand on a Roman statue or a Renaissance painting. Not sharp or aggressive. In peace. Intelligent. *In her way.* There is something about *her* in this hand gesture. Even in death.

The fingertip is completely red down to the joint in the middle, as though it has been dipped neatly into a can of paint. The index finger, spattered and streaked, is crossed over the third. In hope. For help. Even when she is dead.

Her right hand is similarly composed. But clean. A few smudges, drier stains maybe. Her nails are shiny: professionally glossed and tinted white, a basic standard even for a student, especially in the land that invented looking good. On her wrist there is a black band; her arm is straightened by her side.

White cap-sleeve T-shirt. Sea-green psychedelic motif on the front. Ribbed, long-sleeved woollen jumper underneath. The top is scrunched upwards, revealing most of her breasts. Both of them are pulled flatter and outwards by her raised left arm and the slight backwards tilt of her upper body, making them seem smaller than their actual size. The middle section of her top, which should have covered her cleavage, is soaked with blood. Stale blood that has run, even trickled, under low pressure from the artery in the depths of the gash. Blood that should have been going to her head and then back to her heart to be re-energized with life and pumped back into circulation.

Instead, the leaking fluid has spread evenly and gently, over time and under gravity, over her chest. Gradually losing kinetic energy and settling into a natural shape – a rough rectangle between the arch of her breast and the bottom of her neck. Either side of this vertical stripe, the cotton is white and less bloodstained. Lower down, there are spots of blood on the flesh of the cleavage itself. But fewer on the arches of her breast and none on her nipples.

Above her shoulder, her hair is scraggy and bewitched now. Curls flattened into damp clumps, rinsed by blood into sharply defined follicular blades that are stuck to the floor. The worst bits are soaked into a hair-and-blood soup, so black it glistens. Her head is leaning on a brown, soft leather boot. The creases in her earlobe are filled with dried blood. But the inner ear is white – greasy and marblesque. Her nose is blocked with plugs of solid dried blood.

Her eyebrows are thin and neat. In life she was well groomed but now her face is streaked and spattered with fat, ugly droplets. Blood rolling down her cheek, more squirrelly-chubby than high bone structure, but still pretty. This time from powerful jets of oxygenated blood from a severed artery on the right-hand side of her neck. A hole in the main thyroid artery. Near the splice, there is a second knife wound, much smaller than the first. A nick almost, no longer than a thumbnail, on the neck's right side.

The patterns of blood are evidence of the power of her heart. Pumping fresh blood to the neck and head under high pressure. Spurts several feet long, freaking out anyone who may have seen it happening. Making them run away in fright. In surprise. And not return until it's over. Unless they were a battlefield surgeon or natural born killer.

Her teeth are white. Brilliantly clean, straight and strong.

There are photographs on the wall behind her head. Group shots, Meredith smiling with her mates. Backpacking. In pubs. At parties. A family meal with her mum, big, round pizzas filling their plates. Her lips are full and pouting. The shadow of decay has given her a peculiar beauty, like ripe olives on the point of falling. Her waist is slender and exposed, but curves out onto her legs. Long, athletic, smooth. Left leg ramrod straight like a ballet dancer's. The right is bent at the knee, at 100 degrees. Feet are browner than her legs. Her toenails painted shocking pink, but careworn and scribbly. Neglected in winter.

On her neck there is a pair of faint bruises, one each side of her windpipe. Marks left by the assailant's hand, suggesting strangulation before she was stabbed. But the order of battle is irrelevant now. The blood from the first knife wound drips into her windpipe. And creeps along, down into her lungs. Slow. Teasing. But unstoppable. Drowning her in her own life. Until she is dead.

The world is not ready for this horror just yet. The body is shrouded, the shame of it covered by a shabby beige quilt. Only her left foot is sticking out from underneath, and the top part of her head, from the nose upwards. Clothes are strewn around her. Red and white retro Puma trainers, standard student issue. A pair of Levi's. A pocket Collins Italian dictionary. White bra. Brown lacy underwear, with a turquoise apple pattern. A grubby silk handbag containing a W. H. Smith receipt. A paperback by Ian McEwan, *Enduring Love*, on top of a dresser next to letters and postcards home. They're stamped but unposted, the top one addressed to her father. A vampire's costume, left over from a Halloween party the day before, sits at the bottom of a cupboard.

Outside, the wind rustles the trees in the valley directly below her room. An icy, stabbing wind that rushes in from the Steppes, through the Balkans and into the Apennine mountains of central Italy.

Stubbornly, the draught penetrates under her door. Somewhere in the tumbledown farmhouse, a window is open. A shutter bangs against the sill. The moonlight is strong – the full moon was up only five days before – casting a shimmer over the creeping yellow moss on the roof. Like phosphor luminescence on a calm sea. But the murder scene is dark – the curtains are closed.

2

First Clue Found

1 November, 22:30

Meredith Kercher's body might have remained undiscovered for a long time, possibly for ever, if the killer or killers had had time to move it. Only the murderers knew the corpse was there, slowly putrefying under a tatty duvet, in an empty flat. No one, it seems, had been alerted to the crime. No one outside her room had heard her screams, or at least had not come forward. Her secret silenced by the ancient city walls of Perugia that loomed above her cottage. One more unspeakable truth absorbed into the dripping, porous stone. One more lost soul swallowed up by the city's 3000-year history of violence and intrigue.

The lack of disturbance bought vital time for the culprit or culprits. Time to dispose of the body. To clean the scene of the crime. To plot and scheme an alibi.

To run – if need be.

But not much time. No one had taken into account the variable of chance – the sworn enemy of the criminal and the saviour of police detectives. The million-to-one chance that mutates providently into luck.

At around the same time as Meredith was being murdered, an old woman in a neighbouring house received a strange phone call.

'Don't use your toilet, there's a bomb in it,' said the young man's voice on the end of the line, hyper but menacing. Mrs Elisabetta Lana, a prim and rather formal Italian pensioner, was startled. She lived in a well-appointed villa about half a mile away from Meredith's house. Firstly, she was taken back by the rudeness of someone calling so late. In the manner of the older generation, she was disapproving of 24-hour texts, mobiles and emails. It was 22:00 on Thursday, 1 November 2007. To make matters worse, today was a holy day. And, like many Italians, she was a devout Catholic who observed it quietly. Then, as she thought about it more, Mrs Lana panicked, in the way that old people are prone. 'I've just been told my toilet might explode.'

A younger person, tired and not long in from work, might have written it off as a prank call and put it out of their mind. Perugia was, after all, a university town, full of high-on-life students not averse to practical jokes and rag-week mischief. But she was old and she was a stickler for the correct procedure. Mrs Lana called the police.

Like policemen all over the world, hassled and working through the graveyard shift, the officers who arrived at the blackened iron gates of Mrs Lana's house had better things to do. The usual backlog of calls was mounting up – drug addicts kicking off in the town square, burglaries, domestic disputes . . . never-ending, petty, provincial town crime. In addition, down the winding road at the bottom of the hill, Meredith Kercher was in the process of being killed or had been killed. But they didn't know that yet.

The last thing the officers needed was a cranky old woman convinced that Al Qaeda was carrying out operations in her bathroom. As they waited for Mrs Lana to come to the door, one of the police officers studied the coat of arms painted in gold and pink on a ceramic white tile above the intercom. The square and compasses, the universally identifiable symbol of freemasonry, signifying morality and the control of desire. This symbol was stamped on buildings, ancient and new, for miles around. Perugia was a freemasons' town. The controversial secret society had dominated the hilltop fort for hundreds of years. More recently, powerful local members had been accused of taking part in and covering up a string of horrific sex murders. The murders went back a quarter of a century, but the possible connection of a prominent local doctor had come to light in 2003 and the investigation had wrought havoc among the upper classes of Perugia and Florence.

Mrs Lana opened the creaking gates and the policemen politely checked her bathroom. They gave her the all-clear and calmed her down: 'No bomb in there. It was hoax call,' one of the officers presumed. 'Probably a student who still thinks it's Halloween.'

The festival of the occult had been marked the previous evening on 31 October by a stream of fancy-dress parties. Trick-or-treat was now a big deal, even in Perugia, especially since the influx of exchange students from America and the UK who brought with them their traditions of mayhem and an excuse to get drunk. The officers were right first time. The police would eventually trace the call to a youthful prankster using up free credit on his mobile phone before it ran out. No big deal.

Even so, in line with procedure, they told Mrs Lana that she was free to make a statement the following morning to the Postal Police, who specialize in telephone and internet crime. Again, a younger and busier resident might not have followed through. But Mrs Lana felt it was her duty – and what else did she have to do?

As Mrs Lana left for the Postal Police station the next morning on Friday, 2 November, fate intervened that would trigger one of the biggest murder investigations of modern times in Italy. At around 10:00 she noticed an Ericsson mobile phone lying on her garden path. Innocently, she thought it must belong to one of the police officers who had come round the previous evening. The chain of mundane events that had started with a hoax call was now gathering meaning of a momentous nature, although at this point she couldn't have possibly known that.

Mrs Lana took the mobile with her to the Postal Police station. While she was making her statement, complaining about the irresponsible teenagers who had ruined her night, her daughter popped around to her house. While Mrs Lana's daughter was walking in the garden she came across a second mobile phone, a Motorola, near where the first had been discovered. The Motorola, too, eventually turned up in the police station. The police officer took out the SIM card and put it in a test mobile to see if he could trace the owner. Expertly, he plucked out the digits and 'span' them through a central computer. Italy's police have a wealth of personal information at their fingertips. Controversially, unlike the UK force, they can tap into phone conversations more or less at will.

Bingo! The name of the owner of the first phone, the Ericsson, popped up on the screen: Filomena Romanelli, a legal assistant living in at 7 Pergola Road, at the bottom of the hilly pass where Mrs Lana lived. The second belonged to Meredith Kercher, a 21-year-old exchange student from the suburbs of London in England, who lived in the same digs as Filomena.

'It looks like there's been some kind of robbery,' the Postal Policeman explained to a bemused Mrs Lana. 'The thief probably stole these mobile phones from this house at the bottom of the hill, where these girls live. Ran up to your villa at the top, where it's quieter, realized they're of little value and tossed them over the cliff to dispose of them. They may or may not be related to the hoax call.'

The copper continued with his hypothesis: 'It was probably dark when they threw them. They've missed the ravine, and the phones have landed accidentally in your path.'

Mrs Lana's backyard overlooks a steep slope that falls sharply into the valley below. It is heavily overgrown with trees and bushes, an ideal place to dispose of evidence. If the phones had fallen just a few yards further, they would have certainly gone over the edge of the cliff, down into a 50m gully, straight into a thick scrub of nettles, and probably been lost for ever amid the untidy piles of fly-tipped masonry and plastic detritus. And the officers of the Postal Police might never have gone to Meredith's home that morning of 2 November 2007.

The police left Mrs Lana and drove to Meredith's house at 7 Pergola Road. Few police officers might have been so quick to go out on such a trifling job. But for local police it always felt good to reunite an owner with lost property; it was mildly heroic, especially as it didn't happen very often with low-value stolen goods. Most burglary victims settled for a crime number and an insurance claim, never expecting to see their phone again. Anyway, by the sound of it, according to the computer, it also looked like a chance to impress some young ladies and chat them up, one of few perks of being a copper in a provincial town overrun with pretty students.

One of the prettiest was already standing outside the house when they arrived at around 12:30, the time logged on the CCTV across the street. Pale alabaster skin. Laser-blue eyes. Dirty blonde hair, more red than light. Freshly washed, but unconditioned and shaken into an untidy shoulder-length bob. But together. Cool. No nonsense. Amanda Knox, a

20-year-old foreign exchange student from Seattle, USA, was a natural beauty. The all-American Girl Next Door. High cheek-bones, gently winter-pinked by the cold breeze, she was confident and sporty. Her powerful shoulders were balanced by strong, muscled thighs, toned from playing football back home in the States.

Behind the flirty blonde, she presented a forceful image to the world – and could switch in the bat of an eyelash, or so some of her bitchy social enemies claimed. She didn't need to dress up or wear make-up to look beautiful like the glitzy local girls. She wore a street-style green parka that was more Sigourney Weaver than Sophia Loren. But today, like the fur around the hood of her coat, her togetherness was fraying at the edges.

She looked tired and confused. Did she have a hangover? Was she coming down off a heavy session on the skunk the night before – groggy, light-headed and a touch irritable? Amanda Knox, despite her babes-in-the-wood good looks, had an attitude about her. As if something was weighing on her mind.

The policeman told Amanda that he was looking for a woman called Filomena Romanelli registered at this address.

'Yes, she's my flatmate,' Amanda replied in plodding Italian. 'But she's out at the mo.'

The coppers waited, as coppers do, noting that the American looked embarrassed and somewhat surprised to see them. Her flatmate Filomena was a straitlaced 29-year-old law student who worked as an apprentice at a local solicitor's office while she was completing her training. She'd spent the night away with her boyfriend and was just parking up in a car in Perugia town. A short while earlier, before the police had arrived, she had got a call on her other mobile phone from a fraught Amanda saying that she'd found the front door of their shared apartment open. The conversation had been confusing.

Amanda: 'Something weird's going on. The front door was open . . .'

Filomena: 'How can that have happened? What's going on?'

Amanda: 'In what sense?'

Amanda's response seemed disjointed. But she recovered quickly. 'I don't know,' she added. 'I slept at my boyfriend's last night, too. I wasn't here at the flat. But when I got home this morning the front door was open. I was a bit freaked. Then I went inside . . .'

Filomena wasn't surprised that Amanda had gone in and explored on her own. Amanda had bottle, a ballsy risk-taker not afraid to go it alone and experience the new and unknown. An ex-boyfriend said she woke every day just excited to be alive. Cocky, her detractors would say. Amanda continued with Filomena but unexpectedly dropped a bombshell. 'Inside I found . . . some blood in the bathroom.'

Filomena sprang bolt upright in her car seat, as her friend Paola Grande was trying to squeeze their vehicle into a space. 'Blood?' she exclaimed. 'Are you sure?'

Amanda: 'Yes, blood. I found a bloodstain.' An awkward silence. 'Then I had a shower.'

Filomena furrowed her brow in surprise. 'What?' she said. 'You found blood in the bathroom after you found the front door open, and you didn't run away or call the police. You had a shower! Mmmm?'

Amanda appeared to go on the defensive: 'Well, I needed to get ready and get out. I had stuff to do. Then at Raffaele's . . . I'll get him to come over.'

She sounded confused, as though she was half-heartedly trying to tell a story but not succeeding. Raffaele, her boyfriend, was standing next to her. He was already at the house.

Filomena: 'But Amanda, I don't understand. Explain to me because there's something odd. There's blood. Where's Meredith?'

Amanda: 'Errr, I don't know. I'll call her straightaway. Anyway, I don't know whose blood it was or why it was there. I'm just a little scared right now, that's all.' It would be suggested that this was her falling back on her babes-in-the-wood routine.

Filomena cut across her, curtly taking charge of the situation from this strange American airhead. 'Call the police or the Carabinieri, now,' Filomena advised. Ominously, Filomena was in the middle of visiting a local festival to mark All Souls Day – The Fair of the Dead.

More than twenty minutes after their first chat, the police arrived. Frustratingly, in the meantime, Filomena had been trying to get through to Amanda. Their conversation had freaked her out slightly and she wanted to know more. Finally, Amanda picked up. Filomena breathed a sigh of relief.

In their second conversation, at 12:34, Filomena instructed Amanda to have a good look around the flat to see if anything been stolen. She buried her plans for the Fair of the Dead and headed back home, her pal Paola at the wheel. On the way, Filomena called her boyfriend, Marco Zaroli, who lived close to Pergola Road, and asked him to meet her there. If there'd been a burglary, she might need his help.

As Amanda talked, and the police looked on, her own boyfriend Raffaele turned away from the trio and sheepishly kicked the gravel on the weedy path leading up to the house. Raffaele Sollecito was a cute-looking 23-year-old rich kid from Southern Italy. Aloof and silent, he oozed upmarket European chic. In stark contrast to Amanda, Raffaele was very preppie. Black cashmere crew neck, perfectly accessorized with an orange woollen scarf. Well-cut jeans. Soft, brown leather shoes that exactly matched the shade of his hair, which was, of course, expensively styled, fading into neat stubble across his jawline. His boyish features were hardened by a pair of designer steel-rimmed glasses, giving him a slightly Germanic appearance. He reminded Amanda of Harry Potter – one reason, it has been said, why the fantasy-obsessed Grade A student had fallen in love with him a fortnight earlier.

Following Filomena's instructions, Amanda decided to take a second look around the house. She turned to the police officers again. 'Sorry . . . but why exactly are you here?'

They peeked into Filomena's room. Amanda put her hands up to her face. 'Oh, my God!' The house had been burgled. Filomena's room had been turned over, her possessions rifled. The window was smashed and clothes were strewn all over the floor.

Amanda: 'I don't think anything has been taken from my room. But look at these bloodstains on the carpet. What are they? I saw them whilst I was showering earlier.' The police officers exchanged glances.

Then Amanda told them about another strange incident. This time in the apartment's second bathroom near their other flatmate Laura Mezzetti's room. Amanda said: 'When I came back earlier there was shit in the toilet in the big bathroom – and now it's gone!'

'We girls, the girls who live here, always flush the toilet,' explained Amanda. Though a little confused, the police officers weren't fazed. Burglars, especially drug addicts, frightened and pumping on adrenalin, often lost control of themselves. Like foxes they leave their mark . . .

But one of the coppers wasn't so sure: 'If there's been a burglary here, why hasn't that been taken?' he asked, pointing at an expensive camera, 'on offer' as they say in the trade, in the kitchen. Amanda and Raffaele were lost for words.

Moving on, Amanda and the policemen then tried to open

Meredith's room but the door was locked. 'No big deal,' Amanda said, 'she always locks her door.'

Filomena rang Amanda, and they spoke for a third and final time at 12:45 to confirm the bad news about her room. The Postal Police were snooping about but couldn't get a grip on events until Filomena turned up in person. While they waited, Amanda and Raffaele were like cats on a hot tin roof, flitting in and out of Amanda's room. Whispering. Scoping.

Meanwhile, Filomena and Paola's boyfriends Marco Zaroli and Luca Altieri arrived at about 12:46. The lads spent a few minutes explaining the ownership of the phones to the police.

Raffaele looked on but was unable to hear the conversation. His agitation appeared to reach a peak at around 12:50. He decided to take matters into his own hands, attempting to take control of the emerging chaos.

Rich Italians have often been accused of using their influence unwisely. Commentators have observed that privileged citizens in tricky situations often override due process in favour of personal contacts. The powerful have defended their informal networks, saying they are only circumventing sluggish and unjust bureaucracies. Whatever the reason, Raffaele slipped off into Amanda's bedroom, clocked by Luca, and called his sister Vanessa, a 31-year-old Lieutenant in the Italian military police, to report the break-in.

Italy has two police forces – the Polizia, everyday officers trained in general civil duties, including specialist branches like the Postal Police, and the Carabinieri, an elite force connected to the army that runs parallel but independently. Raffaele's high-achieving sister had once been the Italian army's first female military pilot, an astounding achievement in the notoriously sexist military. Vanessa, whose success had overshadowed his own, some of his friends claimed, told him to call the

Carabinieri emergency number 112 immediately. He made two calls. The first was at 12:51 but he was put on hold for what seemed like for ever. Three minutes later, at 12:54, he made the second call and connected. The call lasted one minute. But by then it was already too late, his hope of calling in his preferred investigators was gone. As the Postal Police were already on the scene, in accordance with the first-come-first-served internal competition laws between rival forces, the civil police had bagged the job. Later, this episode would look bad for Raffaele – the police arguing that he was calling the military police simply to cover his back, to make himself look good. 'I've done nothing wrong. Got nothing to hide. I even called the Carabinieri, before and while the normal police were there. Why would I do that if I was guilty of doing something bad?'

3

The Body Discovered

Filomena arrived at the house in a state of panic. 'I hope Meredith is OK. I hope the poor girl is safe,' she said. Inside the house was cold, colder than normal. The grating gear changes of the cars taking the bends on the hilly pass outside seemed louder and more aggressive. An ominous dread hung over everything. Instinctively, she rushed to her room.

'Oh, my gosh!' Filomena exclaimed. The shock of seeing her room ransacked hit home. But after a few seconds her studious, logical brain began to carefully unpick the wreckage around her. 'Thank God my laptop hasn't gone!' she said, fishing the computer from on top of a pile of clothes on the floor. 'And my jewellery, it's still here.' Breathing a sigh of relief, she realized that the scene *looked* a lot worse than it actually was. 'Excellent! They haven't taken my video camera,' she said. In fact the intruders hadn't taken anything. Even her collection of CDs – standard smack-head robber fare the world over – had miraculously survived the burglary.

Standing behind her, Inspector Michele Battistelli, one of the Postal Police officers, pointed out the rock that had been thrown through the window, presumably to break in, and had landed under a chair. 'But look, that's odd,' he said, nodding towards the scattered shards. 'The broken glass from the pane is *on top* of the clothes rather than underneath it.' Observers might expect that the window had been broken first and so the glass would lie under the clothes, on the assumption that these had been thrown about later

Filomena, not understanding the significance of the observation, interrupted him. 'Yes, there was glass on top of the computer as well,' she confirmed. 'But more importantly, have you found Meredith yet? It's strange that's she's locked her door. She never does that.' Battistelli glanced at Amanda, more questioning than accusing. Her blue eyes lowered momentarily.

'But the American girl has just said that Meredith *always* locks her door,' the policeman said. An awkward smile, weaker than her complexion, broke across Amanda's lips. *Is she nervous? Is she lying? Is she flirting?* Battistelli couldn't get his head around this strange American girl.

Both Battistelli and Filomena paced quickly up the corridor to Meredith's bedroom door. A ruffled Battistelli made an announcement – as a policeman, he personally couldn't break down Meredith's locked door because he didn't have a warrant. 'Regulations,' he shrugged.

Amanda repeated the words. 'Break it down?' she asked, appearing slightly freaked. 'Do you really have to?' Later it was claimed that she had a set of Meredith's keys in her own room. If she did, she did not mention it to the police. One of the policemen sensed her unease. 'Don't worry, there's no body under the sofa,' he joked. Who wants to upset a beautiful girl unnecessarily?

Filomena had no time for small talk – she told her boyfriend Marco and his pal Luca to kick it in. 'I'll take responsibility,' said Filomena determinedly, as Luca gave the pine door the full-on Seventies-cop-show treatment. As he got into position, Amanda turned to Luca, reinforcing her earlier claim: 'Meredith locks her room even just going for a shower.'

What was she playing down? What was she delaying? Luca got on with the job, pleased to be of service.

Had Meredith glimpsed the dark side of the house before her death? The fragile beauty of its limestone walls and moss-speckled apple trees had cast a spell on her two months before. It had lured her in, like a honey trap. An alpine farmhouse, set on a rocky outcrop, on top of a valley. The terracotta roof tiles resonated shabby chic like a cracked, oil-painted backdrop for a Tim Walker fashion shoot. The elliptical back garden, which ran down to the valley floor behind, was wild and mature, a perfumery of Italian herbs – parsley, sage, garlic, basil. In the distance, wild mushrooms and truffles covered the Umbrian hills, the narrow valleys funnelling the currents like a natural wind tunnel, swirling the musty but exotic odours directly into Meredith's room above them.

In the morning, mist settled over the fields of soldier-like rows of olive trees, wisps of wood smoke rising from the farmhouses. In winter, the gently curving landscape was powered with a fine coating of snow, like caster sugar on one of Perugia's world-famous chocolates. In autumn, the fading yellow of the leaves, amplified by a sheen of glistening moisture that clung to ageing walls, highlighted beauty.

But in Perugia, darkness is quick to descend and is never far away. Behind the façade of crumbling grandeur, there's an overriding sense of decay that infects everything it touches like a wasting disease. The stone of the bridges and tunnels is black and scrofulous. The steady rain of the winter months penetrates every nook and cranny like a gnawing swarm of insects, and the dark clouds heighten the impression of a city being reclaimed, overgrown, eroded by nature.

Up close, the magic of Meredith's house falls away like a fraud. It's shabby and cold and there are cracked veins in the unpainted cement. Gouges in the mouldy bricks. Plastic bags and sun-bleached Fanta multi-pack wrappers, litter from the disrespectful drivers on the hill pass, growing on the trees. The gates at the entrance to the driveway are made from cheap tubular steel, and are rusting. The gravel is patchy and weedy. The fence-post is a cut-down tree with a blooming crown of fungus on top. It stands next to a torn wire-mesh fence – a half-hearted attempt to stop people falling into the valley below. The fields are peppered with disused wells, like gaping mouths ready to swallow up the dirty secrets of the town. Ideal places to dump a body. How many problems have been solved by these drain-reeking sewers over the years?

Under the portico, there is a milk crate with a blackened mop in it, and a brush mismatched with an old pan. An old guitar, filled with rainwater, dark brown stains where the frets had once been, its strings long gone, has been thrown away near the path. A crude DIY skylight had been sawn into the tiled roof, to release the smells from the grimy student bathroom. Lazy tenants that had gone before had long abandoned the garden, and it was now overgrown with nettles and ugly, spindly trees – tall firs, scarred and misshapen with brown patches, diseased but looking as if they had been burned.

Meredith's house may have looked like an Italian rural idyll to a Leeds University student used to shoebox halls of residence or scummy digs in places like Chapeltown. But to the native Italian eye, over-indulged on beauty, it looked rough and exposed. Nothing more than the converted cowshed it really was. Perugia – a poor man's Florence. But compared to Chapeltown, where the Yorkshire Ripper had murdered a series of young women thirty years before, or the sterile, dusty halls of residence where he had killed again in 1980, 7 Pergola Road was a safe haven. Nothing evil like that could happen here. Not in a million years.

Luca Altieri kicked down the door and went white. Behind him Marco yelled: 'Blood! Blood!'

Filomena glimpsed a blurry image of Meredith's foot sticking out from underneath the duvet, crying, 'Oh, my God, Meredith!' Shielding her, Marco turned her away. 'Go! Go!' he said. Paola Grande recoiled in horror.

Inspector Battistelli, who stood at the door for thirty seconds, could see the marks on her neck, and the blood, so he knew how she had been killed. But, significantly, he later claimed that he had said nothing about the details he had witnessed. By not sharing his observations with other potential witnesses, he hoped not to influence them.

He closed the door, not noticing whether Amanda and Raffaele, who were at the back of the queue, had snatched a look. Unusually, they didn't seem too bothered. Curiosity had not got the better of them. Their position in the queue was plain to see – they were at the back of it, almost in the kitchen, even though Amanda was closer to Meredith, in terms of her age, background and university situation, than anyone who was there.

4

On the Case

Police Investigation: Day 1

2 November, 13:00

Like a chain of bonfires across the Apennine peaks, police phones from Perugia to Rome began to light up. As the official first responder, Inspector Battistelli was the first link in the process. For two hours at least, everyone and everything would bounce off him: homicide squad, Flying Squad, specialist investigators, forensics, autopsy, crime-scene security, senior officers, interrogators, technicians; the mind-boggling array of units that a modern police force can deploy instantly to a murder CSI.

Today he was on point, and though he wasn't exactly in command of the operation, his job was to guide everyone through the killer's labyrinth, partly to keep contamination to a minimum – his DNA was unavoidably already in the area because of his earlier presence, and why ruin it further with other officers' traces? – and partly because he was familiar with the layout of the house.

He took a deep breath, trying not to let the pressure show. This was his moment, his opportunity to do the right thing. Calmly, he palmed one of his two mobile phones from the kitchen table, his own that he'd put down earlier, and called his boss, Commissioner

Filippo Bartolozzi, head of the Postal Police section.

Bartolozzi, no messing around, immediately recognized the seriousness of the case and said: 'This is one for the heavy brigade. I'll get on to the Flying Squad right away.' He called the Chief of Police, the *Questore*, one of the most important men in Perugia, and then the Flying Squad. Like their namesake in the UK, the Italian Flying Squad are a fast-response team of elite detectives with wide-ranging skills and a general remit, flipping between serious cases such as murders and armed robberies with professional ease.

The police station in Perugia is a severe glass-and-concrete bunker-style building reinforced to withstand bomb attacks during the height of the anti-Mafia investigations. But like many things in Perugia it is a facade – the grand exterior hides a warren of narrow corridors and mean offices. Perugia was never a Mafia town.

Chief Inspector Chiacchiera, the heavy-set Flying Squad deputy, answered the phone. 'A murder?' he repeated, slightly startled. But he lost no time in diving straight in. 'What's the cause of death?' he asked.

Bartolozzi: 'Looks like a knife wound.'

Chiacchiera: 'Make sure no one goes anywhere near the place until I get there, including the ambulance crew.' Instinctively, he knew what to ask for. 'Are there any witnesses?'

Bartolozzi: 'Yes, there are a few people, students who lived in the house, and their boyfriends.'

Chiacchiera: 'Get their names and addresses. Check their ID cards.'

Not letting up, Chiacchiera made sure that the first responders followed procedure. He said: 'Watch her flatmates and the people there like a hawk. Don't let them go anywhere near the place. I want to keep the place clean for the forensics.'

Chiacchiera knew you lived and or died by your DNA tests these days. End of story. Or end up getting bollocked by your bosses. Or worse still, walloped later in court by a fancy defence lawyer. The upshot was simple. Cock up the DNA and it often meant career over. Not worth thinking about.

Chiacchiera was in his late forties, with thinning dark hair. His Latin good looks were fading fast – long hours, lack of sleep and there goes another weekend. He hadn't even got out of the lift when the first journalist, a local hack, got in his face. Where did he come from? Chiacchiera, slightly taken aback, was not happy. Eyes rolling. He hadn't even seen the body yet, but was being asked to comment.

The reporter fired a question. 'Is it another smack-head, an overdose?' he asked, notepad in hand.

No comment. Chiacchiera got nervous. Hoping it wasn't a taste of things to come.

In the car. On the phone. Down to business. Chiacchiera wasted no time. He called the Postal Police. Battistelli gave him an idiot's guide to the layout of the house: 'Imagine an L-shaped flat, with the foot of the L dug into the side of the hill. The vertical leg of the L contains three bedrooms in this order – Filomena's, Amanda's and Meredith's. Next to Meredith's room is a small shower room. The foot of the L contains a living room and a fourth bedroom belonging to a Laura Mezzetti. Then there's a utility room and a bathroom proper.'

The 40-year-old woman put on her disposable gloves, a hairnet and blue plastic shoe covers. She wasn't starting a shift at one of Perugia's many chocolate factories. Monica Napoleoni was the unlikely head of the city's Murder Squad. The face-mask disguised her TV-cop good looks. Like the unflattering forensics garb, her professionalism belied a curvaceous figure. She took her first step into the crime scene, cool and dark still. Napoleoni had seen her fair share of dead bodies. However, as she lifted the quilt off Meredith's corpse she winced – astonishingly, it was difficult even for someone of her experience to look at the wounds, so ferociously had Meredith been cut.

Ambitious but not driven by name-making, Napoleoni's only concern was to get the job done, right first time. She moved methodically, slowly even, as though she didn't have to think about anyone or anything – except the higher virtues of truth and justice. 'Look at this,' she murmured to Chiacchiera, snooping at her side. To the untrained eye, the mark next to Meredith's body looked like a random smudge of blood. 'It's a footprint.'

Napoleoni's experience gave her an enviable mix of technical skill and compassion. The cheap plastic flowers that had been stuck to the front of Meredith's white Ikea wardrobe to brighten it up, a faint sign of the girl's attitude to life, filled her with sadness.

But at the same time a tingle passed through her neck hairs. Anticipation. This scene was going to throw up a lot of clues, she surmised, no doubt about it. Blood, footprints, DNA everywhere. But are they the right clues, she wondered? Would they in turn throw up the identity of the killer or killers?

A few minutes earlier the team had inspected Filomena's room and asked Battistelli to explain what he had first encountered.

'To be honest, something's not right,' Battistelli mused. Right off the bat. Showing off. Not mincing his words. I could have been a detective, too, was the underlying message. But at the same time couching the report in deferential humility to his senior officers. 'Straightaway, I thought it's an attempt to make it look like a burglary, as opposed to being a real one,' Battistelli went on. He told Napoleoni why – none of Filomena's valuables was missing. Simple as that, was Battistelli's conclusion.

Chiacchiera nodded in agreement. But he deftly switched the focus to a solid piece of evidence. 'It's certainly a big stone to come through that narrow gap between the shutters.' He was still miffed after hearing that the ambulance crew had possibly entered Meredith's room against his wishes. 'Sorry, we were just checking that she was dead.' He was familiar with the old routine. Chiacchiera put the potential breach of procedure to the back of his mind and quickly got on with the job. He focused on the rock on the floor and smashed window above it. The gap between the two halves of the exterior green shutters was 15 cm (six inches) – just enough to be able to see the road outside.

'You'd have to a be a good shot to throw a four-kilo [10 lb] rock through a gap like that,' Chiacchiera said. 'It looks as though the rock is wider than the gap itself. How is that possible, I wonder?'

One of his detectives, who stood outside on the other side of the window, chipped in. 'Better than a good shot,' the detective mused. 'A magician. And you'd have to be a mountain climber to get up this wall and in through a window like that. Outside the wall is four metres high, with nothing to grab on to; just flat concrete.'

The detective turned around to face the hilly pass in front of the broken window. He wanted to see whether motorists could spot an intruder climbing in. Or whether the window was blocked from general view.

'It's too suss,' he concluded, shouting inside to Chiacchiera. 'Anyone driving past would spot you right away, from the road. Put it this way, if you're a good thief, and you're going to screw this house, there are easier ways to break in.'

Chiacchiera appreciated the appraisal but was too busy for bar-room theorizing just yet. 'Let's crack on,' he ordered.

With green shoe covers and gloves, Giuliano Mignini, one of Perugia's senior prosecutors, was the fourth senior member of the initial search team. He was a government lawyer whose job it was to guide the police investigation gently, so that the detective team gathered enough evidence to build a meaningful court case.

Mignini's bald pate was framed by a ring of curly grey hair, crowning a chubby face, giving him a slightly jovial appearance. His green quilt riding jacket, more Pall Mall than Perugia, struggled to cover his belly, and was often mismatched with crumpled stripy shirts and jeans. But behind the avuncular facade was an experienced lawyer not afraid to follow the evidence, even if it led him into trouble with the rich and powerful.

He examined a smudge of blood on Meredith's door-handle, a cheap brass-effect fitting that went well with the door's decor. Then he followed the clues into the shower-room next to Meredith's room, where he found a clear blood print of some kind on a blue bathmat. Next up, Amanda's room. Nothing extraordinary grabbed his attention, at first instance. It was generally untidy. Amanda's guitar was on the floor. A photo, presumably of an American boyfriend, on her desk. By now, the investigation was gearing up to breakneck speed. He could hear it through the thin walls. The adrenalin was flowing. The horror was unfolding. The confusion was being ordered and created at the same time.

Then Mignini returned to the bathroom, where the visible bloodstains were highlighted – the drips on the door and the light switch. The smell of blood. The trail of evidence. The hunt was most definitely on now.

In the light of the sheer volume of biological evidence, it was decided that the search be handed over to the various forensics squads. The first on the scene were local police units lead by Chief Inspector Claudio Cantagalli. He sent two of his best technicians over in a pale-blue and white police Subaru. Everyone was asked to leave the scene while they donned their Noddy suits, before looking around and laying down numbered and lettered labels to indicate the bloodstains and potential evidence. In Meredith's bedroom, in the corridor, in the living room where a train of circular bloodstains formed a line.

It wasn't long before the floor began to look like a giant puzzle of markers and symbols. The officers soon felt overwhelmed by the amount of evidence. They called for back-up. When officer Gioia Brocci arrived at the police station after her lunch break, Cantagalli told her to get another forensics case ready and they took the Chief's car to Pergola Road. A makeshift office was set up under the portico outside the front door. Hundreds of photographs were taken.

First, Brocci took a walk around the house, following the established drill of examining everything outside the immediate crime scene in an anti-clockwise pattern. She took a photograph of the wall outside Filomena's broken window. No signs of mud on the wall, she noticed, and yet her own shoes had got dirty within a few minutes. Curiously, she observed that the foliage near the window looked untouched. There was no sign that the nettles growing against the wall had been flattened by an intruder. Had there been an intruder at all, she mused?

Then it was her turn to go inside the house while her boss Cantagalli thought about his next tactical move. It wasn't long before he realized that he needed extra back-up and more specialized scientists. He keyed in the number of the Chief of Police, who in turn looked up the number for the head of the Scientific Police in Rome, Commissioner Intini. He called.

'You've simply got to get up here,' said the *Questore*. 'There's too much for us to handle.' Meanwhile, Gioia Brocci had been ordered to write a detailed report of everything she'd seen so far. She moved from room to room, again in an anti-clockwise direction, noting the time at 14:30 on Friday, 2 November 2007.

The vanguard of the Scientific Police Forensics Squad, a fingerprint team from Rome, arrived at 17:00 after a long drive in their cramped Subaru Forrester. Agatino Giunta is a softly spoken man of slight build and greying hair. A chemist by training, his expertise lay in highlighting fingerprints no one would suspect were there. He brought more cameras than the gathering press pack and eagerly unloaded his chemicals, dusters and sprays. But when he saw the state of the house, his heart sank a little – he would have to put his main fingerprint search on hold; there was simply too much blood. Procedure determined that blood sampling came before fingerprinting. Testing visible evidence came before invisible. The delay could have been avoided if the Perugian squad had been more specific. Every minute lost was a setback in the world of precision detection.

Giunta immediately summoned a second squad from his Rome HQ, this time consisting of biologists and DNA specialists. 'There's too much blood and it's covering the fingerprints,' he explained. 'There's no point in us going anywhere near the body, so get up here fast.'

Another Subaru left the Scientific Police headquarters at 17:30, while Giunta began his work in the room with the least amount of evidence – the bedroom of the fourth flatmate, Laura Mezzetti. Laura was away on a break for the holy day. Her room, the jumping-off point, also happened to be the first room in the anti-clockwork direction, starting from the heart of the house – the kitchen/dining area.

Agatino Giunta's team had arrived at the same time as

Commissioner Domenico Profazio rolled up. He was head of the Flying Squad and Chiacchiera's boss, and had been summoned back from holiday to get on the case.

'I've just had my hair cut so I won't go inside in case I contaminate the scene,' he told the forensics team, his professionalism fighting an overpowering urge to get stuck in, to satiate his detective's natural curiosity. While the forensics people from Rome were getting ready to go in, he asked Amanda a few questions. She came across to the police as cool, even cold. She hugged Raffaele constantly. He invited the couple to come down to the police station for a chat later, as witnesses rather than suspects.

On their way, too, was the Scientific Police Biology Team, led by Dr Patrizia Stefanoni, a middle-aged woman with dark hair, a thin, determined mouth and a long nose. She brought with her 500 filter-paper swabs, evidence bags, stickers, latex gloves, shoe covers and, of course, the head-to-toe white paper Noddy suits. Her secret weapons included crime scope and scene scope industrial lights, so powerful and angled they could highlight even the smallest trace, the slightest irregularity on a smooth surface.

Biological forensics was a head-wrecker of a job. The TV image often showed beautiful American women investigating clinical mob murders in palm-fringed mansions, platinum mobile phone in one hand and Petri dish in the other. They fed a tissue sample into one end of a computer and out popped the name of the killer from the other. Stefanoni certainly looked the part – she often wore chic, tight-fitting business suits, well cut and finely detailed, in respectable but fashionably unpredictable colours such as grey-green. She wasn't afraid to set them off with frilly, low-cut blouses in an Italian way that didn't detract from her understated authority. But that was as far as the TV comparison went. In reality crime scenes were often degenerate,

haywire places covered in blood and shit: the evidential equivalent of a combat firefight where microscopic evidence degraded
by the minute into useless non-evidential mush. Locations rav-
aged by atmospheric conditions and natural breakdown
processes on the one hand, and contaminated by dumb, over-
enthusiastic first responders on the other.

Dr Stefanoni's primary task was to bring order to the chaos –
by preserving the integrity of the crime scene – and then to
extract its secrets using super-sensitive chemical tests, knowing
that the difference between guilt and innocence could come
down to a single molecule.

No sooner had she got into the passenger seat of her van, Dr
Stefanoni started directing the local police by remote. Her
mobile phone was cupped to her ear and she strained to hear the
person at the other end above the rushing wind on the motorway. She was told that the local forensics squad, less well
equipped and trained than her own, had joined Napoleoni,
Chiacchiera, Mignini and Battistelli on the scene. Better than
nothing, though, she thought. She had respect for the Perugian
squad.

'What's the weather like?' Stefanoni asked. 'Is there any evidence that is hard to protect, either from the atmosphere or
from the public, such as footprints on a stairway or bloodstains
in the road?' Stefanoni began instructing the local officers on the
phone to prioritize evidence at risk. She also told the local police
to start photographing the footprints inside and where possible
to protect them. 'If there is delicate evidence such as clothes or
condoms lying around,' Stefanoni said, 'photograph them now,
leaving a number sign in their place for further reference.' Better
interfere with evidence than lose it altogether, was her motto for
today.

She ordered elimination samples to be taken from everyone

who had visited the crime scene: the finger- and footprints of the first responder, Battistelli, the ambulance crew, all of the residents and their boyfriends, so that later they could be compared with the traces found in the room and excluded from the list of potential suspects.

Stefanoni arrived at 19:00, her sky-blue designer laptop bag slung over her shoulder. Darkness had drawn in fast, forcing the dozen-strong squad of Scientific Police to deploy a bank of lights. Over the next four hours Stefanoni insisted on being briefed by everyone who had been into the house, before taking a single step inside herself. She ran her fingers through her hair, trying to take in the mass of information. Her hair was long and thick, and reached down almost to the centre of her back.

At one point there were four white-suited Scientific Police surrounding her. One smart-looking, grey-haired officer wore a blue coordinator's bib over an expensive grey mac and a white gingham shirt. Local coppers came, said their piece and then peeled off from the group, immersed in thought and keen to get back to their post. She took a deep breath. Finally, when she did go inside, she began her investigation with the long orange-and-white-tiled bathroom next to the utiltity area and Laura Mezzetti's door. This was completely separate from the shower-room at the opposite side of the house, next to Meredith's bedroom where the bloody bath-mat and blood trickles had been found. She lifted the lid. A thin, unflushed piece of faeces sat halfway up the bowl, a scrunch of white toilet tissue stuck to it. Amanda had said the faeces had mysteriously disappeared, but it was still there. Stefanoni had never been so glad to see human excrement – she knew it would reveal a lot of clues. After Laura Mezzetti's bathroom, Stefanoni went around the flat in an anti-clockwise fashion. Eventually, she came to Meredith's room.

The team had numbered and registered all the articles found: the bra with the torn strap lying next to the body under the duvet, the small tin of Vaseline on the desk . . . there were hundreds of items. They identified trace evidence, put dry articles into plastic bags, and wet ones – including blood-drenched filter paper – into paper bags to avoid humidity creating mould on the sample.

Down to the bloodstains. It's good, very good, Stefanoni thought. Evidentially, at any rate. The drops under the desk, the flood beside the wardrobe, the five arch-like shapes on the side of the wardrobe. Knife-shaped bloodstain on the mattress cover. Yes, it's very good, very good indeed, she repeated to herself.

The balls of stress in Stefanoni's shoulders began to ease – potentially there was a lot of material to work with here. A biologist who had made DNA her life, she knew everything there was to know about Watson and Crick's mysterious coiled helix. Her expertise had won her control of the biology unit, as well as leading the CSI team. Along with her line manager, Agatino Giunta, she was one of Italy's secret weapons in the fight against serious crime. If anyone could find the killer, she could.

Eventually Stefanoni removed the duvet, exposing Meredith's body. The grand finale. The money shot. Evidentially, the body would be of greatest use.

Someone has carved another mouth – gouged *a second mouth – on the left side of her neck. A flap of flesh, which should cover the gape like a lid, protrudes from her neck like a tongue . . .*

The shadow of decay has given her a peculiar beauty, like ripe olives on the point of falling. Her waist is slender and exposed looking. But curves out on to her legs. Long, athletic, smooth. Left leg ramrod straight.

The team looked on. Emotions gone. Years ago. Nothing as dead as a dead body. A thousand things spinning through their heads. This head-wrecker of a job. How it could wear down the senses so completely? Draining them of feeling. Filling them up with science in return. And other structured thoughts such as procedure, and decisions, protocols and worry, piled on top of each other. The spectre of a fancy defence lawyer always looking on over their shoulder. Smiling on. How often should I change my latex gloves? What elements do I collect now and what will I have to wait for? These were the mundane questions at the forefront of Stefanoni's meticulous mind.

Luminol will be the last test because the chemical make-up dilutes the very blood it is supposed to highlight. Life and death choices: do I dust for fingerprints first or do I dab for blood? The dust will contaminate the blood. Doing one may interfere with the other. Always compromises and contradictions. Never exact. Never simple. Will what I do now be used against me in the future? Smiling defence lawyers. Trawling and studying. For mistakes. For choices gone wrong. For a not guilty. Sometimes wishing I was invisible. Stefanoni knew that her very presence interacted with evidence, even damaging some. Crime archae-ologists: they are there to establish who did what and when. No time for feelings.

Stefanoni didn't protect Meredith's hands with a plastic bag, though usually that is the first thing to be done to preserve evidence such as skin and hair from under a victim's fingernails. Did Meredith fight back? A question that could be answered if the assailant's skin was found under her cuticles. Stefanoni left that until after the pathologist had had his first look.

At last the pathologist, Dr Luca Lalli, was let in at midnight. He examined the body for cuts and bruises and signs of rape. Her eyes were open and her eyelids were pink – a typical sign of throttling, he noted. He moved the body to see where the blood had collected after the heart has stopped pumping. Her body lay on a pillow with clear bloodstains on it.

Whilst turning the body over, he inadvertently let the skin touch the wardrobe. Luckily the contact was noted so the contamination wouldn't confuse later tests. It's that thorough, Stefanoni thought.

Meredith was taken away in a green, rectangular body-bag by five Scientific Police officers dressed in white Noddy suits and an assistant wearing a black Puma sweatshirt, jeans and white trainers. The bag was put inside a zinc coffin on a waiting hearse.

With the body gone, painstaking forensics continued in earnest. Quick decisions had to be made. Every time Stefanoni intervened on a trace, she modified it. Whenever a swab was used the sample was diluted. The police used large swabs, while Italy's other force, the Carabinieri, preferred cotton buds. Silver black fingerprint powder interfered with invisible blood traces. The video cameras kept rolling.

The key exhibits were bagged and tagged. The clothes collected from the bedroom included Meredith's underpants and her bra. Both had been removed from the body and placed to the south, near her feet. While Stefanoni focused on the molecules on the fibres, Napoleoni zoomed out and comtemplated the bigger picture, particularly the bra. The bra was heavily bloodstained. Did that mean it had been taken off Meredith before or after she was stabbed? The bra clasp had been torn or cut off the straps. Did that mean the attacker had ripped it off during a frenzied sexual attack? Or, thinking more laterally, more subtly, had the bra been clinically snipped using scissors or a knife? If so, before or after the attack?

Other pieces of material evidence included toilet paper, hair collected from under the body, a white towel drenched in blood and a sheet with bloodstains on it. And of course, the quilt that had covered the body. Napoleoni pondered for a moment. What kind of person covers up their dirty work? Someone who is ashamed or frightened of it? Good meat for a profiler or a psychologist. Unfortunately, the Italian police didn't tend to use them as often as the British or the FBI.

Then a major breakthrough occured. A shoeprint came under close scrutiny. The tread on the shoe consisted of nine concentric circles, clearly showing the grip of a training shoe at the ball of the foot. Then they found another matching shoeprint. Then another. Astonishingly there was a trail of shoeprints, as though the wearer had walked from Meredith's body and out of the flat. If they could identify the shoe they could identify who was present at the time of the murder. Finally, they collected 108 fingerprints, leaving doors and tables, handles and armrests covered in little black patches where they had spread silver black dust.

The pack moved in for the kill. First on the scene were local reporters from the *Umbrian Journal*. Former financial journalist Giuseppe Castellini was running the desk while his two reporters crunched gravel on the ground.

Then came the spearhead of the British invasion. Nick Pisa was a British tabloid journalist based in Rome. Straight as a die but cunning as a fox. His dad was an Italian café-owner in Crawley. After serving his time on the *Sunday Mirror* Nick moved his family to Italy to make hay. He'd made his reputation on the Fred West House of Horrors case in Gloucestershire. Nick was known in the trade as a Big Top Operator. A murder like this was his bread and butter. Richard Owen from *The Times* joined the fray. Fiorenza Sarzanini and Meo Ponte of *Corriere della Sera* and *Repubblica* turned up in the city almost immediately.

Castellini ran his fingers through his hair and pulled on his Tuscan cigar. His office is stark and dingy, papers spread all over the place. But he had noticed a chink of light on the horizon. Within hours he had realized that the police investigation was already heavily skewed towards forensics. Too skewed, in his opinion. Where were house-to-house inquiries? Where was the hunt for witnesses, the fingertip searches? Where was the good old-fashioned police work? As an ex-number-cruncher he understood that the big numbers often had big failings. And that trusting science and experts was a gamble. After all, when he was a city reporter, no economist had predicted the credit crunch. The police investigation was already flawed. Castellini saw a gap in the market.

5

Strange Fruit

First Police Interviews

2 November, 14:00

For Amanda and Raffaele, the blood of the murder scene was eclipsed by the blaze of autumn colours that burst from the trees. Amanda looked radiant, her pale palette melding perfectly with the yellowing backdrop. Raffaele stood out, sharp and powerful, his arms protecting the girl he loved from the unfolding horror. Inside, the stench of death. Outside, a lovers' tryst. The shadow of decay on the leaves washing the scene with a peculiar beauty. Inside, hollow stomachs, pressure, stress. Outside, sweet nothings, tongues and temptation.

For the press photographers and TV cameramen the shots of the couple were crime-scene gold. The pack snapped the pair canoodling, snatching the lovers with long lenses from a high-up vantage point, on the top floor of a small multi-storey car park on the opposite side of the road. Amanda and Raffaele played their parts like leads in a Hollywood scary movie. But with a cool, somewhat post-modern twist. Raffaele looked protective, but not in a macho way. More businesslike, exuding the confidence of a successful young executive in an ad shot, the breeze from the Umbrian valley fanning his hair. He wouldn't have looked out of place amid the steel and granite towers of Milan, or Munich or Canary Wharf in London.

Amanda pouted, but carefully couched her flirtation with a delicate lostness. Pulling her Renaissance man close to keep warm. For reassurance. For deliverance. His jeans rubbing hard against her. The spectre of sex and death leering down from the ancient walls.

Inside, death and desperate middle-aged men and women. Searching and sweating. Outside, youth and beauty. Free. The leaves bursting over them, like tears for the friend they have lost. Amanda and Raffaele, Beautiful People caught up in a tragedy. Stumbling into a situation that the privileged should never have to witness. Like tourists who have taken a wrong turn into the dark side of town. Raffaele sad that Amanda's beautiful eyes should have to see such things. White middle-class kids should-n't have to go through this. But soon it will all be over. The police will guide them back out into the light again. And let the Beautiful People go back to living their beautiful lives.

Photographed from an angle the location of the house looked isolated and rural. But look behind the picture postcard, and the image is no more than cityscape mirage. The property was hemmed in from all sides. An ugly multi-storey car park on one side, unkempt, dirty ravines on the other. To the rear a busy, dangerous road, and in front a recycling dump.

Look deeper and the danger signs are obvious. The house was a mere 50 metres from the town's main junkie hangout, a sunken basketball court called Grimana Square, frequented by dealers, punters and drop-outs. The dealers used the public recycling bins and the overgrown wasteground near Meredith's gates to stash their gear, so that they didn't have to carry it around. If a student from the University for Foreigners, opposite the basketball court, came to score some pot or coke, the dealers ran down the steps to the hilly pass outside Meredith's house, took a wrap out from their hidden stash and ran back up to the waiting punter to close the transaction.

To the untrained eye, Meredith's house looked normal. To a criminologist 7 Pergola was a classic example of boundary crime. A house built on a border between a nice neighbourhood and the wrong side of the tracks. There are always higher instances of burglaries and violence at the line where the poor come to prey on the relatively rich – the interstitial zones, where the druggies burgle houses. Where the black hustlers prey on the white middle-class kids – or so the politically incorrect police officers claimed. Meredith was a street-smart girl from a bustling metropolis. She could take care of herself. But she was in unfamiliar territory, not yet acclimatized to the subtler, more hidden dangers of the Italian provincial underworld. Moreover, Meredith was blinded by its apparent beauty. A fatal flaw. She would have been oblivious to the topographic nightmare that surrounded her.

The cold wind from the Steppes blew in. The leaves fell to the ground. The cameras stopped rolling. Amanda and Raffaele came back down to earth with a bump. The police began questioning them immediately. Not as suspects – yet. But as potential witnesses, simply helping with inquiries.

Amanda breezed through her story again. 'I stayed the night in Raffaele's flat.' She let the image hang there for a second, so the middle-aged officer could salivate, if he chose, over what the euphemism 'stay the night' really meant when it involved a beautiful young student in full flower. The officer looked at Raffaele, the blank expression thinly veiling his smugness.

Coyly, Amanda continued: 'And then I came back home to have a shower.' She let the image hang there, giving the officer a glimpse into a world he could only fantasize about. Now that all eyes were on her, Amanda switched the tone: 'When I got home I asked Raffaele to come along to take a look around.' Her delivery bright and bubbly now. 'I called my flatmate, Filomena. Raff called the Carabinieri.' Her American optimism unwavering. 'And, yes, Meredith usually did keep the door locked.' Supremely confident that her story would be believed.

Meanwhile, the wheels of administration began to turn slowly. By now the Preliminary Investigating Magistrate had been informed. Claudia Matteini had the job of overseeing the probe on a higher level. If it was the job of Prosecutor Mignini to conduct the investigation on a tactical level, getting deep down and dirty with operational details, it was her job to step back and be somewhat more strategic. Making sure that everyone's rights were respected, procedure was complied with, dealing with issues such as prison remand and legal representation. She instructed the police to find out who their victim was so they could notify next of kin immediately.

Meredith had been a student at Perugia's world-renowned University for Foreigners for two months, reading European Politics and Italian. The University for Foreigners is a fading red sandstone building 200 metres' walk up the hill from 7 Pergola Road – very convenient for both Meredith and Amanda. The neo-classical décor, broad-stroke and gold-painted nineteenth-century wood, is in the same style as a Viennese music school or an old British ballet academy. The rooms are an atmospheric blend of green walls, patterned marble floors and Arabian-themed frescos.

Amanda Knox studied Italian and Creative Writing there, while Meredith had won a place on the Erasmus programme, an international scheme run by the European Union to bring together the brightest and the best from around the globe, in the long-term interests of harmony and cultural understanding. Amanda was on a study-abroad programme organized by her own university in the USA. Meredith had come from the University of Leeds in Yorkshire and Amanda from the University of Washington.

The police called the Dean. The Dean called the British consulate in Florence – someone was going to have to break the news to the family. British students were urged to come forward with information about Meredith. Her three closest girlfriends – Robyn Butterworth, Amy Frost and Sophie Purton – revealed that they had seen her on the previous evening, before she was murdered, then broke down in tears. After visiting the crime scene they headed to the police station on the mini metro train.

Amanda and Raffaele cadged a lift to the police station with Paola Grande and her boyfriend Luca Altieri, who had been there when Meredith's body was discovered. Night was closing in on Perugia's maddening streets, narrow alleyways that went round and round like a medieval maze. Heightening the tension. Dragging in the gloom. For some, a trap of no escape.

Once the police were out of sight, Raffaele asked Luca what he had told the police. He began firing questions at Paola and Luca about the murder scene. Amanda's face hardened. Tense glances were stolen in the rear-view mirror. Suddenly he wanted to know what the police had been asking, his breath fogging the cold air. Nervously, Paola wiped the steam from the window. She couldn't see where she was going. Outside, just dark corners, hidden cloisters, looming walls. Haunting Perugia.

Raffaele pressed Luca for what he had told the police, the heat of his breath on the back of his neck. The streets ahead folding in. The people gone. The doors closing.

Round the corner, sunlight. Paola hit the brakes. Thank God. At last, they had reached the police station. Raffaele's interrogation stopped. Paola and Luca jumped out and breathed in deeply. A sigh of relief. A shudder. In a flicker, Raffaele regained his charming manners. He took Amanda by the hand and smiled, then walked calmly into the station.

Paola and Luca were frightened. So cautious that they dived back into the car to check that Raffaele and Amanda had not planted incriminating evidence inside. Amanda and Raffaele's strange behaviour had made them deeply suspicious, guarded enough to search their own car. Perugia, a haunted place. A place of suspicion. Of paranoia.

The police wanted an informal chat – no lawyer, no official translator, no notes – to get to know the victim's circle of friends. Experience led them to believe that the culprit was likely to be one of them. Robyn was inconsolable. But oddly, Amanda sat with her feet in Raffaele's lap, keeping him comfortable while they waited on the plastic chairs. Under the neon lights she looked tired and venal, her eyes darting from face to face. She poked her tongue out at Raffaele and made faces. While the others mourned, Amanda laughed.

The oppressive, claustrophobic atmosphere of the police station was slowly closing in. Deep within the belly of the bunker, phones rang eerily. Shifty eyes poked from behind doors. Whispers drifted out of stark, tiny rooms.

Amanda fought the dread. She started showing off to people on the phone. 'I found the body!' she was overheard saying. 'Do you realize it could have been me?'

Sophie and Amy were shocked. Robyn found it difficult to be around Amanda. Raffaele grinned, egging her on. Sophie Purton asked Amanda what she had seen at the house. 'I saw Meredith in the closet,' shot back Amanda, quick as a flash, confident.

Luca's ears pricked up. 'How could she have seen her in the closet?' he puzzled. 'She was behind me and Marco, and the cops, and Filomena and Paola. She was too far back in the queue when Meredith's door was broken down. There's no way she could have glimpsed that,' he thought, but he said nothing. After all, Amanda's behaviour could have been down to shock. And this whole thing was certainly a strange experience. Who could blame a young girl far away from home for acting out of sorts?

Sophie picked up the baton. She noted that Amanda had used the word 'closet', the American way of saying 'wardrobe'. Based on Amanda's observation, she assumed that Meredith's body must have been found either in or near the wardrobe in her room. But how could Amanda have known that if she hadn't seen it with her own eyes? The question was: had Amanda been into Meredith's room before the door was broken down at 13:15?

'I hope she didn't suffer,' said Robyn Butterworth, with another pal, Natalie Hayward.

'What do you think?' Amanda left it hanging there, as though she was deciding whether to say more. Unable to help herself, she unleashed a bizarre volley. 'She died a terrible slow death with her throat cut,' Amanda stated. Once again, people wondered how she knew that. And to speak about such gory details in an inappropriate manner was to add insult to injury. The girls turned away.

Amanda was revelling as the centre of attention, they thought. With Raffaele proudly looking on. But giving nothing away. A policeman walked by and told Amanda to sit up. 'This isn't a place for funny faces,' the officer said.

Amanda's information had got everyone thinking, and Filomena mulled over the morning's events. Why was the washing machine warm when she got home, as though a cycle had just finished? Amanda hadn't mentioned putting on a wash after getting her shower. And why did it seem to be full of Meredith's clothes? The suspicion was mounting.

During the informal chats, aided by a cop who spoke English, a sketchy picture of Meredith's life began to emerge. She often went out with Robyn, Sophie, Amy and the other English girls. Her pals revealed that Meredith had a boyfriend called Giacomo Silenzi. He was a student from the Marche region of Italy and he lived in the flat downstairs at 7 Pergola.

Below Meredith and Amanda's L-shaped apartment, there was a lower floor, cordoned off into a separate flat and also rented out to students. Suspiciously, not one of them was in on the day the body was discovered. Were they the culprits? Flying Squad boss Profazio thought. Had the boyfriend, the usual suspect in such cases, fled the scene? Earlier, Chief Prosecutor Mignini had authorized the police to break into the boys' flat to see if they were hiding in there. They weren't.

The English girls quietly confirmed that Meredith was obviously having regular sex with Giacomo. While the police hunted him down, they inquired about other men who were interested in Meredith. There was Juve, an internet café owner originally from Argentina. One of Meredith's pals chipped in: 'Juve had a tendency to be a bit too touchy-feely with Meredith when he was drunk.' Then there was Hicham, a Moroccan cook who hung around the bars after work.

'Did anyone visit the house?' the police asked.

'No, not really,' Filomena answered. 'Amanda's boyfriend Raffaele had only started coming to the house about one week before around the 26th October.'

'What about Amanda?' the police inquired in a separate room. 'Did Meredith and Amanda get on?'

Amanda's suspicious behaviour in the waiting room

prompted Robyn. She said: 'There were many things that Meredith didn't like about Amanda.'

'Really?' said the police officer, 'What like?'

Robyn referred back to conversations she had had with Meredith. 'Amanda was always attracting people's attention. That annoyed Meredith, even if she tried to be friendly and do things together with Amanda, such as go shopping or to the chocolate fair together.'

Robyn began to voice the suspicions that all of them had felt in the waiting room, trying to convert their hunches into some form of solid data the police could understand.

'Amanda brought too many strange men home,' one of Meredith's friends said. 'There was one who was older than us, whom Amanda met at an internet café. Meredith complained that he always tried to kiss her.'

The police had got a snapshot of their victim's lifestyle – a middle-class girl from a reasonably well-off English family, serious about her studies, clean.

But Robyn began to give them the nitty gritty.

'Giacomo was Meredith's boyfriend. They slept together. He even asked her to water his cannabis plants.'

So she wasn't a complete square then, thought the Italian officers.

Filomena filled in the basics. She explained how they had all become flatmates. At first, Filomena had found 7 Pergola with Laura Mezzetti, who was also a legal assistant like Filomena, training up to become a barrister. Meredith and Amanda had moved in later, just before their courses started.

The police soon turned up one of the boys from the lower flat, Stefano Bonassi. He told them that the lads who lived there had all gone away for the holiday weekend. Meredith's boyfriend Giacomo Silenzi was on his way back – so on the face of it he had a good alibi. In addition, Stefano gave the police a helpful list of visitors who frequented their flat. He said: 'There was a guy called Peppe, a boy called Body Roga and a black man, a South African, I think, a body-builder they called The Baron. He really liked Amanda. He got so drunk one night . . .' Student antics. Transitory characters. Nothing unusual. The police lost interest.

Robyn's information on Amanda had begun to colour her character in the eyes of police. Officers questioned her again: 'OK, Miss Knox, you've told us about last night. But how did you spend yesterday afternoon?'

Amanda was ruffled: 'Raffaele joined us after lunch about 4 p.m. at my place at 7 Pergola. Meredith had got up late and she still had some of that fake blood on her chin.'

'Fake blood? Why?' The officers asked.

'She'd been out to a Halloween party the night before,' Amanda explained. 'She dressed up as vampire and messed about with some joke-shop blood.'

'Where exactly was Meredith when you saw her then?' the officer asked.

'Meredith was in her room,' Amanda said. 'As I said, she got up late and got dressed. Raffaele had just turned up and we were going to have something to eat. She wasn't hungry and she was going to meet up with her friends.'

'You stayed there at Raffaele's all evening?' the copper asked.

'Yes,' replied Amanda. Her honest-looking blue eyes gazed straight into the investigator's, just to underline the point. She had an alibi.

Sollecito was being questioned separately in another room. But little cracks began to appear. He said that after their late lunch he and Amanda had gone for a walk down Corso Vannucci, the buzzing main street in town. Raffaele's trainers were examined by police. They found nothing untoward and, because he wasn't a formal suspect yet, handed them back to him. Many of the group, including Amanda and Raffaele, were kept overnight.

That very same night, Domenico Profazio, the Flying Squad chief who had cut short his holiday, summoned his team to his office. Chief Prosecutor Giuliano Mignini honoured them with his presence. They all knew that the first few hours would be decisive in identifying probable culprits. After that memory fades, sensations get mixed up and judgment gets less acute. Further pressure was brought to bear: the Head Prosecutor, Nicola Miriano, had promised the British Embassy that the case would be solved quickly. Patrizia Stefanoni was invited to give her first impressions.

Mignini was gracious and made sure that everyone knew he had total confidence in the officers before him. Patrizia Stefanoni joined the meeting, as did a new character, a suave police officer from Rome. Edgardo Giobbi was the boss of the violent crime unit of the Rome Central Operations Service. Mignini introduced him, although everyone knew who he was. Dark and dapper, he oozed self-confidence and experience. He had looked many a Mafioso in the eye and brought them to justice, and the killers of Meredith Kercher would be his. He was sure of that.

'So, what's the latest?' Mignini asked.

Profazio asked Chiacchiera, as the first senior officer on the scene, for his first take on the findings so far. He pulled no punches.

'The break-in is staged,' was Chiacchiera's shock reply. 'There's glass *on top* of the clothes and it's almost impossible to throw a stone through those shutters.'

He went on: 'In any case, if the thief had climbed in that window, the shutters would have been left open, and not almost closed, with a small 15-centimetre gap, as we found them.'

He rubbished the idea of a burglar climbing up the wall from the garden at the bottom of the house. 'You'd have to be Spiderman,' he said, smiling dismissively.

Chiacchiera concluded that any burglar worth his salt would have broken in through the terrace around the back the house, because it was not visible from the road. He signed off with his conclusion: 'Basically it's completely illogical that a thief broke in through Filomena's window.'

Although burglary was ruled out, in the interests of justice the possibility had to be checked. Mignini pondered.

'Meredith's flat is close to Grimana Square where the pushers hang out,' the Prosecutor said. 'Could it have been one of them? Drug addicts often behave irrationally.'

Profazio shook his head and said: 'No, I don't think so. Granted, sometimes they hide their stuff in the bushes down there, but usually in the gas-meter boxes. They're all ripped open; you might have seen it,' he continued. 'But I don't think this is the work of one of them.'

Chiacchiera chipped in: 'Yes, but Meredith herself did complain that she saw someone in the bushes down there four days ago. Marco Marzan, one of the boys from the downstairs flat, also said he had found syringes in the driveway.'

The investigators agreed to shake down their informants and run through the CCTV camera at the entrance to the car park opposite.

Mignini put his pipe in his mouth. Although it's illegal to smoke in public offices, nobody minded. This was time to refocus what they did know. He puffed and then turned to Napoleoni.

'OK. So the break-in is staged,' Mignini said. 'What does that tell us?'

Napoleoni cut to the chase. She said that the culprit was someone the girl knew. 'Someone who had the keys to the house,' she added.

From that moment on Amanda Knox became the prime suspect, if not officially on paper, at least in the minds of the people who mattered. Raffaele was falling in a close second.

Chiacchiera began to paint a demeaning picture of their characters. 'They were odd,' he said. 'Very odd indeed. Showed no emotion, all that hugging and kissing . . . But she also went into a bit of a shake when she was taken down to the station for her fingerprints and saliva swab. Chatted to D'Astolto a lot.' Police officer D'Astolto was born in Australia and spoke English.

'All that kissing wasn't very normal,' interjected Naploeoni. 'And did you see what she was doing downstairs while they were waiting to be questioned?' she asked.

'Yes,' agreed Chiacchiera, 'the other girls were shocked.'

Profazio enquired whether the police could tap into Amanda and Raffaele's phones. Mignini promised to ask the judge for authorization.

Patrizia Stefanoni closed the meeting with a round-up of the science.

'Yes,' she stated, 'I would say that the break-in is staged. The amount of blood indicates that the victim probably died of blood loss, but until the autopsy is complete we don't know that. We have found blood in the small bathroom and a good footprint, as well as a number of concentric circles that may be from a shoe. There is little we can say immediately, of course . . .' She had little more to add. Her science wasn't making the difference for the time being.

6

The Gilded Generation

The gargoyles screamed and hissed in the wind. Rain dripped from their rotting stumps stained red and black by the medieval stone. Whispers of Satanism. Rumours of sacrifice. Gossip on the Devil's radio, already.

Rape. Sex. Slashing. Young students rushed home to escape the closing gloom. The fog closing in, the moon blackening, the footsteps behind, tapping on the shiny cobbles. Perugia was in the grip of fright and murder.

A tattered note went up on the University message board: 'Looking for new flatmate – ours has just left us. Preferably girls. Ring 075 2 11 07' – the date of the murder.

The portraits of Amanda Knox and Raffaele Sollecito that appeared in the press the following day were a ray of sunshine amid the darkening clouds. The photos, taken outside the murder scene, knocked the celebrity shots off front pages around the world.

Picture editors liked the images. Amanda and Raffaele were young. They looked posh. They were, in short, Beautiful People.

But not so beautiful that they couldn't mourn. Or cry. Or be dignified towards their dead pal. The papers hinted that their unruffled behaviour was suspicious. But above all else, these images would come to characterize the case of Meredith Kercher – the first notorious murder of the Big Brother Generation.

Readers wanted to know more, particularly why Amanda and Raffaele were kissing instead of shedding tears. Suspicions were raised. Was Amanda Knox simply oblivious? Was she in shock? Or did she exercise a high degree of control over her emotions? The ravens were circling. Closing in for the kill. Cracks were starting to appear. Journalists began to delve into the background of the latest TV media stars. To find the fault-lines.

Amanda Knox was born in Seattle on 9 July 1987 into a lower-middle-class family. The foundations were far from stable. Like millions of aspirational American families, the Knoxes' social status balanced precariously on the cusp between blue-collar worker and middle management. A worrying place to be in America, not least because of the inherent vulnerabilities they faced. The family fortunes were exposed to the rapacious vagaries of the US job market, although having safe jobs at least meant that both parents had health insurance; living in Seattle they also enjoyed a more flourishing local economy than in many American cities. However, parents were expected to put aside for expensive extras like college fees. Her father, Curt Knox, was twenty-six when Amanda was born. He worked in the Macy's central headquarters in Seattle. Her mother, Edda, was a 24-year-old schoolteacher.

Amanda Knox had been born with a plastic spoon in her mouth. However, there was hope and ambition in ample supply. One of the few comforts was that their life path to betterment was a well-trodden one. Millions of hardworking people had successfully achieved the American dream through hard graft and prudence, even though life had a steelier edge than it did in Europe.

The Knoxes' marriage had the air of a shotgun wedding. Amanda had been conceived out of wedlock, a minor scandal for her deeply religious mother, and the couple rushed to get married halfway through the pregnancy.

When Amanda was two years old the strain became too much for her father. Edda was about to give birth to their second daughter Deanna. He was out of the house when she delivered – a bad omen. Later, he left for good.

Edda was left alone to bring up her two young children on a teacher's wage, always short of money and constantly worrying about childcare. She became a full-time maths teacher at a primary school. The unrooted feeling of coming from a lower-middle-class background, a kind of social no-man's-land, may have left Amanda with a looming identity crisis. Though exposed to a kind of mediocre reality, Amanda developed a rich imagination to make up for it – and rich tastes. She set her heart on going to one of the city's top private schools.

Following her divorce, Edda began taking life more seriously: she had to fight where before she had relied on Curt; she had to rise above the emotional and material loss, in turn impressing a stern upbringing upon her daughters. Amanda's grandmother had been part of a second wave of Northern European immigrants to emigrate to the great West following the Second World War. Amanda was constantly aware that her roots didn't run deep. They had left family in Germany. Edda knew from experience that if she were to survive her marriage break-up she had to get back to basics. She was hard-working, Catholic and serious. To stop the family from falling apart, Edda became a strict mother, bringing up her children in a more disciplined way than was fashionable in the post-baby-boomer generation.

Her experience with Curt left Edda in no rush to find another man. Their marriage had lasted just two years and he had quickly found another woman. The struggle shows in her face – tired and careworn, sallow, with a pasty complexion. Her busy-mum, no-nonsense, shoulder-length hair is frayed at the ends and there are dark circles under her eyes. But she is dignified and tries not to let it show in her demeanour. Diminutive and wide-hipped, she wears plain but smart clothes. Loose and value for money in a very American fashion.

Edda turned to her own family, imprinting on their favourite granddaughter a love of the German language and a desire to escape. Edda had been born in Germany and moved to the States when she was six. Her mother, from Hamburg, had fallen in love with a US servicemen based there.

One of the few advantages the family had lay in their faith – a fast track to a good education, if mom could play the system. Edda made sure that Amanda attended Mass and Bible classes, while she networked with prominent local Catholics. Even without the pushy-mum leg-up, Amanda would have shone. The girl set her sights on the upmarket Seattle Preparatory School, a strict $6000-a-year Jesuit-run college, 15 miles away from her home. She was bright. To the family's delight, Amanda landed a place on a partial scholarship. Even during the US equivalent of infants' and primary school, she was a good student, well behaved and excelling in languages.

American girls often express their ambition through sport, as it is funded and supported by the schools system. Amanda excelled in the gym and on the track, more of a tomboy than a little princess. Sport was a cheap, democratic way of showing off her self-control and her conformity, and she was able to channel her fierce competitive spirit in a positive way. Amanda quickly became obsessed with soccer.

She was picked out early on as a future winner in life and her teachers worked hard to push her. Catholics are proud of their schools and proud of the pupils, even during the early years. The Jesuits follow the teachings of Saint Ignatius of Loyola, who said: 'Give me a youth and I'll turn him into a Christian', stressing that the first seven years are the most important in terms of character building.

At Seattle Prep Amanda discovered a happy marriage of rigour and tolerance, obligation and love, rather than the repression and obsession of the old days. When the family situation became difficult, the school waived fees and handed on used clothes.

Amanda's early days were regimented compared to those of her friends, who were allowed to watch more television and spend more time playing. Amanda and Deanna went to school, came home, did their homework and went to bed early. Day in, day out. Curt moved into a house around the corner with his new wife, where he set about building a new family. In the earliest years after their separation, court records show that Edda had to turn to lawyers to get his financial support. Edda led from the front. She instilled a strong work ethic in Amanda by staying busy herself – she played in two women's soccer teams and went back to university to earn a master's degree in education.

The Knoxes lived in a large corner-lot house in a quiet working-class neighbourhood of detached clapboard bungalows in West Seattle. The gardens were spacious and unfenced, giving way to wide, tarmacked cul-de-sacs. The driveways were cluttered with pick-up trucks, small business vans and unused boats and motorbikes. Car-repair shops and small industrial units lined the side streets. Amanda grew up in her mother's modest pale-yellow house, which was proud but frayed around the edges. Both Amanda and Deanna's childhoods were happy, spent walking backwards and forwards between their parents' houses.

Amanda was feisty but not violent or badly behaved, although she was fiercely protective of her sister. When she was seven, Amanda punished a bully who was picking on Deanna, giving him a bloody nose. But she also had a sensitive side and couldn't bring herself to kill spiders. She knew her own mind, at seven already independent-thinking and confident.

Meanwhile, 5800 miles away near Bari in Southern Italy, the young Raffaele Sollecito's upbringing was a stark contrast of fortunes. He was handed a good start in life and a silver spoon in his mouth. The 26th of March 1984 was a joyous day in the Sollecito family history – the day their first son was born. But from the beginning there was pressure on the young Raffaele. Pressure to live up his macho father's expectations. Pressure to be the perfect Italian son to his needy mother. Pressure to succeed. High hopes were invested in the boy from an early age. Hopes that he would uphold the family's prestigious name. Hopes that he would achieve as much as his gifted seven-year-old sister Vanessa. Hopes that he would save his parents' crumbling marriage.

Despite differences in personality, there were some similarities with Amanda's circumstances. Raffaele was born into a Catholic family. However, the Sollecitos' faith was more extreme and right-wing than that practised by the Knoxes and their provincial convent-style school. Raffaele was named in honour of an angel, a messenger, and at his birth the name held deep significance. Raffaele was born to a couple whose marriage was in crisis. As a successful urologist with a growing practice, his father worked night duty at the local hospital. His workload put a strain on the relationship.

For many years, Raffaele's parents had patched up the cracks for the sake of their wealth. Both Francesco and his wife came from rich, powerful families. Southern Italy in the 1980s was essentially a developing agro-economy, rife with poverty and corruption, and the Sollecitos consumed conspicuously – big houses, expensive cars, the finest clothes. Francesco boosted his social mobility by joining the freemasons, even though the Italian branch of the controversial society was immersed in a damaging scandal at the time, in which secret lodges had seized political and military power.

Unlike Edda Knox, with her puritanical brand of New World Catholicism, Raffaele's mother was sucked into a more mystical side of the faith. She was also rich, but her family was plagued by a history of depression and heart disease, making her a suitable follower of – some say ideal target for – the cult of Padre Pio, the saint blessed with the Stigmata who could read devotees' minds and often, some said, performed miracles.

Unlike Amanda, who reacted to her family's problems by confronting the world head on, Raffaele sought sanctuary within himself. He was very shy. He was quiet and studious at all times – even during catechism classes, when traditionally noisy Italian kids ignore dry religious instruction in favour of jokes and gossip. Some people viewed Raffaele's sensitive nature as a weakness, a direct result of his mollycoddling mother.

Luckily, like his parents, he was bright at school, even at an early age, inheriting his intellectual gifts from his mother.

Raffaele spent five years at the local primary school, where he had two teachers – one for the literary subjects of Italian and History, and one for the scientific subjects such as Mathematics.

As the reporters covering Meredith's murder compiled standard newspaper backgrounders, general similarities began to emerge. Both Raffaele and Amanda were born around the same time, into families with relationship problems and Catholic influences to varying degrees. The vague likenesses even extended to the victim's family.

Meredith Susanna Cara Kercher was born on 28 December 1985 in Southwark, London, to John and Arline Kercher. The Kerchers were a cosmopolitan London family, John a successful freelance showbiz journalist, Arline an exotic-looking housewife, born in Lahore in 1945 and, unusually, a Pakistani Catholic. Meredith was their fourth child. Their large brood and multicultural background gave the Kerchers a slightly bohemian air. John worked when he could, often unusual hours, and they were happy to take what life brought them.

Meredith's oldest brother, John, was born in 1976, Lyle in 1979, and Stephanie, her older sister, was one year old when she was born. Life in the cramped Kercher household was hectic. John was at the height of his career, writing for the *Daily Mirror* and the *News of the World*, covering the big showbiz stories of the day and following the likes of Madonna and Guns 'N' Roses from one celebrity party to another.

John looked for a more stable income stream, and one that would keep him at home so that he could help with childcare. He started writing pop music annuals for kids including a Madonna special, Michael Jackson, Culture Club, A-Ha, Wham and Bros. He expanded the format to cover TV shows such as *Bread* and *Home and Away* and souvenir editions for royal weddings. On sport he covered BMXing and American football. Then he penned several successful biographies on stars such as Warren Beatty, Arnold Schwarzenegger and Joan Collins.

Like many young families, the Kerchers moved to the suburbs to get more room and a garden. John's eyes fell on the small town of Coulsdon in the borough of Croydon. There was a good private school nearby, the Old Palace of John Whitgift School.

By the age of seven Meredith was showing impressive academic potential. But she often hid her talent, especially for English, under a bushel. She was always quiet and polite, and never boastful or teasing, pals say. Family friend Elizabeth Crofts, whose daughter was friendly with Meredith's older brother, told how she beat off all of the adults and kids in an educational word game.

Mrs Crofts recalled: 'One night Meredith's family came for dinner at our house. I was struck how quiet and polite all of them were. They were a beautiful family. Meredith was very well behaved, as were the other three. John and Arline were very kind, very calm. We played a board game called Dingbats, which is quite a difficult guessing game. Meredith was leaving the other kids standing, even beating the parents. Meredith was very clever, even at that age, very on the ball.

'The Old Palace School is extremely academic. The headmistress then was a real bull terrier and she never let the girls get away with anything. They got rid of the girls who weren't clever. But Meredith knew her own mind, even at seven and eight. She was decisive, and that was important in that school. If you didn't make your mind up what you were doing, in terms of courses and study, the headmistress made the decision for you, fast, and that was it.

'But they didn't need to make sure she succeeded – Meredith was academic. I used to see her father pick her up from school. It's very sad to look back at it now.'

In order to pay the bills John had to return to the treadmill of Fleet Street. The family was to pay a high price for John's involvement in celebrity culture. Like many creatives, he had highs and lows. Increasingly he spent nights out to cover his celebrity stories, leaving the home front entirely to

Arline. Eventually they separated under the strain and John moved to a residence in Croydon. John junior and Lyle were finishing school. Stephanie and Meredith were still young girls.

7

The Autopsy

Police Investigation, Days 1–3

Friday–Sunday, 2–4 November

The Detective of Death entered the crime scene. As the forensic pathologist, Dr Luca Lalli's job was to find out how Meredith died. Clinical in one sense but almost spiritual in another, his role is that of an ombudsman for the dead, to speak for those who no longer can. The unpleasant irony of his trade was that he would have to invade Meredith's body to a greater degree than the killer. This last violation was the price of revealing her secrets, no matter how unspeakable. The price of bringing closure for the family, one of the sole comforts of a very cold profession.

Gravely, Stefanoni granted him permission to begin his medical examinations where the body fell. He was allowed to perform several basic but vital operations to gather evidence solely from the corpse. Firstly, Dr Lalli took the body's temperature: 22 degrees centigrade compared with 13 degrees in the room. The data would be used to estimate the time of death. Though the body was still warm, rigor mortis had set in.

Secondly, Lalli swabbed the vaginal area looking for signs of sexual or violent activity. He quickly found a small fibre and removed the sample from the body using a vaginal swab. As potential biological evidence, the strand was more use to forensics than to himself, so he immediately delivered the clinically bagged swab to Patrizia Stefanoni.

Thirdly, Lalli carefully examined Meredith's fingernails, taking material from under them, before covering her hands and feet with plastic bags to ensure zero contact with environmental surfaces, and to catch any falling debris.

Finally, Lalli studied the blood patterns around the body. A fortune teller claims to see the future in the settling of tea leaves at the bottom of a cup. By studying the seemingly random shape of a pool of blood, Lalli could look into the past. At once he noticed the phenomenon of hypostasis – blood collecting in places where gravity pulled the liquid after the heart had stopped pumping. He noted lots of blood in the areas where the body touched the floor. The pools moved when pressed, showing that the blood was still fluid. Hypostasis also occurred on and within the buttocks lying on the pillow that the murderer or an accomplice had placed under the body. Oddly, he observed, there were no pools on her breast, only small globules of blood.

In a few hours Meredith's home would be the autopsy lab, a clinical room of sterile white tiles and stark steel dissection tables. A grisly but practical place, where the edges of mortuary tables are lined with angled lips to prevent body fluids dripping and large central drains to wash away embalming chemical. She would be more alone than she had ever been in her life. Her body still owned by the Italian state. In the company of strangers. A horrifying kind of limbo.

But for now Meredith was still in her dark, cluttered bedroom. All the signs of full and happy life around her. Electrical wires and extension cables criss-crossed the low-cost ceramic floor tiles, a common sight in Perugian student flats where the electrics and plumbing are often haphazard. A Chemical Brothers CD balanced on a thin wooden shelf above her desk. Study stuff and girly things littered her workstation – a glossy white laptop, lecture notes, a silver plastic hairdryer, a cream woolly scarf and a hairbrush entangled with dark-brown strands, signs of the last time she had got ready to go out. A to-do list written in longhand in a reporter's notebook, evidently used to plan her year in Italy, was open on her desk. The title on the first page was 'Erasmus', along with an Italian phone number and a bill for £106.92, possibly for her plane ticket from London, scribbled next to a mobile number and an email address for a friend called Tim.

Recent signs of life included a pocket-sized tin of Vaseline, scrunched-up tissues and a clear plastic make-up bag, all jumbled up on the desk. A curious mixture, indicating that Meredith was highly organized, yet the signs of a girl going out to enjoy herself, too excited to tidy up, making the most of her year abroad.

Meredith's right leg was bent and had to be pushed hard to get it into the coffin that took her away at 1 a.m. to the Monteluce hospital, where Luca Lalli had his laboratory. The first part of the post-mortem, which took place while the body was still in the green bag, was the external examination, a detailed recording of the basics – the clothes were inspected and described, the position of body studied, photographs taken. Then Meredith was bathed in a bluish ultra-violet light and scanned for evidence not visible to the naked eye. The body was measured – 164 centimetres from head to foot. The mortuary assistants, known as 'dieners' in the profession, then removed the body from the bag.

Later that morning on Saturday, 3 November, a small group of investigators and doctors examined the corpse again. This time Patrizia Stefanoni wanted to definitively establish whether Meredith had been raped or not. A gynaecologist called Dr Luigi Epicoco was on hand to give a second opinion, as Dr Lalli performed a close internal inspection. Further vaginal swabs were taken and fingernails re-examined. Lalli found small scratches on Meredith's inner labia and bruises to her lower belly. The unnatural markings suggested that there could have been rough, quick sex and that the labia had not had time to protect itself with the usual secretions. 'Does that mean she was raped?' the police observers asked. Not necessarily. Similar scratches were observed nearby.

Luca Lalli then continued the visual autopsy to the whole of Meredith's body. His stubble had grown almost into a beard behind his operating mask. His balding patch amid otherwise thick hair was hidden by a green surgeon's hat. Meredith's naked body lay before him. The dieners had removed her clothes.

The next step was to make a visual inspection of the whole body, carefully cleaning the skin and exposed tissues selectively as he went. The objective was to identify every single wound and to reveal any injuries obscured by blood and dirt. Lalli counted no fewer than twenty-three wounds, describing each of them verbally into his tape recorder. Most significantly, there were four knife holes – three in the neck and one in the hand. Five scratches on her neck and face also drew dark frowns from Dr Lalli.

The biggest cut was on the left-hand side of her throat (Stab A) – 8 cm wide and 8 cm deep, about the size of an average human mouth. The cut penetrated backwards and upwards into the head, from the direction of the left side of her lower chin, through the flesh and into the mouth. Eight cm deep in all, from the neck to the oral cavity. The conclusion was self-evident: a blade or a portion of a blade, the length of a credit card or the average length of an index finger, had stabbed her under the chin in an uppercut, thrusting way.

Once he had cleaned the blood away, another knife wound became apparent on the neck. Bruises also became visible. The second knife wound (Stab B), on the right-hand side of her throat, was smaller in width and shallower, and at first glance appeared to slice the carotid artery. The bruises on the neck showed she was also strangled. Her pink eyelids were clear signs of asphyxia, meaning that the supply of oxygen to the body had been cut off by choking. Conclusion: Meredith Kercher had been strangled and stabbed.

Bruises to her right forearm, and on her left thigh, were visible to the naked eye. Scratch marks on her face and a smaller knife prick to her chin. Her hands bore the signs of scratches and a knife wound on her middle finger and palm. Conclusion: Meredith may have tried to fight off her attacker, at the same time as they were trying to muffle her screams.

Having already carried out a detailed investigation of her private parts, Lalli made a second sweep of the area to make sure nothing had been overlooked. No signs of rape were found on further exploratory swabbing, but the samples were bagged and tagged carefully.

DNA sampling to find evidence of the killer's tissue on Meredith proved more difficult. The bruises on her throat were a potential DNA goldmine, as the hands of the murderer or accomplices had been pressed against these spots just a few hours earlier. However, despite microscopic probing of the area, the site was lost to contamination after Lalli was forced to wipe away the blood to uncover the wound. More scrapings from under Meredith's fingernails were taken in search of DNA or fibre traces. Routine blood samples were also extracted from Meredith's tissues.

Meredith's body spent the night alone on the slab, thousands of miles from home. The internal examination was carried out the following day, Sunday, 4 November, after the body had been cleaned thoroughly. Dr Lalli was to begin his terrible but clinical journey into the depths of Meredith's corpse. The words of a pioneering eighteenth-century pathologist Giovanni Morgogni adorn autopsy labs all over the world:

Let the conversation cease,
Let the laughter flee,
This is the place
Where Death delights,
To help the living.

As the invasive part of the procedure got under way, the avuncular Giuliano Mignini and Commissioner Domenico Profazio steeled themselves. Rigor mortis had disappeared and the body's temperature gained equilibrium with the room. The hypostasis was fixed – the blood had coagulated.

The examination started with the head. The following bruises were further inspected and photographed: bruises on the right nostril and lips, cuts and bruises to the left cheek and chin, and bruises to the left and right throat.

A full examination of the gaping wound (Stab A) in the left neck got under way. The hole was positioned 8 cm below the left ear and 1.5 cm towards the front of the neck. The wound exposed the oral cavity, fatty tissues and throat glands. Lalli noted that an important jaw muscle had also been severed. The cut ran obliquely from left to right, almost parallel to the jaw, and extended from left to right and slightly upwards. The second stab wound (Stab B), on the right-hand side, was 1.5 cm wide and extended 4 cm backwards into the flesh. Conclusion:

the smaller incision supported the idea that a second knife was involved.

The team proceeded downwards and identified bruises to the right elbow and forearm, small cuts to the right hand and bruises on the left leg.

Lalli then began to cut open Meredith's body using a powered circular saw and a scalpel. Starting with the head, he removed the scalp by making an incision from ear to ear across the top part of the head. The front flap was peeled away and the back was pulled down across the back of her neck. Lalli cut away a circular piece of skull, in the form of a cap that can be pulled off and replaced, and verified that there were no signs of head damage. He sawed through the skull and opened up the cranium: the brain was pale in colour, indicating that Meredith had suffered from poor circulation whilst alive.

Using surgical instruments Lalli began to peel away the flesh around Stab A on the left-hand side of her neck. Astonishingly, as he began to scrape away the connective tissue around the multiple veins, arteries and nerves, he unearthed an unexpected surprise. The wound had not severed the jugular vein or the internal carotid artery, or even the inferior thyroid vein as first assumed. Nor indeed had the facial nerves been shredded. Conclusion: Stab A *looked* a lot worse than it actually was. In fact, the knife had completely missed a key bundle of life-giving tubes that are on the left-hand side of the neck.

Lalli had hit a brick wall. For a moment he pondered. If the left-side blood carriers had not been pierced, then what had caused the massive loss of blood? There was only one answer: what about the arteries and veins on the opposite side of the neck? He quickly transferred his probe to the right-hand side of the neck. Suddenly, the cold steel of his instrument picked up one half of a seriously ruptured artery – the deep wound on the left side of the throat had been so savage that it had passed through the middle and severed the right thyroid artery, which would have led to massive blood loss.

Surprisingly, the smaller cut (Stab B) on the right-hand side had not severed the external carotid artery, or the internal jugular vein. Stab B was bad but essentially cosmetic.

Opening the throat exposed the hyoid bone, a small and fragile V-shaped structure at the bottom of the tongue. Conclusion: further indication that pressure through strangulation had been exercised on the throat or that the bone had been sliced by the knife.

Now it was time to open up the chest. The dieners placed a body block underneath Meredith's back that pushed the chest up, making it easier to dissect and inspect. Lalli then peeled back her skin and breasts by making a Y-shaped incision from each of the shoulders, joining at the sternum at the base of the rib cage and then on to the pubic bone, deviating to the left of her navel in line with convention.

The Stryker saw sliced through the sternum at the centre of the ribs and the doctor's protective goggles and mask were lightly spattered with bone dust and residue. Shears were used to cut awkward bones. But there was no bleeding as there was no blood pressure. Mignini and Profazio looked on in horror, a stomach-churning sight they would never forget.

Parts of Meredith's heart were scrutinized and a blood sample taken from the inferior vena cava chamber. Major blood vessels were cut open and routinely inspected in case Meredith suffered from a complaint that might have weakened her. None was found.

The lungs were exposed next. Meredith's windpipe contained a piece of mushroom, probably from her last meal. The lungs were weighed in at 340 grammes each. Their foamy consistency suggested that blood had flowed inside. Conclusion: the blood had stopped air from being absorbed into lung cells. In effect, Meredith had drowned in her own blood.

Other alveoli – the special tissues that trap pockets of air for absorption into the body – were white and elongated. Conclusion: signs of suffocation from strangulation.

The liver, spleen and kidneys were removed and found normal. The contents of the stomach were examined. Meredith's last meal consisted of 500 cc of green-brown jelly substance. Lalli identified the matter as partially digested mozzarella cheese, discoloured by intestinal juices and enzymes.

Blood samples and extracts from the liver and kidneys were handed over to the forensics squad. Tests for drug and alcohol abuse proved negative. Conclusion: Meredith was sober when she was murdered and in general was a clean-living girl.

Dr Lalli mulled on his conclusions overnight and on the following day, Monday, 5 November, returned to the hospital to brief Mignini. Dozens of journalists besieged him in his car.

'Dr Lalli, was Meredith raped?' a reporter asked.

'Dr Lalli, how did Meredith die?' another TV journalist inquired.

Italian law is clear: information about an ongoing criminal investigation, technically classified as sub judice, is absolutely confidential. Lalli followed procedure, smiled and said nothing. The pressure continued. In the spirit of cooperation, Lalli threw the pack a bone: 'After I've met with the Chief Prosecutor, there might be a press conference.'

Maybe some kind of statement could be made.

Behind closed doors, Lalli presented his findings to the Chief Prosecutor. Mignini took it all in slowly and nodded. Then the legal fencing began. Frustratingly, Lalli couldn't say whether Meredith had been raped or not.

He lifted his palms in a very Italian way, to indicate doubt, and then he elaborated. 'Slight bruising of the labia happens in normal sex,' he replied. 'If the woman isn't sufficiently aroused.'

'The bruises to her inner thighs could have happened just after death,' Lalli said clearly. He wasn't budging on the idea of rape.

It didn't stop Mignini, whose job was to keep on probing for the definitive, wanting to know what the *likelihood* was that she was raped then.

Lalli: 'Fifty-fifty until we have the DNA results. No sperm from what I can see . . .'

Under the fingernails had drawn a blank also. Moving on to the cause of death, Lalli was on firmer ground. 'Multiple causes,' he said. 'Drowning, strangulation. The hyoid bone in the neck was broken.'

Giuliano Mignini knew all about the significance of the hyoid bone. His other ongoing murder case in connection with the Monster of Florence and the Freemasons involved a body with a broken hyoid bone – an indication of strangulation. But there were still complications, especially in connection with the severed thyroid artery.

Lalli explained: 'Severed, yes. But not fatal. She may have lost a lot of blood, but she didn't die of blood loss. The blood got into her lungs and she drowned.'

Mignini wasn't ecstatic. Why wasn't anything ever simple? he mused.

However, Lalli had saved something of a pay-off until last.

'There are some interesting things to say about the rest of the body. I'd say she fought her attacker. She has a knife wound on the hand and scratch marks to her face, which indicates she was pushed to the ground. The bruise on her left thigh might mean she fell.'

But just as Mignini thought he was getting some detail, Lalli tailed off: 'You know that's not my job. There are forensics experts for that.'

'Anything else?' asked Mignini.

Lalli did have one last thing: 'You might be interested to know that I think she was dressed when she was killed.'

Mignini's ears pricked up.

Lalli responded: 'Well, there's a triangular shape on her chest, which indicates that she had her bra on.'

Mignini recalled that Meredith's bra had been found next to the body. So if Lalli was right, that meant the killer or killers had stabbed her then removed it when she was dead or dying.

Lalli had further evidence to back up the fact that the bra might have been removed as Meredith was actually dying. 'There are small droplets of blood on her chest which are probably from when she was coughing.' Coughing up small amounts of blood as she was choking.

'Time of death?' Mignini asked.

'The last thing she ate may have been mozzarella cheese,' Lalli responded. 'Which we found in her stomach. It takes a couple of hours for food to go through the stomach, so it was within a couple of hours of when she ate the cheese. From the body temperature, and the fact that the body had entered rigor mortis when I got there, so at least twelve hours before.'

Mignini decided to give the media a wide range: 'between 9:15 in the evening and 4:00 in the morning.' He wanted someone out there to feel safe.'

Luca Lalli got up and shook the Prosecutor's hand. The Prosecutor left and the doctor was there alone to face the press.

'How did she die?'

'I can't tell you,' Lalli said.

'Was she raped?'

'I can't tell you,' he repeated. 'There are certainly signs of sexual violence.' Lalli batted off the rest of the questions but a reporter from Italy's main commercial news programme was waiting for him by the car.

'Off the record, do you think there was rape?' the reporter asked.

Lalli: 'No, I don't think so. It's hard to say. There are no clear signs. It's not that simple . . .'

Harmless words. But ones that would come back to haunt him.

8

The Lab Detectives

Forensics: Police Investigation Days 1–3

Friday, 2 November–Sunday, 4 November

As Meredith's body was being cut open on the slab, Amanda Knox whispered seductively in Raffaele's ear. 'I'm going to take you home so we can have wild sex together,' she said. In one hand she held a G-string, and in the other a revealing silk camisole. On her face she wore a smile. Amanda put an arm around her lover's neck and pulled him close for a long, passionate kiss.

On the morning of Saturday, 3 November, Amanda and Raffaele had gone out shopping for, of all things, lingerie. They acted out their seduction in public, Amanda throwing back her hair provocatively, white American teeth biting her lips in playful frustration. The shop owner, Carlo Maria Scotto di Rinaldi, looked away in embarrassment as Amanda rifled through piles of sexy underwear and laughed out loud. Raffaele, dressed in a smart, camouflaged hunting jacket, nipped at the waist, gripped her from behind. Amanda was wearing a black college-style hoodie, which made the wound under her chin harder to detect. She needn't have bothered. The wound was healing rapidly. Her exhibitionism, in full view of the till staff and waiting customers, struck the lingerie shop owner as odd.

Meanwhile, at the murder scene, the forensics teams were working doubly hard in the hope of making up for the previous evening's delays. Some of the fingerprint officers had gone home at 02:00, leaving the blood squad to race on.

In the small shower-room, almost an ensuite to Meredith's bedroom, the murderer or murderers had desperately tried to wash themselves and their weapon(s) clean. Forensics officer Gioia Brocci discovered an unusually long streak of blood that began at the rim of the washbasin and dripped all the way down to the plughole and another following the same dynamic in the bidet. She took the lot on her filter-paper swab. The attackers had also left a smear on the tap. A clear print, of a bare foot soaked in blood, was found on a cheap blue bathmat woven with a sea shell pattern. Patrizia Stefanoni advanced a theory to fit and explain the shower-room blood spats, moving her arms around kata-style to map out the movement of the murder weapon.

'This is the knife moving around,' she said, extending her right arm away from her hips in an arc motion, as through she was throwing a frisbee. 'These blood drops on the tap were left by the knife. Too many droplets and look, the blood in the basin and bidet is paler, so it's the knife that has been washed at that particular point.'

Pointing to other drops, she continued: 'The drops on the box of cotton buds and the basin are dark. This is blood before being washed.' Stefanoni cracked a thin professional smile, lips closed, to reinforce the breakthrough. As always, she was all business.

But the success was short-lived. In Meredith's room, as the night drew on, Gioia Brocci's concentration waned. She yawned and carried on numbering the artefacts. Meredith's bra clasp, found underneath the bloodied pillow, looked lost amongst the debris. Officers were now climbing all over the busy scene. Someone called her from inside the house for assistance. Amid the confusion she left the item without an individual marker, assuming it would be collected later, along with the larger bra that was close by.

Morning brought bright sunshine streaming through the window, and renewed vigour. As fresh shift officers bolstered the flagging team, the hunt for the murder weapon was immediately prioritized, as so far none had been found. The pathologist's estimate of a blade longer than 8 cm was passed down the line to the coal face, in a bid to focus the officers' attention. The dimension matched two bloodstains found on Meredith's white bed sheet that looked like the outlines of a blade. The kitchen drawers were full of knives. But the sheer volume of evidence now being extracted, or piling up for further processing, was taking its toll. The officers were getting sloppy. In the rush to move on, only two of the kitchen knives were taken away for examination. An unusually low number, critics would later say.

Suddenly a rush of excitement pierced through the ranks. A separate batch of kitchen knives had been discovered in a bag in Amanda's room. However, a false alarm was declared almost at once – they were still sealed in their original packets and, at first glance, were more than likely unused. For the sake of completeness the knives should have been taken. Astonishingly, the police left them where they were.

Disappointment was rapidly disintegrating into frustration. As is the case with many crime-scene investigations, the law of diminishing returns was depressing the early highs and sapping morale. The officers needed fresh leads, virgin territory, more space. Some went outside, glad of a breather. As if by magic, drops of blood were observed on the steps that led down to the flat below, whose door Mignini had ordered broken down by policewoman Lorena Zugarini earlier. Maybe they had given up on Meredith's boyfriend and his flatmates too easily, the officers concluded. Hopes grew when the bloodstains, similar in appearance to Meredith's, led into the living room of the downstairs flat and on to the sofa. 'This is looking promising,' one of the coppers said with a smile. More incriminating evidence was found in the corridor – seven cannabis plants. An old penknife was quickly unearthed in the garden. They collected the duvet on the bed and shook it softly to see if there was anything of interest on it.

Back in Meredith's room above, the massive drop of blood on the door handle presented no fingerprints, so was swabbed for DNA analysis instead – often the two tests are incompatible because of chemical cross-contamination. Meredith's bedroom was desolate. Her stripped bed was exceptionally grim-looking, the mattress covered with an ill-fitting bottom sheet and strewn with trinkets from her life mixed with the detritus of murder. A black-and-white sock was draped over the handle of her bulky tan leather WAG bag. The matching one, stained with blood, lay next to her body. A white bloodstained towel was also on the bed, similar to the other soaked towels, including a green one, found under her body.

Stefanoni looked pitifully at the prison-style bed made of black tubing and thin wood slats. Underneath, there was a cheap black nylon suitcase waiting to be packed for her Christmas trip home, now just a few weeks away. Meredith would have celebrated her 22nd birthday over the holiday. Strewn around the case, there was more evidence of her busy lifestyle – lecture notes, a textbook, untidy multi-plugs, a biro.

The bra and underwear near the body were taken away for

DNA testing, as well as her jeans, parts of which the attacker might have touched, such as the waist and the pockets, and the cuffs of her jumper. The handbag on the bed was tagged and taken away too.

A macabre handprint in blood on the wall, assumed to be Meredith's, became a focal point but disappointingly Giunta declared it was useless fingerprint-wise. He was confident, however, that he could get a match from the 'nice handprint' on the pillow that Meredith's body had rested on, next to what looked like a shoeprint. In the interests of completeness, the scientists returned to their starting point to see if they had missed anything – the room of the fourth flatmate, Laura Mezzetti.

Meanwhile, Laura had returned from her long weekend in Montefiascone. Immediately, after reporting to the police station, she became concerned by Amanda's claims to have found the body. Laura, pensive and suspicious now, drilled Amanda with her eyes. Looking, thinking, sussing. Bang! Immediately she picked up on the scratch under Amanda's chin. She didn't have that two days before, Laura thought.

She was also alarmed by Raffaele's behaviour. He just walked up to her and started to tell her about specific timings, as though he wanted her to believe his story. She too raised a few questions about Amanda's relationship with Meredith. Laura echoed the suspicions that were being voiced by the English girls. That morning Amanda and Raffaele had been back to the police station. They had gone down with the English girls on the mini metro train. Their dislike of Amanda grew. She was noisy, callous.

'All the way down here,' Robyn Butterworth told the police. 'Amanda kept on telling me she knew everything about how Meredith died.' Robyn drew breath. 'Don't you think that's odd?'

Next up, Amy Frost painted some interesting colour on Amanda's character assessment. Amy said: 'Meredith didn't like the fact that Amanda kept a beauty case with a vibrator and condoms in full view.'

Afterwards Amanda had been brought back to the flat for more questioning. There she met a new face from Rome, Edgardo Giobbi, the head of the violent crime department, as well as forensics. He was powerful, sleek and articulate.

Not all the investigators were convinced by Laura's suspicions, and those of others, including the English girls. It didn't add up, they concluded, simply because Amanda didn't seem to have a motive. In addition, she had returned to the crime scene voluntarily that day, accompanied by detectives, and had been very cooperative to boot. Though the questions during the visit weren't aimed at her and she wasn't put under pressure, Amanda had done well to answer many personal and probing questions about Meredith's private life, honestly and in detail.

On the whole she gave no grounds for suspicion. However, there was one slip up. Giobbi recalled how he handed Amanda a pair of shoe covers before entering the boys' apartment below her own. Amanda swivelled her hips and said, 'Oopla.' The unusual display made him turn his 'investigative attention' on her.

Then, also during a second round of police interviews on the Saturday, Filomena Romanelli dropped a bombshell, revealing that shortly before the murder Amanda and Meredith had a clash of personalities. 'As of mid-October, for the last two weeks, they weren't on good terms,' Laura told the murder squad. 'Before then, they were always together. I mentioned it to Laura.' During a five-hour stint at the station, Filomena added: 'I said to Laura that I thought that Mez was a bit fed up with Amanda. Probably because Amanda was excitable and exuberant and Meredith was quiet and hard-working.'

The final straw for Amanda came when Mignini got the results back from the autopsy. The section on the neck injuries confirmed his worst fears. 'How could Amanda have been *so certain* that Meredith had her throat slit?' he asked his colleagues. 'Did anyone tell her at the crime scene?'

Sunday, 4 November

The mourners bowed their heads as the haunting notes of the Italian version of 'The Last Post' drifted across the square. At Perugia's war memorial, soldiers had gathered to honour the dead on Army Day. The impeccable uniforms of Italian soldiers, often tailored by the country's world-renowned designers, contrasted with the shabby, crumbling marble of the fountain. The Scandanavian pines swaying noisily above them jarring oddly with Mediterranean palm trees that had been arranged neatly. Perugia, a city of contrast, even in its vegetation.

Though it was a public holiday, the forensics team was still hard at work, testing samples of hair, tissue and toilet paper, at 7 Pergola Road. Mignini pondered deeply on how to play Amanda Knox in the coming hours. Today, he was sure, would be a make-or-break day. Knox was fronting it out, he felt, and if she did have something to hide, it didn't look as if she'd fold under questioning any time soon. In addition, her story was being backed up by Sollecito, and vice versa. Fortunately, police officers the world over have a few tricks up their sleeve to deal with this particular state of limbo.

This investigative phenomenon, when a witness is teetering on the edge of falling into the realms of suspect status, is a common one. In Britain, the police often serve up suspicious people to the media, persuading them to do televised appeals.

Seeing how they cope under fierce studio lights and a grilling from reporters unrestrained in their questioning by the Police and Criminal Evidence Act sometimes throws up something new to go on, especially when an investigation has reached an impasse. Detectives often plant awkward questions with compliant journalists, about issues they couldn't bring up themselves without formally arresting the suspect.

In the case of Tracie Andrews, who murdered her boyfriend Lee Harvey in a fake road-rage attack, the police gave her enough rope in this way and she hanged herself on TV by being inconsistent. In the US, officers are allowed to lure their prey into complex honey traps to facilitate confessions. In Italy, Mignini settled on a subtle psychological trick – to rattle Amanda by taking her back to the murder scene once again, but this time focusing on *her own* movements on the day of the murder.

To make it look routine, the police invited Filomena Romanelli to go through her possessions again to check if anything had been stolen. Fortunately, she was tired after having spent five hours with the police the day before, and exited the scene quickly, leaving Amanda centre stage and alone.

At first she held her own without difficulty. Whilst being questioned in the garden, Amanda stuck to her line admirably and added a sprinkling of new detail, giving the tale more credibility.

Then Amanda's surefootedness appeared to slip. She began using hand gestures to reinforce lame points. At first, she put her hands together and then moved them up and down. And she began to struggle to remember certain events. She was thinking *too hard*. She showed anxiety and stress. Profazio scratched his head, sensing there was something wrong. In parts of her story, she was too clear and emphatic. In others, she was too flaky.

Generously, Profazio thought the inconsistency might be down to cultural differences.

Mignini arrived on cue to take up the baton – and go deeper into the mystery. To go inside the house. He put out his pipe, smiled and asked Amanda to put on latex gloves and shoe covers. Slowly, they walked past her own bedroom and Mignini deliberately let her see that officers were checking for finger-prints. Heads turned. Eyes peered. Gioia Brocci looked up ominously, a bloody swab in her hand.

In the kitchen, Mignini suddenly opened a drawer.

'Are there any knives missing, Miss Knox?'

His words had scarcely left his mouth when Amanda broke down. She put her hands over her ears and began trembling. She couldn't answer. She just shook.

Mission accomplished. In police terms, her reaction spoke vol-umes, as far as they were concerned. Mignini put his arms around Amanda's shoulders and took her back out into the fresh November air, before letting her go back to Raffaele's.

'What do you make of that?' he asked Domenico Profazio.

'Bad, Mr Mignini. Looks very bad – for her, that is.'

Mignini relit his pipe.

It was the end of the day when Patrizia Stefanoni could at last report the latest to the Prosecutor. She adjusted her hair while she waited for Mignini to free himself from his incessant round of *ad hoc* consultations. Her hair was brushed over her brow, her long fringe curving inwards, her curls covering her cheeks.

After detailing the more obvious samples, Stefanoni revealed:

The best footprints, the ones with the concentric circles, are a trail going from the victim's room, through the corridor and living room, out through the front door. The path you would follow to flee the scene. We think they are Nike Air Force One, size seven or eight.

Next to the body, there is a clean square patch of space on the floor. Blood is all around it, except this area is clean. This indicates that something was there when it all happened. Probably the Italian dictionary.

There's also a long stringy stain between the sofa and the table, in front of the fridge in the living area. We've got blood on the lavatory cover too and on the drainpipe going into the wall, apart from the blood in the basin, bidet and on the light switch.

Just then Mignini was interrupted. Important news had arrived from London. A British Sunday newspaper had published an exclusive interview with Raffaele in which he gave a different version of events leading up to the murder. Mignini scribbled down four points of difference in his pad:

- On the night of the murder, Raffaele said he was at a party with Amanda and not at his flat as previously stated.
- He said that Amanda had gone back to 7 Pergola Road the following day at around midday, instead of two hours earlier at 10 a.m., as Amanda had just told him.
- Raffaele claimed that *he* had tried to knock down Meredith's door, and because he had failed, that *he* had called the police.
- Finally, it seemed to the police as though Raffaele was trying to deflect suspicion away from himself by claiming that the killer had come through Filomena's window.

'There were drops of blood everywhere in the bathroom,' he had told the *Sunday Mirror*.

Meanwhile, inside the house, fingerprint boffin Agatino

Giunta made his final throw of the dice in an effort to seek out the last of the near-invisible marks. The cyanoacrylate test he selected involved vaporizing a superglue base chemical over the surface of the wardrobe doors. This is then baked under special tungsten lights, to reveal even the faintest prints. Giunta removed Meredith's wardrobe doors and placed them on chairs to perform the procedure. It was worth it – several previously undiscovered prints emerged from the reacting chemical cocktail. Overall, however, the picture wasn't so rosy – of the thousands of fingerprints tested for, only 108 were found to be readable and of these, only forty-seven complete. And then there was that bloody hand print on the pillow no one could account for.

Back at the Postal Police offices, an officer reported in to Bartolozzi. 'Sir, something strange here. I've been studying Sollecito's telephone traffic and he received no calls after nine on the night of the 1st; in fact a message was delivered to him at 6:02 in the morning. His standard routine is that he makes calls until late into the night, but that night nothing. He picked up a message his dad sent that night at nine at just after six.'

9

Talk of Death

Formal Interviews: Days 4 and 5

Monday, 5 November–Tuesday, 6 November

'Bad news.' Patrizia Stefanoni rang Mignini with the results for the blood trail to the downstairs flat first thing in the morning. 'It's a red herring,' she reiterated. 'Just cat's blood from one of their pets.'

Mignini's heart sank. He looked at the photograph on his desk – his three daughters, who were just a little younger than Meredith Kercher.

A weary Domenico Profazio then briefed the prosecuting magistrate on the latest versions of Amanda and Raffaele's alibi, gleaned from the previous day's events.

'Raffaele and Knox say Meredith got up late on the day of the murder, skipped breakfast, and then went out to eat. After smoking a joint together at 7 Pergola, Amanda and Raffaele then say they went out at about 6 p.m. But here's the interesting bit.' The Flying Squad chief shook his head in amazement. He continued: 'Knox says they went to Sollecito's place. While Raffaele says they went for a two-hour walk around the old town, Amanda then says she went home and read Harry Potter in German! And Raffaele says all that stuff in the papers about going out. Then we have the fact that his phone was off, and so was Amanda's.' Profazio then went back to the murder scene, leaving Mignini alone in his office.

Mignini's spirits lifted slightly. He picked up the telephone and dialled Edgardo Giobbi to discuss the inconsistencies with him.

Mignini: 'It isn't much, but it's at least something to go on.' As Mignini mulled it over, the Roman police officer took the initiative. At 21:20 on Monday, 5 November, three days after Meredith's body had been discovered, he ordered Commissioners Chiacchiera and Napoleoni to get Raffaele in for a more formal interrogation. 'And make sure you put pressure on him – I want the real story.' He drove up to Perugia to make sure.

Raffaele and Amanda had just finished eating a pizza together when they received a call from Chiacchiera ordering him in. Raffaele drove his black Audi A3 down to the bunker-like police station and parked in the courtyard. Some of the lowly paid officers looked on. There were sneers about the 'poor little rich kid'. Raffaele was oblivious – Amanda was sitting at his side. She had chosen to accompany him to give him moral support and was there under no obligation; the police had only asked for Raffaele. It was 23:00 when he entered the small room where Commissioner Profazio awaited him.

After twenty minutes of taking his personal details, asking other routine questions, and setting up the recording instruments, the questioning started blandly: 'Did he know Meredith? What did he think of Giacomo Silenzi, Meredith's boyfriend? What did he think of the fact they had found cannabis plants downstairs? Oh, and do you ever smoke it?' Then the pressure started.

Raffaele handed over his phone as Profazio turned up the

heat. Career criminals can often withstand hours of interrogation by keeping their body language neutral – back straight, palms up on each knee, eyes focused on a single point in the room, repeating 'No comment' over and over. Raffaele had been cool as ice to begin with, mainly coasting on his intelligence, but in reality, when the chips were down, he was easy meat. He was a student whose daddy had bought him a tasty sports car; not a buck Mafioso who has spent his life in and out of police stations. The officer's plan was to niggle the arrogant kid – and let him hang himself.

Round one involved hijacking Raffaele with their secret intelligence about his lack of alibi: mobile phone off about 9 p.m.? Why was that? Oh, and do you carry a knife with you?

'Yes, I have collected knives since I was fourteen,' he rebutted, weakly at first, totally caught off-guard, bemused by the accuracy of their inside info. 'My dad collects guns . . .' Vainly, he tried to pass off the weapon-collecting as a normal family pursuit.

'Do you have one with you, by any chance?' the interrogator asked. Shaking his head in disbelief, Raffaele had no choice but to show them his flick-knife. A look of guilt passed over his face.

Then the officers chipped away at his personal weaknesses, quickly taking the high ground over his heavy dope-smoking. Subtle snipes that his behaviour was incongruous, however slightly, with his family's standing. And all the time, as if to underline the point, soberly reminding him that he was being questioned about the death of a human being. Guilt, the police pondered, can be a useful burden that sharpens the mind.

Amanda was biding her time in a nearby room. Astonishingly, she was performing acrobatics. A policeman walking by commented on her fitness. 'Oh, that's nothing! Watch this.' Oblivious to her surroundings, Amanda leapt into a cartwheel, flipped on to her back in the crab position and pushed up with feet and hands. The grand finale was the splits. The police looked on stunned. Officer Lorena Zugarini told Knox it was not the right place for such activities. Profazio said it was inappropriate. Napoleoni called her downright 'odd'.

But nothing was to keep them from their focus – pushing Raffaele psychologically until he broke. Napoleoni took away his shoes away for a proper forensic examination. No big deal. But for the hunted, it felt significant. A finger was being pointed. A screw was being turned.

Raffaele went pale. His neck tightened. The chase was on. At first, he gave good sport, tracing through his story and swerving to avoid trapping himself.

'As I said, Amanda and I went back to her place at 7 Pergola for something to eat at about 2 p.m. Meredith was still in bed, sleeping off the Halloween party. When she got up she got dressed and we joked about the fact that she was wearing her ex-boyfriend's jeans.'

Then, he deftly laid down new details. Like a new scent, momentarily throwing the officers off his track. Policemen are always excited by fresh information.

'Amanda and I had something to eat and we smoked a joint. Then we went out at about 6 p.m., when it was getting dark. We walked along Corso Vannucci and we decided we wanted something to drink so we headed for the pub House of Delirium but it was closed. Then we went home. It must have been half past eight or nine when we got home. I went on my computer to work.'

But it wasn't good enough. Raffaele's shoulders hunched. His eyes looked for a way out. It was time for the interrogators to move in for the kill.

'Raffaele, tell me, are you sure you were with Amanda on the evening Meredith was killed?'

He didn't know which way to run. In the confusion, he threw up another new revelation, presumably to muddy the tracks.

'At 8:15 p.m. Amanda got a call from her boss at Le Chic to say she needn't go to work so we went home.'

Raffaele explained that Le Chic was the bar where Amanda worked part-time as a waitress.

'But,' the policeman asked, 'did you stay with Amanda all night, Raffaele? That's what we really want to know.'

Raffaele suddenly seemed to give up the struggle.

'At least I went home. I can't remember if Amanda was with me. I think Amanda told me she was going to the Chic anyway to meet up with some friends. I remember she came back at 1 a.m.

'To be honest I do a lot of dope on holidays and I'm confused. I can't remember if she went out . . .'

Finally, the quarry had been brought to bay.

Significantly, for the first time in nearly four days Raffaele Sollecito had stopped giving the love of his life a solid alibi. It was now midnight on Monday evening, and in the light of this new twist, Monica Napoleoni ordered the interrogation to switch to the acrobatic American in the corridor.

All day a growing tide of suspicion, buoyed by her strange but cool demeanour, had been eroding Knox's reputation. A second set of press pictures, taken the day before when she had returned to the murder scene, were splashed all over the papers. The images had reinforced the unique selling points of the story so far in many people's minds. Viewers and readers seemed to be mesmerized by Knox's enigmatic appeal. All over the world Amanda Knox was becoming an object of warped sexual desire, as often happens when attractive young women become figures of suspicion in murder cases. Commentators drew comparisons with Joanna Lees, the attractive but misunderstood girlfriend of Peter Falconio, the backpacker who had been mysteriously murdered in the Australian bush. Lees had been smeared unjustly for her private life. Faint echoes from another recent case were also setting the tone. The media was still reeling from the Madeleine McCann case, in which a three-year-old girl from a middle-class family had disappeared from a foreign town. Maddie's mother Kate had become a figure of fascination. Later, the red-top obsession turned to vilification because of her perceived unemotional demeanour.

Now, in Perugia, Raffaele's new evidence had given detectives an excuse to poke away behind the image of the clean-cut young student to see what dark secrets might be lurking behind it. In addition, rumours were circulating that Meredith was killed after she refused to take part in a sex game. In fact, detectives were briefing off the record that she was stabbed resisting the advances of a group of people involved in a drug-fuelled orgy. No one could prove it yet but that was the best hypothesis. Today they were determined to extract facts that stood the theory up.

Knox smiled as she motored through her alibi for the night of the murder. The officers ticked off the events.

'So you slept at Raffaele's that night. He cooked fish. The pipes under the sink broke and the kitchen flooded. You had sex, you watched a film, oh, two films. You smoked dope.

'We need the details, Miss Knox.'

Her coping strategy differed from Raffaele's. The on-top American wasn't going to play the victim. She wasn't going to make herself the hunted.

'Well, yes, we got home to my place about 4:30 or 5:00 and had a bite to eat. We smoked a joint, just one, and then came back to Raffaele's. We were there all evening. We had sex and I read a book, Harry Potter, in German. We watched a French film called *Amélie* which finished around 11 p.m. We were there until 10:30 in the morning.'

Amélie, the kitschy feel-good rom-com about a young girl who lives with her head in the clouds.

Amanda seemed more agile in her thinking than Raffaele. She took cues from her interrogators and seemed to spin them round to her advantage. She mirrored behaviour with perceptive ease. She searched for pointers. The policewoman picked up Amanda's mobile phone and began scrolling down the messages in search of the text she had received at around 20:15, the one Raffaele had mentioned. And to look for any inconsistencies that the phone might throw up.

Amanda struck the police as worried. She fidgeted. The tone darkened. The interpreter tried to calm her down with small talk to Amanda in English. 'Memory is a strange thing. I broke my leg a few years ago and my mind just completely cancelled it out.'

Amanda nodded as though this had given her an idea. When the questions resumed, Amanda suddenly told the officers that she couldn't remember anything.

Napoleoni countered deftly. A policeman walked past her brusquely. Amanda thought she'd been hit on the head.

'Well, what's this message at 8:18 saying, "See you later"?' she asked.

At first Amanda played it neutral. 'It's from my boss, Patrick Lumumba. He owns the bar Le Chic where I work on Tuesdays and Thursdays.'

Napoleoni nodded and let her finish, before firing back: 'And so what's this at 8:32 p.m.? You reply back: "See you later, *buona serata* [in English, "Have a nice evening"]. What does that mean? Did you have an appointment?'

Amanda looked confused, opening the way for Napoleoni to play her trump card – without warning she told Amanda that Raffaele wasn't backing her up any longer. A sense of betrayal coloured the dialogue. But she didn't spend long contemplating defeat. Amanda's mind went into overdrive. She began to shiver.

'Yes, I seem to remember.' She looked at the phone, as if to take up the cue. It was 01:45. 'Yes, I remember we met up with Patrick to go home. He wanted to meet Meredith. He wanted to get to know her.'

Her temporary amnesia was gone. She looked at the text. A catalyst sparking the past into life. More of the story came flooding out.

'I seem to remember something. He was in her room. Oh, my God! And yes, I could hear the screams. He was in her room and had locked the door. I was in the kitchen. I had to put my hands to my ears to block out the screaming . . .'

The police sterographer wrote it all down in a statement Amanda would be required to sign. Napoleoni had made a major breakthrough. She was exhilarated at finally getting Amanda to open up, but her enthusiasm was tempered by a curious mixture of frustration, impatience and worry that every police officer will be familiar with once a suspect has began cooperating. The overwhelming urge to motor on, and to get every cough and spit out of the interviewee while she was still onside, must be restrained so that the statement can be taken in compliance with the law. Frustration – from the wait. Impatience – not knowing whether the suspect will clam up given time to think or refuse to say more after a lawyer has got involved.

Monica Napoleoni knew the implications of what she had just heard. She was disciplined and stopped Amanda in her tracks, admirably curtailing her own curiosity.

'Amanda, I'm glad you've remembered, but the law now requires me to do two things. You have now become a suspect as an accomplice to murder and you have to tell the Prosecutor what you have just said. Are you ready to do that?'

The tables had turned. Everyone was now dancing to Amanda's tune. She was about to serve up the name of the alleged killer, officially and on a plate – a mystery man called Patrick Lumumba. Who owned a bar. Who was black. The details were sketchy, but in the dim recesses of the early hours, and with extreme pressure to solve the case building up, it was enough to make a possibility of a fairy-tale ending. The posh white kids were now off the hook for yielding the killer blow – and a seedy black bar-owner was now firmly in the frame.

The early-morning call to Mignini woke his wife, dog and daughters. He got dressed in the dark and stumbled out into the cold. At the station he immediately ordered a strong coffee, and then the arrest of 'this Patrick Lumumba, whoever he is'. He made the decision after reading the statements of both Raffaele and Amanda, who were still there. For the second time in three days both of them had spent the night at the police station.

Although she was technically now a suspect, and therefore had no obligation to make any further statements, Amanda asked to be questioned again. At 03:30 she repeated her remarkable story to Mignini. She said that at 21:00 on the night of the murder she met with Lumumba at the sunken basketball court at Grimana Square, opposite 7 Pergola, and returned with him to see Meredith at the house. Mignini said nothing. But word was beginning to spread around the station. The Lumumba line was certainly a cute move, the officers couldn't deny it. Not only had she saved herself; in one stroke, she had plugged the weakness in the line by explaining away Raffaele's alibi wobble *and* believably blamed the murder on a stranger. In addition, there were bonuses. As far as her credibility was concerned, she had stopped some of the rot caused by her earlier bad behaviour and, if she played it right, her stock was potentially on the way up. At the same time, she was also shoring up her drippy Italian boyfriend. If nothing else, this plucky American girl was capable and industrious or at worst, as she would claim later, simply confused under pressure.

At 05:54 the session ended. Amanda was offered a breakfast bun and a vending-machine drink. Cheerfully, she asked a passing policeman for a piece of paper and wrote down her statement: When the policeman passed by again, she gave it to him. 'Here's a present for the Prosecutor.' The statement read:

> I can't remember. I want to tell you what happened because it's left me really shocked and I'm terrified of Patrick, the African boy who owns the Le Chic pub where I work sometimes. I saw him on the evening of 1 November after I replied 'See you' to his text message. We met at about 9 p.m. on the basketball court in Piazza Grimana and went to my place. I can't remember if Meredith was already there or if she turned up later. What I can say is that they went into the bedroom. The only thing I can say is that at a certain point I heard Meredith screaming.
>
> I was scared and put my hands over my ears. I can't remember anything else . . . I was in shock, but I could imagine what was going on.

10

Electronic Fingerprint

Things were looking up for Amanda and Raffaele. Though both of them were detained at the station for further inquiries, and crucially while Mignini decided what to do with them, the Lumumba revelation had definitely helped their position. Their prospects turned even rosier when details of emails and phone calls from Amanda began to emerge. The story so far, as told from Amanda's point of view to her friends and family, threw a completely different light on events – a light that cast her in the role of an angel, and a wounded one at that.

On the morning of Tuesday, 6 November, a few hours after her confession, a few hours after she had thrown an unknown black barman to the lions, police recovered an email that Amanda had sent two days before, on Saturday, 4 November.

To: My Close Friends
From: Amanda Knox, Perugia.

This is an email for everyone, because Id like to get it all out and not have to repeat myself a hundred times like I've been having to do at the police station. Some of you already know some things, some of you know nothing. What Im about to say I cant say to journalists or newspapers, and I require that of anone receiving this information as well. This is [my] account of how I found my roommate murdered the morning of Friday, November 2nd.

The last time I saw Meredith, 22, English, beautiful, funny, was when I came home from spending the night at a friends house. It was the day after Halloween, Thursday. I got home and she was still asleep, but after I had taken a shower and was fumbling around the kitchen she emerged from her room with the blood of her costume (vampire) still dripping down her chin. We talked for a while in the kitchen, how the night went, what our plans were for the day. Nothing out of the ordinary. Then she went to take a shower and I began to start eating a little while I waited for my friend (Raffaele – at whose house I stayed over) to arrive at my house. He came right after I started eating and he made himself some pasta. As we were eating together Meredith came out of the shower and grabbed some laundry or put some laundry in, one or the other and returned into her room after saying hi to Raffael. After lunch I began to play guitar with Raffael and Meredith came out of her room and went to the door. She said bye and left for the day. It was the last time I saw her alive.

After a little while of playing guitar me and Raffael went to his house to watch movies and after to eat dinner and generally spend the evening and night indoors. We didnt go out. The next morning I woke up around 1030 and after grabbing my few things I left Raffael's appartment and walked the five minute walk back to my house to once again take a shower and grab a [change] of clothes. I also needed to grab a mop because after dinner Raffael had spilled a lot of water on the floor of his kitchen by accident and didnt have a mop to clean it up. So I arrived home and the first abnormal thing I noticed was the door was wide open. Here's the [thing about] the door to our house: it's broken, in such a way that you have to use the keys to keep it closed. If we dont have the door locked, it is really easy for the [wind] to blow the door open, and so, my roommates and I always have the door locked unless we are running really quickley to bring the garbage out or to get something from the neighbors who live below us. (Another important piece of [information]: for those who dont know, i inhabit a house of two stories, of which my three roommates and i share the second story appartment. there are four Italian guys of our age between 22 and 26 who live below us. we are all [quite] good friends and we talk often. Giacomo is especially welcome because he plays guitar with me and Laura, one of my roommates, and is, or was dating Meredith. The other three are Marco, Stefano, and Ricardo.) Anyway, so the door was wide open. Strange, yes, but not so strange that I really thought anything about it. I assumed someone in the house was doing exactly what I just said, taking out the trash or talking really [quickly] to the neighbors downstairs. So I closed the door behind me but I didnt lock it, assuming that the person who left the door open would like to come back in. When I entered I called out if anyone was there, but no one responded and I assumed that if anyone was there, they were still asleep. Laura's door was open which meant she wasn't home, and Filomenas door was also closed. My door was open like always and Merediths door was closed, which to me [meant] she was sleeping. I undressed in my room and took a quick shower in one of the two bathrooms in my house, the one that is right next to Meredith and my bedrooms (situated right next to one another). It was after I stepped out of the shower and onto the mat that I noticed the blood in the bathroom. It was on the mat I was using to dry my feet and there were drops of blood in the sink. At first I thought the blood might have come [from] my ears which I had pierced [extensively] not too long ago, but then immediately I know it wasnt mine becaus the stains on the mat were too big for just droplets [from] my ear, and when I touched the blood in the sink it was caked on already. There was also blood smeered on the faucet. Again, however, I thought it was strange, because my roommates and I are very clean and we wouldnt leave blood [in the] bathroom, but I assumed that perhaps Meredith was having menstral issues and hadnt cleaned up yet. Ew! but nothing to worry about. I left the bathroom and got dressed in my room. After I got dressed I went to the other bathroom in my house, the one that Filomena [and] Laura use, and used their hairdryer to obviously dry my hair and it was after I was putting back the dryer that I noticed the shit that was left in the toilet, something that definately no one in out house would do. I started feeling a little uncomfortable and so I grabbed the mop from out closet and [left] the house, closing and locking the door that no one had come back through while I was in the shower, and I returned to Raffael's place. After we had used the mop to clean up the kitchen I told Raffael about what I had seen in the house over breakfast. The strange blood in the bathroom, the door wide open, the shit left in the toilet. He suggested I call one of my roommates, so I called Filomena. Filomena had been at a party the night before with her boyfriend Marco (not the same Marco who lives downstairs but we'll call him Marco-f as in Filomena and the other can be Marco-n as in neighbor). She also told me that Laura wasnt at home and hadnt been because she was on business in Rome. Which meant the only one who had spent the night at our house last night was Meredith, and she was as of yet unaccounted for. Filomena seemed really worried, so I told her Id call Meredith and then call her back. I called both of Merediths phones the English one first and last and the Italian one between. The first time I called the English phone [it] rang and then sounded as [if] there was disturbance, but no one answered. I then called the Italian phone and it just kept ringing, no answer. I called her English phone again and this time an English voice told me her phone was out of service. Raffael and I gathered our things and went back to my house.

I unlocked the door and Im going to tell this really slowly to get everything right so just have patience with me. The living room/kitchen was fine. Looked perfectly normal. I was checking for signs of our things missing, should there have been a burglar in our house the night before. Filomenas room was closed, but when I [opened] the door her room and a mess and her window was open and completely broken, but her computer was still sitting

on her desk like it always was and this confused me.
Convinced that we had been robbed I went to Lauras
room and looked quickley in, but it was spottless, like it
hadnt even been [touched]. This too, I thought was odd. I
then went into the part of the house that Meredith and I
share and checked my room for things missing, which
there werent. Then I knocked on Merediths room. At first I
thought she was alseep so I knocked gently, but when she
didnt respond I knocked louder and louder until I was
really banging on her door and shouting her name. No
response. Panicing, I ran out onto our terrace to see if
maybe I could see over the ledge into her room from the
window, but I couldnt see in. Bad angle. I then went into
the bathroom where I had dried my hair and looked really
quickly into the toilet. In my panic I thought I hadnt seen
anything there, which to me meant whoever was in my
house had been there when I had been there. As it turns
out the police told me later that the toilet was full and that
the shit had just fallen to the bottom of the toilet, so I didnt
see it. I ran outside and down to our neighbors door. The
lights were out but I banged [on the] door anyway. I
wanted to ask them if they had heard anything the night
before, but no one was home. I ran back into the house. In
the living room Raffael told me he wanted to see if he
could break down Merediths door. He tried, and cracked
the door, but we couldnt open it. It was then that we
decided to call the cops. There are two types of cops in
italy, carbanieri (local, dealing with traffic and domestic
calls) and the police investigaters. He first called his sister
for advice and then called the carbanieri. I then called
[Filomena] who said she would be on her way home
immediately. While we were waiting, two ununiformed

police investigaters came to our house. I showed them
what I could and told them what I knew. Gave them phone
numbers and explained a bit in broken Italian, and then
Filomena arrived with her boyfriend Marco-f and two other
friends of hers. All together we checked the house out,
talked to the police and in a big [word missing] they all
opened Merediths door. I was in the kitchen [standing]
aside, having really done my part for the situation. But
when they opened Merediths door and I heard Filomena
scream 'a foot! a foot!' in Italian I immedaitely tried to get
to Merediths room but Raffael grabbed me and took me
out of the house. The police told everyone to get out and
not long afterward the carabinieri arrived and then soon
afterward, more police investigators. They took all of our
informaton and asked us the same questions over and
over. At the time I had only what I was wearing and my
[badge], which thankfully had my passport in it and my
wallet. No jacket though, and I was freezing. After sticking
around at the [house] for a bit, the police told us to go to
the station to give testimony, which I did. I was in a room
for six hours straight after that without seeing anyone else,
answering questions in Italian for the first hour and then
they brought in an interpreter and he helped [me] out with
the details that I didnt know the words for. They asked me
of course about the [...] morning, the last time I saw her,
and because I was the closest to her, questions about her
habits and her relationships. Afterward, when they were
taking my fingerprints, I met two of Merediths English
friends, two girls she goes out with, including the [last]
one who saw her alive that night she was murdered. They
also had their prints taken. After that, this was around 9 at
night by this time, I was taken into the waiting room where

there was various other people who I all knew from varous
places who all knew Meredith. Her friends from England,
my roommates, even the owner of the pub she most
frequented. After a while my neighbors were taken in too,
having just arived home from a weeklong vacation in their
home town, which [explained] why they werent home
when I banged on their door. Later than that another guy
showed up and was taken in for questioning, a guy I dont
like but who both Meredith and I knew from different
occasions, a Morracan guy that I only know by his
nickname amongst the girls 'shaky'. Then I sat around in
this waiting room wthout having the chance to leave or eat
anything besides vending maschine food (which gave me
a hell of a stomache ache) until 530 in the morning.
During this time I received calls from a lot of different
people, family mostly of course, and I also talked with the
rest. Especially to find out what exactly was in Merediths
room [when they] opened it. Apparently her body was
lying under a sheet, and with her foot sticking out and
there was a lot of blood. Whoever had did this had slit her
throat. They told me to be back in at 11am. I went home to
Raffael's place and ate something substantial, and passed
out. In the morning Raffael drove me [back] to the police
station but had to leave me when they said they [wanted]
to take me back to the house for [questioning]. Before I
go on, Id like to [say] that I was strictly told not to speak
about this, but Im speaking with you people who are not
involved and who cant do anything bad except talk to
journalists, which I hope you wont do. I have to get this off
my chest because its pressing down on me and it helps to
know that someone besides me knows something, and
that Im not the one who knows the most out of everyone.

At the house they asked me very personal questions about Meredith's life and also about the personalities of our neighbors. How well did I know them? Pretty well, we are friends. Was Meredith sexually active? Yeah, she borrowed a few of my condoms. Does she like anal? wtf? I dont know. Does she use vaseline? For her lips? What kind of person is Stefano? Nice guy, has a really pretty girlfriend. Hmmm . . . very interesting . . . [we'd] like to [show] you something, and tell us if this is out of normal.

They took me into the nieghbors house. The had broken the door open to get in, but they told me to [ignore] that. The rooms were all open. Giacomo and Marco-n's room was spotless which made since becaus the guys had thoroughly cleaned the whole house before they left on vacation. Stefano's room however, well, his bed was strpped of linens, which was odd, and the comfoter he used was shoved up at the top of his bed, with blood on it. I obviously told then that the blood was definatley out of normal and also that he usually has his bed made. They took note of it and [ushered] me out. When I left the house to go back to the police station they told me to put my jacket over my head and duck down below the window so the reporters wouldnt try to talk to me. At the station I just had to repeat the answers that I had givn at the house [so] they could type them up and after a good 5 and a half hour day with the police again Raffael picked me up and took me out for some well-deserved pizza. I was starving. I then bought some underwear because as it turns out I wont be able to leave Italy for a while as well as enter my house. I only had the clothes I was wearing the day it [began], so I bought some underwear and [borrowed] a pair of pants from Raffael.

Spoke with my remaining roommates that night (last night) and it was a hurricane of emotions and stress but we needed it anyway. What we have been discussing is bascially what to do next. We are trying to keep our heads on straight. First things first though, my roommates both work for lawyers, and they are going to try to send a request through on Monday to retrieve important documents of ours that are still in the house. Secondly, we are going to talk to the agency that we used to find our house and obviously request to move out. It kind of sucks that we have to pay the next months rent, but the owner has protection within the contract. After that, I guess I'll go back to class on Monday, although Im not sure what Im going to do about people asking me questions, because I really dont want to talk again about what happened. Ive been talking an awful lot lately and Im pretty tired of it. After that, its like Im trying to remember what I was doing before all this happened. I still need to figure out who I need to talk to and what I need to do to continue studying in Perugia, because its what I want to do.

Anyway, thats the update, feeling okay, hope you all are well, Amanda

Bemused, detectives scratched their heads. Though the text read like a trailer for a scary movie, written in a style that the MySpace generation could relate to, the meaning boosted Amanda's credibility. 'It makes her look like an ordinary kid trapped in nightmare miles away from home,' said one detective rubbing his chin. 'Maybe we are barking up the wrong tree. How would you have reacted to finding your flatmate dead when you were twenty-one? You'd be confused, to say the least.' The question remained, however: how did she know that Meredith's throat had been slit?

Other titbits of evidence emerged that made Amanda look good, or at least poured water on some on the damning speculation that had built up against her. One of the lads from downstairs, Marco Marzan, said that he had never noticed any friction between Meredith and Amanda.

11

Gotcha!

Tuesday, 6 November, 05:00

Sleek and lethal, the special weapons and tactics force silently took up position in the Perugian street. Secret-service-style ear mics, individually moulded and transparent, crackled with last-minute instructions and run-throughs. The men pressed gloved hands against their ears, checked their clunky watches and cocked their guns. Their futuristic body armour and state-of-the-art semi-automatics made a striking contrast against the ancient stone buildings. But armed guards on the streets of Perugia were nothing new. Three thousand years ago a pre-Roman civilization centred around Tuscany had turned this hill fort into a stronghold and trading post. The Etruscans were warlike and superstitious. Their gods were merciless. The giant stone Etruscan Arch, still the main gateway into the city, is a monument to the city's dark history.

Suddenly, at 05:00, the order was given to arrest the new prime suspect in the murder of Meredith Kercher. Flying Squad officers started beating their fists at Patrick Lumumba's door. His Polish wife Aleksandra and 18-month-old child Davide jumped from their beds in terror. A female police officer buzzed the intercom to the fourth-floor flat and demanded that both the main entrance and the internal door be opened immediately. In the confusion, the toddler rushed towards the flat door. 'Let us in or we'll break down the door,' screamed the men in blue uniforms outside, not knowing that it was a kid fumbling at the lock.

Congolese musician and bar-owner Patrick 'Diya' Lumumba, 38, swept his only son into his arms just as the heavy door swung open. 'Wait, I'm letting you in,' he shouted. Commissioner Chiacchiera burst into the apartment. Lumumba, five foot six, chubby and bewildered, just stood there in his underwear while his wife screamed in the background.

At first, because some of men were were wearing normal clothes and carrying guns, Lumumba thought it must be some sort of armed gang about to kill him. But their real purpose was soon evident. 'Patrick Lumumba, we have an arrest warrant for you here . . .' The terrified suspect watched in disbelief as more than twenty officers poured through the door. He claimed some of the policemen hit him over the head and yelled, 'Dirty black'.

The specialist officers in the background stood down when they realized Lumumba wasn't armed and was likely to come quietly. But still they watched him closely while he got dressed, slipping on a pair of jeans and a pullover. Then they put hand-cuffs on him. Taking no chances, Lumumba was then manhandled by two hefty policemen who grabbed him in a lock position under the armpits and shoved him out of the door, as Aleksandra pulled Davide away, screaming.

Inside the police car, cold and claustrophobic, a wave of deadening helplessness overwhelmed him. The windows were misted up. Amorphous blobs of neon light, refracted from the drops of rain on the glass, cut through intermittently. The officers' breath, though tainted with briefing-room coffee and last night's garlic, fogged up in the biting cold. His mind drifted back to when he was five years old. When strange men had came out of the darkness. And his father had disappeared into a steamy Kinshasa night, never to return, paying with his life for the name he bore.

At the police station he was jolted back to reality – sirens blared and press cameras flashed. The security convoy consisted of seven cars. He had seen terrorists being arrested like this on the TV news. Patrick Lumumba had come to Italy twenty years before, just like Meredith and Amanda, to study at the University for Foreigners. To support himself on a Political Science course, he exported Italian shoes back to his family business in Kinshasa. His family had been highly politicized – a distant relative was the anti-colonial leader Patrice Lumumba, who had gone on to become the Congo's first legally elected Prime Minister in 1961. Ominously, Patrice was murdered in a coup. As a result, Patrick had faced being an outsider in his own country, teetering on the edge of danger nearly all of his early life. His mother and father, activists from the Congolese countryside, had been ostracized from court life in the Congo capital, then ruled with an iron fist by dictator Sese Seke Mobutu. As soon as he was able, Patrick had fled to Italy in search of a better life. However, like all immigrants, deep down in his heart he had never felt totally secure in his adopted country – and less and less so in recent years, as anti-immigration tensions across Italy grew following a mass influx of Africans in the 1990s and, later, the Albanian crime wave.

After fingerprints and formalities, Patrick was pushed into an interrogation room. By now, he was in a sorry state: bags under his eyes, his bed-head dreads spiked in cornrows but untidy. An equally exhausted Mignini did not look amused. And he didn't stand on ceremony.

'Lumumba, you have just been accused of being the material perpetrator of the murder of Meredith Kercher.'

The precision of the legal language pierced any hope that Lumumba had been holding on to that this was all a big mistake. The revelation took his breath away. But Patrick was politically savvy, his antennae sharpened by years of careful socialization and delicate compromise in an alien land. Instead of indignation, he reacted with the trademark politeness that had so endeared him to the academic community in Perugia.

'Sorry, who said that?' An African frankness that is often mis-interpreted as naivety or innocence.

But Mignini wasn't going to reveal his hand just yet. 'You need to find yourself a lawyer quick. You are under arrest.'

Across town, ageing barrister Carlo Pacelli, bespectacled and balding, took the call. A cold November morning after the hol-iday, it was bound to be the usual – unpaid traffic fines, a troublesome border dispute, or, if he was very lucky, a petty criminal caught red-handed getting his Christmas money together. So when Lumumba made his desperate call, he shot off immediately, both surprised and excited that a juicy case had finally landed on his desk.

Mignini's questions were terse. But it wasn't all gratuitous. From his bearing, he knew that Lumumba was a rounded, mature guy. He didn't have to kid-glove around as he had been forced to do with the students.

'Mr Lumumba, do you employ Amanda Knox?'

'Yes, two days a week, when I need help in the bar,' Patrick replied.

'Do you also know Meredith Kercher?'

'Yes, she came to the bar twice, I think. We discussed a cock-tail we sell making a Polish vodka . . .'

'Have you ever been to Meredith's flat?'

'No, never.' Patrick was certain in his answer.

'Are you sure, Mr Lumumba? We have a witness who tells us that you have been to her flat.'

'I said no. And I mean never.'

'Where were you on the night of the first of November, Mr Lumumba?'

'In the bar. I opened at nine as usual.'

During routine house-to-house inquiries that morning, a neighbour who lived opposite Le Chic had told the police differently – that the bar was most definitely closed at that time. Patrick's denial fell on deaf ears. Worse was to come. Patrick confidently instructed the police to check the till records to back up his story. 'The time code will prove that I was in the bar from nine till closing time,' he declared confidently.

But the till roll didn't show any sales at 21:00. Patrick's heart sank. He then backtracked by saying that there was a plausible excuse. Sometimes he delayed issuing a receipt until the customer was about to leave and had signed off a tab, rather than ringing in every drink at the time it was served.

'Just like at a restaurant,' Lumumba explained. Some officers unfairly speculated that he may have scuppered himself by his own petty fiddling. Not registering transactions until much later was a small-time tax dodge carried out from time to time by bar-owners, designed to report a lower income.

Now that Patrick had effectively cornered himself, his excuses neutralized, the expert cross-examiner delivered his *coup de grâce*.

'Mr Lumumba,' Mignini asked. 'Why did you delete traces of the telephone call you made to Amanda Knox? The one in which you arranged to meet later, to go and have sex with Meredith?'

Genuinely surprised, Lumumba responded blandly: 'I didn't cancel anything.'

'Well, we'll see about that, Mr Lumumba. Our analysts are

looking at the phone as we speak. They'll be able to tell me for certain whether you did or didn't.'

Lumumba put his head in his hands.

Mignini continued: 'In the meantime, how do you explain the other missing communication, Mr Lumumba?'

'What communication? I don't know what you're talking about,' replied Lumumba.

'Come on, Mr Lumumba. There's a text on Miss Knox's telephone from you, saying, in Italian, "See you later". And yet that outgoing text has been deleted from your phone also. I presume you sent it from your own phone?'

Lumumba shook his head in resignation. 'I actually meant, "See you tomorrow". As in tomorrow, meaning the next day. There was no work that night, so I told her to stay home.'

'But why did you delete that text to Amanda, Mr Lumumba?' Mignini asked once more. 'Did you have something to hide? Did you know we were coming this morning? Did you think it would prove that you went to see Meredith, so you got rid of it? Is that the case, Mr Lumumba?'

Patrick was dumbfounded now. 'I don't know what you're talking about.'

'We don't believe you, Mr Lumumba.' Mignini paused. 'In fact, we know for certain that Amanda replied to you "see you later" proving that this little exchange of texts actually took place.'

Unconvinced of his suspect's reaction, Mignini pressed the attack home.

'You had an appointment at Amanda Knox's apartment to have sex with Meredith Kercher.'

Patrick couldn't believe what he was hearing.

'And Miss Knox has just accused you of being the material murderer of Meredith Kercher.'

'Material murderer? What?' Patrick shouted in disbelief, almost laughing, but not.

Patrick Diya Lumumba looked straight into the eyes of his accuser. Centuries of violence in deepest Africa had not prepared him for this. Nor had the imprisonment, torture and murder of many members of his family. Patrick knew that even in twenty-first-century Europe his colour alone was enough to invite injustice. Especially if the crime in question played up to the oldest and most inflammatory prejudice of all – that of a savage black man defiling a defenceless white girl. He knew that every word, every move was being scrutinized. How would he play it? He had no idea. Lumumba couldn't think of a strategy off the top of his head. Instead, in desperation, he put his fate in the hands of the gods and turned to a simple African faith, in the hope of pulling him through.

He thought of the villages back home, where each one hosts a white hen as a symbol of truth and justice. 'Always tell the truth' is the Congolese saying that underlies the custom.

Finally Lumumba faced down Mignini: 'No. I have never been to Meredith Kercher's flat. I did not kill her . . .'

But Mignini wasn't letting go. He had no time for sympathy and customs. He just wanted evidence. He wanted a confession. 'Come on, Mr Lumumba,' he stated. 'We know that's the exact opposite of the truth – you're going to jail.' The ten-hour interrogation was over.

Later, Patrick complained that at various points during the ordeal he was abused, although today he is more reticent: he still has to live in the city that adopted him. He can't fathom why his neighbour said the bar was shut that night when he could clearly see it was open; he can't believe that the Italian state could move with such swift accuracy on the say-so of a 20-year-old from Seattle. The veneer of Italian political correctness slipped away quickly. The brutality of his arrest led him to think he was suspected of terrorism. Terrorism justifies most police brutality these days, he thought.

'I'd seen it before, I knew it would end. This is not the Congo.'

As he was taken down into the cells, Lumumba thought of the life in Italy that he had struggled to build up over the years, and that was about to be washed away in an instant. On the say-so of a 20-year-old girl. It was incredible. Patrick had worked in music and bars for ten years in Perugia. He had started by organizing the University for Foreigners' band and orchestra – players from all over the world would come together to give concerts for charity. He did it free for five years but then started getting paid for it. His job was to find out who plays what instrument and put them together in the same room to see what music comes out.

The local council had then given him a concession in a local park to host an arts festival and put a few tables out to serve drinks. Le Chic had been born out of this scene, to tide him over the winter, and though the business hadn't been going long, Patrick made it work by organizing wider student nightlife and relying on residual goodwill to bring punters through the door. His piano and percussion playing was also an attraction of his bar, which lies somewhat out of the way compared with the other pubs popular with students.

But years of serving the community were not enough to save him now. Racists and jealous businessmen were now pointing the finger. Locals who disliked the students now turned on the black outsider who was seen as their most visible champion. Provincial bitterness seethed from the town-and-gown conflict. Poor locals had seen their rents and food bills soar with the influx of couldn't-care-less foreign students.

Though the culture is more café society than the binge

drunkenness that mars life in many university towns, especially in the UK, some Perugians openly resent the noisy crowds that occupy the cramped civic area. In summer months life goes quiet again – but relief often mutates into resentment towards the temporary visitors whom they accuse of treating their ancient town like a hotel.

The irrationality resonated in the outside world. In the media, the arrest of the black suspect felt right. Newspaper reporters began to investigate the new accused and he was immediately characterized as a seedy bar-owner who preyed on students half his age. In newsrooms he was painted as a kind of Pied Piper who led impressionable youths into a life of dissolution and hedonism.

For the first time, the police felt confident enough to confirm a motive on the record. Perugia Police Chief Arturo De Felice said Meredith had been killed during a sex attack. He added: 'The motive appears sexual, but Meredith was morally innocent. She was a victim, not a participant.'

Lumumba's fingerprints and a blood sample were taken and he was put in isolation in a sparse 6 ft by 12 ft cell in the town's Capanne prison. Police chief De Felice went even further in his calls for closure, congratulating his detectives and praising their 'magnificent work'. He added: 'We worked around the clock. The city needed a result quickly.' In the remand sentence Claudia Matteini would write: 'The sexual intercourse involving [Kercher] and [Lumumba] must be regarded as violent, given the particularly threatening context in which it took place, and to which Ms Knox must have contributed to.'

There would be no need for another autopsy.

PART TWO

———

The Probe

12

Coming of Age

The new twist in the tale did not dampen the media's appetite. Though Patrick Lumumba's arrest brought an element of closure to the case, and simultaneously deflected heat away from Amanda and Raffaele, the story was still playing out big in the papers. Editors were enchanted by the basic facts – that the plot revolved around middle-class 'gap year kids', one of whom had been killed in a posh-looking Italian town. Umbria was definitely not Tuscany, but the Renaissance stone and the wooded hills gave the backdrop an exotic air. An appeal that struck a chord with more sophisticated readers, who endlessly yearned for and romanticized their Northern Italian playgrounds.

Agency pictures were carefully cropped before distribution, to cut out the industrial town that has spread out untidily across Perugia's slopes, in the hope that they would get 'better shows' and make more money. At dinner parties, the thriller aspect of the case was compared to upmarket novels such as *The Talented Mr Ripley* by Patricia Highsmith and *The Secret History* by Donna Tartt. In short, the murder of Meredith Kercher was a crime that fitted perfectly with a key target demographic. In commercial terms, it was a murder that reached out to, but also struck fear in, a middle-market audience. The fact that a black man was now being blamed only added to the timeless power of the narrative. Ratings and circulation managers were over the moon. As a consequence, reporters continued to dig into the lives of the leading cast.

Between the ages of seven and fourteen Amanda Knox picked up numerous school prizes, often outdoing her better-off but less motivated richer classmates. By the time she was eight, her soccer team-mates dubbed her 'Foxy Knoxy', not because she was a flirt but because of the cunning way she could read a game. Her tricky dribbling drew gasps of amusement and surprise. Her school pals included the daughters of Seattle's millionaire technology elite, excecutives from Microsoft and Boeing. But Amanda had a competitive advantage beyond their grasp – she was cool. Cool in a shabby-chic way like most lower-middle-class kids from Seattle, the avant-garde city that gave birth to the no-global movement. She was West Seattle, the home of Kurt Cobain and spiritual Mecca of the grunge music scene. An association that couldn't be bought by her well-off pals.

Amanda was no slacker, however. At home she had a strong sense of responsibility, like many eldest kids, towards her single mother and younger sister Deanna. Deanna enjoyed a little more freedom, taking advantage of Amanda's willingness to do chores and homework. As a working mum, tired Edda cut her more slack.

But Amanda's cushy routine, and the control over her life that she strived for, was about to be rocked. When Amanda was nine, her mother fell in love with a man twelve years younger than herself. She called a technology helpdesk to help her with her job. Chris answered the call. Edda was thirty-five years old and he was just twenty-three. Chris Mellas was a clean-cut technology whiz-zkid who worked in Seattle's futuristic computer industry, home to the Microsoft international headquarters, among other companies. The romantic Greek-American swept Edda off her feet and breathed fresh life into Amanda's broken family.

Four years later Edda decided she deserved a break. She married blue-eyed Chris and he became the girls' *de facto* day-to-day father, for better or for worse. Amanda was fourteen, with all that delicate age brings with it, in the midst of angst-ridden mental and physical change.

Two oceans away in Italy, Raffaele was growing up. At the age of seven, his mummy's boy traits had been a continuing source of worry for his overpowering dad. He genuinely believed that his son's clinginess, together with his lack of independence, would hold him back in life. Raffaele was often embarrassed by his dad's heavy-handed interventions to protect him or to push him along.

At seven years old he retreated even further into his own world. He did, however, find solace in his local church of San Domenico, a very traditional parish. The church became the centre of his social life, and of much of his learning.

Raffaele could do nothing about his shyness with the girls. At fourteen, he was sent to the mixed-gender Liceo Scientifico 'Einstein', a British grammar-school-style college focusing on sciences and Latin. The curriculum was hard, replete with hours of homework, leaving even the brightest students little time for socializing or sweet-talking members of the opposite sex. On the few occasions he made an effort, his plans for extra-curricular dates were often frustrated by small-town geography – the school was so far from his home at Molfetta that it became difficult to meet up with girls. The isolation exacerbated his sense of awkwardness. Consequently, the only girls he met were the ones who frequented the church playground near his home. Almost all of his school friends came from other small towns around the province of Bari.

When Raffaele's parents announced they were divorcing, his world began to fall apart. The process, drawn-out and poisoned with bitterness, must have been deeply traumatic for the young lad. His mother walked out of the family home and went to live close to his grandmother. Raffaele was torn apart and confused. But it was inevitable that the boy who was still attached to her apron strings would follow her soon enough.

His misery was deepened by the complexity of legal business that plagues Italian divorce cases. He watched from the sidelines as lawyers divided up the family property, calculating Francesco's income and his financial obligations to his wife and children. Relations were strained. Richer husbands, at that time, were expected to keep their former spouses in the same style of life to which they had become accustomed. Separation was often a financial disaster.

The upshot was that Raffaele, whose upper-middle-class lifestyle was destined to shield him from the unpleasant sides of life until much older, was exposed to the turmoil of domestic disintegration. The divorce left him with a lingering sense of guilt: family breakdown represented a moral failure in a staunchly Catholic country. Outside the home the pressure on Raffaele was immense. In his small town, the Sollecitos became the subject of gossip and judgment. Friends took sides, extended family argued and the incestuous mesh that is the fabric of Italian society was damaged. Just the kind of nightmare a shy kid fears most.

Instead of shunning church as many teenagers do, Raffaele found comfort within it. The Catholic solution to guilt is the confessional. By the end of the twentieth century the Vatican had accepted the basics of psychology and no longer inflicted penance on children whose only sin might be having cheated in their homework. On the contrary, the modern church minimizes sin, taking the view that all people are all in the same boat – careful not to judge behaviour but rather bring acceptance. Raffaele's parish priest incited him to have faith and feel free of responsibility for his parents' break-up.

Raffaele's sister Vanessa coped better, getting down and studying hard. Raffaele lost heart. A similar situation had happened to his mother. She had been one of the cleverest girls in her school but had lost her way. She suffered from depression. Her neighbours remember her as an intelligent woman, from an intellectual family, with great potential. But being a clever woman in Southern Italy in the 1980s was frustrating. Women were still seen as either sex objects or mothers-in-waiting. Striving for a career was often laughed off as vain. Even after settling for less, her esteem was dented further. Mrs Sollecito did not need to work and maids took care of domestic duties, contributing to her sense of uselessness and in turn to her depression. She died while Raffaele was still in his teens. There were rumours of suicide but these were unfounded; she died of natural causes.

When Meredith turned seven years old in 1992, Britain was in the grip of a recession. Croydon, however, still remained an unusually busy suburb of London. The town was a hectic meld of mini-skyscrapers, retail parks and giant housing estates, the rumble of the London A roads and M25 motorway never far away in the background. Meredith was a busy, active child from an early age. She went to ballet, liked reading and was generally known for her all-round vitality. When she took up karate, unlike many kids, she stuck to it. By her early teens, she had attained her third belt.

Meredith inherited her father's flair for the written word. At school she wrote poetry and her fiction compositions were highly thought of. But mostly Meredith was known for her bubbly personality and her sense of humour – she had an imaginative sense of the ridiculous, according to her family.

Meredith may have been educated at a £10,000-a-year private school but she wasn't born with a silver spoon in her mouth. Her mother and father sacrificed almost all of their income and savings to give their youngest daughter, as well as her older siblings, the best education they could get. For all four children the fees climbed into the £100,000s over the years. In effect, John and Arline Kercher gave up the family's material aspirations – the dream of owning a well-kept, well-appointed house in a smart part of London, nice cars, expensive foreign holidays, a fat pension to look forward to, a comfortable inheritance to pass on . . .

Arline put her social life on hold. John chose to work instead of taking annual leave. His haymaking years in Fleet Street were dedicated solely to putting his kids through school and university. He did well to keep the whole show on the road on a single freelancer's wage, not only paying his own expenses in Croydon but also contributing to the upkeep of Arline and the kids at the old home a few miles south in Coulsdon. Arline was too busy being a full-time mum of four to go back to work.

Following their divorce, both of them lived in reduced circumstances in order to give Meredith more than they could really afford. But both teachers and schoolfriends alike say Meredith benefited immensely from the school's renowned approach of concentrating totally on the individual and supporting pupils to a degree that the state sector educators can only dream of. A family friend, who knew Meredith when she was in her early teens, said:

> Meredith was the kind of girl who could have coped going to the local comprehensive. She wasn't a snob at all. She was very much heads down when it came to school and home-work, a can-do, resourceful type of person. No moaning or skiving off. She wasn't laid back, by any means.
>
> However, I don't think she would have turned out as well-rounded and confident as she was, if she'd gone off to any old school. I think John was very proud that he'd taken the decision to send his girls to a good one. Everything revolved around education in the family. That was partly down to Arline. She wasn't pushy but she realized the value of qualifi-cations, especially coming from Pakistan, where families want their kids to do well.
>
> I got the impression it was a case of: 'If we give our kids a good education, that's the best we can do for them.'

Though the Kerchers didn't have much money, neighbours remember the house as being full of life. It only had three bed-rooms between four kids and one adult, but it was one of those homes where friends always came to play, because it was wel-coming and exciting. Family friends said that Meredith and Stephanie were always going to parties when they were kids rather than playing out in the street.

The Old Palace School in Croydon is a rarefied oasis in a gnarl of urban sprawl. Meredith's creativity was allowed to bloom in an atmosphere of learning, where pupils are encour-aged to be independent whilst being somewhat protected from the outside world. One former pupil, who graduated from uni-versity just before Meredith moved to Perugia, said: 'I'm not surprised she chose to study abroad. A lot of girls would be put off, but she was quietly capable all along. You learn to be like that at the OPS [Old Palace School]. The school prides itself on churning out self-contained women who can stand on their own two feet, especially when they move into the outside world. It's not like Rodean or somewhere totally up there. But Mez was like that in Years Eight and Nine.'

The Elizabethan buildings, standing in the shadow of Croydon Parish Church, are home to perfectly manicured gardens, an indoor swimming pool and five state-of-the-art IT suites. The high walls and intercommed security gates cut the school off from the local area, a run-down mix of high-density terraced houses and flats, of closed-down pubs and a High Street dominated by charity shops, pound stores and cheap fast-food restaurants. Though the school has a strong religious tradition – founded by an archbishop, supported by a Christian foundation and for 500 years the summer residence of the Archbishop of Canterbury – Meredith wasn't particularly committed. One of the school's mottos is 'For the Church and People of God'. But she did help out with fundraising for the Catholic charity Caritas, through the school's long-established links with international aid programmes. Curiously, one of the suspects later accused of her murder would seek refuge in a Caritas centre abroad whilst he was on the run.

The financial sacrifices took their toll on John and Arline. The family home, a 1930s-style suburban semi in Fairdene Road, Old Coulsdon, where Arline lived with the kids, fell into disrepair. The gutters hung off the roof and porch and Arline made do with tatty black curtains that covered the front windows, the glass bevelling under the weight of the old lead inlays. The street was not in the poshest part of Coulsdon. The residents were a mixture of proud homeowners with tidy lawns, commuters who travelled from South Coulsdon station at the end of the street to good jobs in London, and poorer renters. The situation was exacerbated when Arline fell into ill-health with a kidney condition.

John Kercher moved into a newly built townhouse in a shabby part of West Croydon with a large ethnic population. There is a photographic warehouse at one end of the busy slip road and a large cemetery at the other. Today neighbours complain of the shootings and violence between gangs in Croydon and nearby Thornton Heath. Amid the weedy gardens, littered with abandoned mattresses and bed frames, John Kercher's house stands out as being smart. The walls are covered in creepers and high bushes, preserving a quiet space. He often retreats into his small rear garden to write.

But the sacrifices were worth it. The sight of the Kercher sisters sitting on the bus to school, wearing their smart dark-green school jumpers over light-coloured collared cotton dresses, with their hair immaculately groomed, stuck in people's minds. So much so that after her death one former pupil called Christina from Eastbourne wrote: 'I didn't know Meredith but I used to go to OPS and remember seeing her and her older sister on the bus on the way to school when they were very young. I just wanted to say to Stephanie that I couldn't get the image of you and your little sister out of my head all day.' The other motto of the school is 'The End Crowns the Work'.

Meredith was good at creative writing. The staff remember her as a model pupil, self-disciplined and focused, even in her formative years. A former staff member said: 'Meredith was never in any trouble whatsoever. She was always smiling, just like you see on the photographs. She was very popular. Meredith favoured the humanities over maths or science. She was an innovative, bright thinker. Leadership qualities are encouraged at school and that rubbed off on Meredith. She wasn't a pushover or a follower. She would have gone far in her chosen profession. We knew she would go far.' Though the school is very competitive – it won Independent School of the Year in 2005/06 – and many pupils take their GCSEs early in Year 10, Meredith took it all in her stride. Pals say she wasn't competitive but she did enjoy netball and running.

Almost all of Meredith's friends remember her as 'the girl who was always smiling' or 'the girl with the beautiful smile'. They call her simply Mez. One schoolfriend remembered how Mez pulled her through the stress of coursework and exams at school:

Mez was warm. I'd say the word is cosy or cuddly; she had that kind of aura. She would give you a hug and she was more interested in you than talking about her. I remember when I was burnt out doing revision and Mez helped me get organized. Mez liked doing coursework in English, English Lit and history. Very even-tempered, I don't know anyone who ever fell out with her the whole time we were at school. I think because she was youngest in a big family, she was practical, a quick learner, or rather, well organized.

There were some girls there, proper Surrey girls, who waste their time and get through with extra help. But Mez was hard-working and steady. Her mum and dad weren't rich – she was there to get on.

One memory of her, from younger days, particularly stood out for her father. Meredith really liked Halloween. She made costumes from bin liners, carved out pumpkin lanterns with her family and played trick-or-treat on the neighbours. Later John Kercher would describe it as ironic and tragic that she would die so terribly only one day after Halloween.

13

Freshers

August–September 2007

Amanda Knox's European adventure began when she touched down in Germany in midsummer 2007 to stay with relatives before moving on to Perugia. She was bursting with excitement. Like many American college students, her dream vacation was to backpack around old Europe, visiting the places that under-graduates had been travelling to for decades. Amsterdam coffee shops, Roman ruins, the Alpine peaks were not only must-sees on the well-trodden independent traveller trail. Some of the sights had been part of campus folklore in USA since Ivy League freshmen had discovered their magic in the 1930s and '40s, later followed by the hippy generation of the '60s. Amanda wanted to be part of that, even though by now it was somewhat of a conservative tradition.

Not only was Amanda finally free to make her dream come true, she could go one better. She had a whole year of explo-ration and romance to look forward to. This was her version of Alex Garland's cult novel *The Beach*.

Amanda oozed backpacker chic. She wore a charity-shop

floral summer dress with trainers, topped off with a beanie hat. With a Lonely Planet guide in one hand, a sports bottle of water in the other and a Gauloise between her lips, Amanda looked the part. Europe was a blaze of the new. The attack on the senses was almost overwhelming. She drank in the nuances that made travelling in a different country delightful. She idled away hours drinking coffee in the shady sidewalk cafés. She absorbed the new fashions. She was blown away by the ancient buildings.

After staying with her relatives in Germany, her sister Deanna flew in from the States to help her get set up for her adventure of a lifetime in Perugia. They flew to Rome and jumped a train down to Florence. Amanda got stoned with a handsome Italian boy en route. Breathlessly she blogged her exploits. She was having the time of her life.

Plane was chill, and the train wasn't hard. In fact, met a guy named Frederico on the train to Florence from Milan, and we ended up hanging out together in Florence, where he bought both Deanna and I dinner and then, when Deanna went to bed, we smoked up together, my first time in Italy . . .

Like many backpackers, Amanda wasn't really that interested in the cultural sites, or getting to grips with the philosophy that had underpinned Western civilization for 2000 years. The statues and fountains were just a means to an end, touchstones that could be conveniently ticked off the sights-to-see pages of her travel guide. The real goal was to have an 'experience' based around like-minded people, cool hang-outs and eating and drinking, which never really left the comfort zone of what she was used to back home.

Amanda raced through the history bit. She wrote: 'Took pictures early the next day of Neptune's fountain and naked David, conveniently located right next to each other.'

After chilling out in Florence, Amanda and Deanna travelled to Perugia with the aim of scouting a flat, securing it with a deposit before hitting the trail again. Within two hours of arriving, Amanda, now tanned, her hair sun-bleached, was hit on by a pervy Italian motorist twice her age. The second admirer in as many days who wanted to take her out for dinner and into bed. Amanda batted him off with humour, but not before cadging a lift to their distant hotel. Both sisters seem to be enjoying a girly, giggly holiday. Amanda's mischievous sense of humour shines through her diary, a particularly American worldliness: sharp but at the same time not cynical.

Then the train the next day to Perugia, wasnt bad. Had a little adventure trying to find our hotel though. Carrying everything on our back, Deanna and I buy a map and discover that the hotel booked for us is actually as far on the edge of the map as it can get on some random little road that doesnt list it's whole name. 2 hours of hiking up and down Perugia's hills, we were lost. Deanna was drowning in her own sweat, and I was pissed to say the least. Or at least hot. I just wanted to find this place, but it was ridiculous. Then some 40-something Italian guy pulls over and looks at our map. He offeres us a [ride] when he explains that it's another 20minutes away by CAR and there is no bus to it. Alright, Ill risk my life to get to my hotel. So Deanna and I pile in and we do indeed get to our hotel alive, the only awkward part is when I have to try to explain to our driver in broken Italian that we aren't interested [in] going out with his 40-something year old self this evening. We check in and our brains check out.

Amanda recounted her experience at an exciting pace, peppering her entries with lively American slang. It wasn't over the top and her lack of self-consciousness gave it an undeniable charm. Amanda didn't need to impress anyone with her streetsmarts. She knew she was on it, unaffected and natural.

The next three days are great. We figure out how to find a bus somewhat close to our hotel that will take us downtown. Once there we make friends with the two workers at this cafe that we visit everyday. Deanna wants to shop some more, but I need to find a place to live, so I search desperately through Italian classifieds. I also buy a phone. Then, when we walk down a steep road to my university, we run into a very skinny girl who looks a little older than me putting up a page with her number on the outer wall of the [university]. I chat it up with her, she speaks English really well, and we go immediately to her place, literally [2 minutes] walk from my university.

Most conveniently, Amanda had bumped into Filomena Romanelli, who was putting up a notice to rent a flat at exactly the same time that Amanda was hunting for one. Filomena was newly installed at 7 Pergola Road herself, along with her legal-eagle workmate Laura Mezzetti. The pair had agreed with the landlord to help sublet the remaining two bedrooms in the top flat. Like all viewers, Amanda was immediately spellbound by the enchanted cottage that would alter her life, from dream to nightmare, irrevocably.

It's a cute house that is right in the middle of this random garden [in the] middle of Perugia. Around us are apartment buildings, but we enter through a gate and there it is. Im in love. I meet her roommate molly [*error for Laura?*]. The house has a kitchen, 2 bathrooms, and four bedrooms. not to mention a washing maschine, and internet access. Not to mention, she owns two guitars and wants to play with me. Not to mention the view is amazing. Not to mention I have a terrace that looks over the Perugian city/countryside. Not to mention she wants me to teach [her] yoga. Not to mention they both smoke like chimneys. And, she offers me one of the open rooms after we hang out for a bit.

Amanda didn't mess about. She knew what she liked and she was decisive. She cut through the administration like someone who understood that they only had one life and lived it to the full. There wasn't any backpacker haggling. Or student pettiness. The 300 euro rent may have seemed to some like a rip-off. The landlord was raking in at least 2500 euros a month from both floors of what was, in reality, no more than a converted animal shed stuck on top of a nice hill. Amanda shook on the deal there and then and paid up.

We exchange numbers. I put down a down payment. Im feeling sky high. These girls are awesome. really sweet, really down to earth, funny as hell. Neither are students, they actually both work [in the] same law office, and they are desperate for roommates because the two they had decided they wanted to disappear all of a sudden. They are relieved to meet me believe it or not, because aparently everyone else they have met have been really not cool. An rude, uptight German guy, and girl who cant speak English or Italian. Only Japanese, and an Italian guy who wont answer his phone. That, and a bunch of others who had to 'think about it'. The rent for this HOUSE is only 300 euro a month, whereas, Ive looked at

holes in the wall 'apartments' with nothing going for them
for 500 euro a month. Fuck that. Im hooked. We hung out
for a good long time the day before yesturday, just laughing
about crazy people and in general getting to know each other.

With the benefit of hindsight Filomena and Laura may have
wished that they had held out for one of the other candidates.
But now there was no going back. Amanda was bursting with
anticipation. She was high on life and horny – or at least in the
mood for romance. Whilst on the way back to a local bar, she
got the hots for a striking black man she met in the street. She
was ballsy enough to chat him up on the spot, but mature
enough to do it in a cool way. They pencilled in a date a couple
of weeks ahead when she returned from a planned pre-school
excursion. As he turned away, she pretended to punch the air in
glee.

Then, Deanna and I went to grab a sandwich at the same cafe
and I bumped into the most beautiful black man I have ever
seen. He said he'd see me when I come back from Germany.
Eheheheh and our waiter, Nerti, from Albania, hung out
with us a bit and talked politics.

Amanda had been in Perugia for less than a week, but already
she had found her feet. Moving effortlessly through the cosmopolitan culture, hanging out with people from countries she'd
only ever seen on a map. She did it with style, as though she'd
been there all her life. Amanda was a social chameleon. As with
everything, she worked hard to get the most out of a given situation.

But who was the mystery black man? Was he a college student like herself? Was he one of the immigrants who worked in

one of the local restaurants for less than minimum wage? Or was he one of the cool townies who hustled a lifestyle out of the students, dealing them a bit of weed, shooting pool for drinks and impressing the posh girls with their street-side escapades? As she headed north to visit her relatives in Austria, Amanda giggled with Deanna about extra-curricular activities that awaited her once she returned to enrol in mid-to-late September.

In early September, while Amanda was still enjoying her holiday, Meredith Kercher landed in Italy. On the train from the airport, she put her head out of the window to let the wind rush over her face and through her hair, temporary relief from the torrid heat of the Italian summer.

The gently undulating countryside, some of the most beautiful in Europe to rival Provence, Scotland or Scandanavia, eased the stress of the flight. Though Gatwick Airport was just a stone's throw from her Coulsdon home, at this time of year the lounges were manic with families returning in time for the school term and last-minute package tourists flying out. The journey had been especially tiring because she was laden down with all her bags. Now she could sit back for a couple of hours. The dark green of the fields in the north, sprinkled with copses of familiar European oaks and birches, soon gave way to the yellowing Mediterranean bush of the south. Ominously, in the distance Meredith saw the Apennine mountains for the first time, black but gentle, and shrouded in mist. This mysterious range, which had played such a key part in Italy's tumultuous history, would be her new home for the next year. A tingle of anticipation went through her body. She'd read up on her new country. The Apennine mountains were the backbone of Italy that ran all the way down to Calabria on the southern tip. Created by a violent clash of continental plates, the raw power

of the Apennines had destroyed the lives of many brave enough
to make it their home over the centuries. Mount Vesuvius had
laid waste to Pompeii in AD 79. But, in contrast, the mountains'
natural fortifications had also protected many civilizations from
invasion. Perugia was an excellent example – the town had
avoided the wrath of almost all marauding armies over the years
because it was hidden, and off the beaten track that led to the
bigger prizes of Florence or Bologna.

Meredith alighted at Perugia's charming train station, a pic-
ture-box building that looks as if it has been ripped from the
pages of a pre-war spy novel. She dragged her clattering wheelie
bag across the polished tiles of the platform, taking in the ochre
walls, the pretty bunting trim on the wooden roof and the
arched windows above the ticket office. Perugia resonated with
romance from a bygone age.

After checking into a cheap hotel, Meredith began her flat
search. Before flying out, she had done some research. She
had found an ad for 7 Pergola Road on the University for
Foreigners' web site and emailed Filomena to tell her that she
was interested. From her hotel in Italy, she followed up with
a call. At the viewing she hit it off with Filomena and Laura
at once. Filomena again spoke of her annoyance with previous
callers who were either rude or unreliable. The mores of the
University were dropping fast due to the high turnover of
students.

Meredith instead surprised Filomena with her kindness and
good manners. She was exactly what the Italians imagine a
British student to be – well-spoken, cultured and genuinely
interested in learning about Italy. They took to her immediately.

Meredith relaxed. Fat blobs of rain from the end-of-summer
thunderstorms speckled the baked stone walls. The narrow
streets, a natural humidity trap, freshened up. A clean-smelling

but musty odour filled the air. Meredith welcomed the drop in temperature to pleasant levels, a foreigner unused to the unforgiving heat of the Italian summer. In the fields below her new house, the grapes ripened on the vines and the bees buzzed in the hives. The cacophony of clicking crickets, which reached a crescendo in high summer, slowly dampened in response to the changing climate. The farmers contemplated the coming truffle and mushroom season with glee. Meredith, the cosmopolitan girl from one of the most hectic cities in the world, unwound with the simple pleasures of life – wholesome food, good company and plenty of conversation. The finest ingredients that Italian life has to offer.

Raffaele Sollecito rolled up in Perugia late, stoned and disorganized. He'd spent the last year, his third on his Computer Engineering degree, in Munich as part of an Erasmus programme. He'd had a great time, falling in love with the German way of life that contrasted so much with the Mediterranean upbringing he'd rather forget about. Germany had seemed like a new start. He'd come away with a great respect for its people, with their bent for reserve and privacy, which complemented his shyness well and allowed him to be who he was without judgment. The experience was a breath of fresh air for someone coming from a small Italian town where nosy neighbours and gossip were hot currency. His new enthusiasm for all things German would endear him to Amanda, who was also quietly proud of her German heritage.

However, unlike the Germans he so admired, Raffaele was not a good timekeeper. He had been late submitting his application for the halls of residence where he had stayed for the first two years at Perugia University. Raffaele panicked. He was lazy and barely able to take care of himself without some form of help. The halls of residence were a kind of upmarket hostel, only open to the sons of doctors, who were invariably well off. The building had its own canteens, cleaners that serviced rooms and a private launderette. An ideal home for a mummy's boy. But it was also oversubscribed and now he would have to leave his comfort zone and find a flat off campus.

For Raffaele, university life in Perugia didn't have the same glamorous appeal that it did for foreigners like Amanda and Meredith. He was bored. Could he face another year, he asked himself? Though academically the institution was highly regarded, Perugia was in reality a backwater, no more than a poor man's Florence. Studying in Perugia was the equivalent of going to university in a quiet market town in eastern England, say Norwich or Ipswich, or a provincial place such as Preston, Bangor or Aberystwyth. He knew that Perugia could be a difficult place for students to get their head around. On the one hand, the town had one of the lowest average ages in Italy, because of its 40,000 students. The chat rooms were awash with claims that there was lots of sex to be had and that girls outnumbered boys. But on the other hand, students moaned that they were beset with lethargy or were on the verge of dropping out. Raffaele had also been infected by a lack of motivation that seemed to hold back many students in Italy. University is free and applicants don't necessarily have to get good grades to get in or even graduate. Students can drift into the system, they don't have to sit exams until they feel ready, and some don't leave until they are thirty. The most ambitious were accused of using higher education as little more than a networking opportunity, to the detriment of their studies.

Raffaele didn't want to think about it. Finding a new flat was traumatic because the process required effort and dealing with people. He cut through the red tape by securing a self-contained box on one of the most exclusive streets he could find. Who cared? His dad would pay anyway. Nightmare over. Party on. The first thing he did, after moving his bags in, was spark up a joint.

14

Sex, Work and Simmering Feuds

October 2007

Following her jaunt to Austria, Amanda returned to Perugia on 21 September to move into Pergola Road and enrol on her course. She got on well with Meredith, both Anglophones who could speak only basic Italian.

The atmosphere was like a rerun of Freshers' Week, but this time round the fun was more hardcore and edgy – Erasmus students are older and far away from home. Amanda jumped in head first. She cultivated a friendship with the boys downstairs because there was free homegrown cannabis to be had. She began looking around for other male company. In her diary, Amanda wrote that she felt attracted to many of the good-looking men that now surrounded her, exotic species from far-flung countries that were rare on the bland streets of West Seattle. However, she also admitted to still holding a torch for a mystery boyfriend that she had left behind in the States. David Johnsrud, whose only defect, Amanda said, was that he hadn't had sex with her. He preferred rock-climbing to romance, Amanda moaned. She lost no time in making up for it.

Meredith too was experimenting, but preferred to dip her toe into the pot-fuelled bohemia, rather than lose herself in it altogether. She thought the boys downstairs, particularly Giacomo Silenzi and Stefano Bonassi, were great company. They grew their own cannabis plants. She was pushing her boundaries, trying things she had never done before. She began smoking some dope. She told Filomena that she was loyal to her boyfriend in London and considered unfaithfulness a weakness. She fancied Giacomo Silenzi, but did no more than flirt with him at first. Giacomo had once been a grungy bass player with a Seventies-style centre parting, lank long hair and semi-flared trousers to match. Now he sported a close crop, a designer beard and a large button earring.

Still, Meredith wasn't sleeping around and she often felt uncomfortable when Amanda brought back strange men late at night. On 6 October Meredith pointed to a man who had just entered the Merlin pub. She called him the 'Internet man'. He was of average height, well built and casually dressed, but the dark, brooding stubble across his face made him appear creepy. Meredith flagged him up to her English drinking pal Amy Frost. Amanda had brought him back one night and he'd tried to hit on Meredith or at least touch her up. 'That's the man who always came round to the flat,' Meredith told Amy. 'And he tried to put his arms around me.'

Amanda was soaring high on her new-found freedom. On her MySpace website page, under her seventh-grade nickname 'Foxy Knoxy', on 15 October she wrote:

I'm actually at one of my happiest places right now. I've made plenty of friends here, and I have a lot of fun. I love things like good wine, rock climbing, backpacking long distances with people I love, yoga on a rainy day, making

coffee, drinking tea, and lots of languages. I'm twenty
years old and I like new things. Ooh, and soccer, and
roller coasters, and Harry Potter.

On her MySpace, her Seattle rock heritage came through loud
and clear in her list of likes and dislikes, mixed with standard
head music fare. She listed the Beatles and Led Zeppelin as her
favourites while her taste in films ranged from the Beatles movie
Help! to James Bond and *Fight Club*. She would do yoga when
she felt stressed and strum on the guitar but always the same
chord, she blogged.

Academically, Amanda was coasting, making do with little
more than attending her Italian language classes. Meredith studied harder after lectures, determined to make her Erasmus
placement count towards a good degree and not be just an excuse
to party. She enjoyed Italian history and seminars on Italian
cinema. At Leeds she was reading European Studies, a branch of
international affairs that focuses on the European Union – a
subject that can only be mastered by someone who is really interested in the serious study. The syllabus covers treatises,
administration and directives, dry subjects that require determination, application to study and good language skills. Meredith
was following in the footsteps of her sister in studying Italian. She
relaxed by reading John Le Carré novels at the kitchen table.

After the novelty had worn off, and the weather turned rainy
and cold, some students became discontented. In the cold light
of day, they could see Perugia for what it was – a gloomy and
incestuous light industrial town, where everyone got to know
each other quickly and one street led into another in a perpetual
puzzle. Students joked that when they went out for a walk to
take a break from their studies, they went round in circles. There
was no easy escape, nowhere to catch your breath; it was a hot

house that could be oppressive. There was no room for cars in the old city, so students felt hemmed in. Less disciplined students who didn't get their heads down like Meredith quickly turned to drink and drugs. Trips arranged by the University came as a welcome relief.

Like Club 18–30 holiday reps, the Erasmus coordinators organized pub crawls and coach excursions to the brash superclubs that had sprung up on the out-of-town industrial estates. At the Red Zone, which was 30 km from Perugia, Giacomo hit on Meredith for the first time. Meredith was glad to get out of the glare of the club's ubiquitous red lighting when she climbed back on to the coach, tipsy and tired, in the early hours. She and Giacomo sank under his coat.

Not to be outdone, Amanda had picked up Giacomo's cousin and took him home as well. He wasn't a student and thought Amanda and her pals were prissy intellectuals, faffing around because they couldn't hack it in the real world. The next morning he told Giacomo he had had sex with Amanda.

On 26 October, a week before Meredith's murder, Amanda met Raffaele Sollecito at a classical music concert. He joked that Amanda only had two settings: slow and fast. She was attracted to his Harry Potter looks and made the first move. Amanda took control early on – after a few days there was little she didn't know about him and a lot he didn't know about her. She liked the fact that he had a sporty Audi A3. Somewhat self-consciously Raffaele whisked his new trophy girlfriend off to Assisi to visit the tomb of St Francis.

The nights were closing in. The drop-outs who couldn't handle the hot-house atmosphere were going home. University life in Perugia had always had a shady side bubbling under the surface. Palestinian radicals at the time of the PLO attacks had attended the University for Foreigners. Colonel Gadaffi's son had played for Perugia football club and lots of hardline Libyans had taken a break from the Green Revolution to study there. Ali Agka was a Turkish member of the extremist Islamic group known as the Grey Wolves. He had shot at the Pope but had first come onto the radar of Italian secret services as he passed through Perugia. The Italian approach to such under-the-table dealings was relaxed.

After a month of partying, Amanda's funds were running low. As for many students from similar backgrounds, money was a constant worry. She wasn't exactly broke, though, and her rent of 300 euros a month wasn't a critical problem just yet. She had worked two jobs back in Seattle and saved prudently to fund her year abroad. She had the generous punters of the World Cup bar, in the port area of Seattle, to thank for much of her study-abroad fund – she had made good tips, grafting and flirting hard in equal measure. She had also worked in a second-rate art gallery to pay her fees. Now, once again, she needed a top-up and some pocket money. So she trawled the bars looking for work.

She inquired at the Bear's Lair pub, run by an attractive English woman called Lucy Rigby, a 33-year-old from Shrewsbury, and her 36-year-old Argentine husband, Esteban Pascual. They had just hired someone but directed Amanda to a new bar down by the law courts called Le Chic, which their friend Patrick Lumumba had just opened. Amanda combined her first visit with an opportunity for a drink, dragging Meredith along. Ironically, Patrick was more impressed by the English girl and would have hired her without hesitation if she had been looking. Meredith pointed out the special make of Polish vodka Patrick kept behind the bar.

'I used it myself instead of rum when I was a barmaid making mojitos back in Britain,' Meredith told him. Patrick was surprised she was English as her skin was so dark.

'As she and Amanda headed off to chat with the rest of their group of girlfriends,' Patrick recalled, 'I thought how close-knit they all seemed. It was a Latin and reggae night, and they danced happily, attracting the attention of all the guys around them.' After getting his attention, Amanda asked for a job. The next day Patrick hired Amanda to collect glasses for two shifts a week from 20:00 to 03:00.

One evening after work Amanda went to the downstairs flat to see the boys and cadge a joint. A tall African lad, who had had too much to drink, was lying back on the sofa. He looked a bit like the mystery black man whom she'd been smitten with on her first visit to Perugia. Was it him? Who cares? It was all a haze now. And the novelty of good-looking men had worn off a long time ago. After all, she had tasted the temptation several times since being here. But she did vaguely recognize him from the sunken basketball courts over the road from their flat, opposite the main entrance of the University for Foreigners. She remembered his physique, sinewy and cut-up, particularly his six-pack, which was slashed like an athlete's. Amanda also remembered that he'd tried to chat her up in one of the bars. She smiled coyly and exhaled. The Italian lads excitedly introduced their shadowy new guest as The Baron.

A white slash of teeth smiled back mischievously, forcefully streaming out a grey swirl of pot fumes. He revelled in the shady connotations of his nickname. He liked the strong identity, which made him stand out from the students. He squinted as the clouds drifted upwards over his red eye. Amanda sensed the danger. The basketball courts were the dark side of town, the centre of the local drugs trade. She was turned on. She felt a connection with The Baron. After all, wasn't she also a streetwise kid from an American city? They stole glances while the others weren't looking. Amanda threw him an 'I know you fancy me' smile, a glint of yearning in her stoned, passive eyes. The Baron thought he was on. The lads giggled – just minutes before Amanda had arrived they'd been fantasizing about having group sex with her, trying to convince The Baron that this girl was up for it.

Half an hour later, when Meredith popped in to say goodnight, the room went quiet. The Baron's jaw dropped. Never mind the American, he thought the English girl was breathtakingly beautiful, momentarily eclipsing the chase for Amanda. Meredith smiled, said a few words and left to go to bed. Amanda followed. Meredith was unattainable. He was drunk and doped up. He found his way to the bathroom, did his dos and dozed off in there. He was woken by another of the lads who needed the toilet. He made his way to the sofa and asked his mates if he could crash there for the night. At 05:30 he fell asleep on the sofa with the boys' cat. Flatmate Marco Marzan found him there later that morning.

One day not long after that, Meredith woke up to find that Amanda had left a sex toy shaped like a rabbit sticking out of her see-through make-up bag. She had also left packets of condoms lying around the flat as though she might need them at any instant. Meredith was embarrassed but didn't flag it up out of courtesy. But the sex toy was enough to make Amanda the target of gossip from Meredith's pals.

The British girls said that Amanda was getting a reputation for being a slut. Visitors to 7 Pergola began to pick up on Amanda's selfishly stoned attitude, her flakiness. Even Filomena's mother thought she was odd.

She said that Meredith 'was always very sociable with our daughter and the other Italian girl in the apartment. The other girl, the American, was always very cold and distracted; she seemed to be in a different world.'

As the house grew dirtier and more cluttered, tension grew over Amanda's slovenly attitude to housework. Filomena Romanelli remarked: 'Amanda never cleaned the house, so we had to institute a rota.' Meredith was too polite to confront Amanda, but she did confide in her pal Robyn Butterworth. Robyn winced in disbelief when Meredith said the pair had quarrelled because Knox often failed to flush the toilet, even when menstruating. Filomena began noticing that Amanda could be odd, even mildly anti-social.

'Amanda,' Filomena concluded, 'was someone with quite a lot of interests. She liked music, sports, yoga, languages. Sometimes she had unusual attitudes, like she would start doing yoga while we were speaking, or she would play guitar while we were watching TV.'

Although they had initially got on at a surface level, Filomena was struck by how different Amanda and Meredith were turning out to be. Meredith was fastidious about cleaning and never brought back boyfriends. Relations started to deteriorate.

'At first they got on very well,' Filomena said. 'But then things began to take a different course. There was tension over the cleaning roster in the house. Amanda and Meredith had their own bathroom and Laura [Mezzetti – the fourth flatmate] and I had the other. I know Amanda missed her turn a couple of times. She didn't always respect them.

'Then she would also bring strangers home – both she and Meredith were young and pretty and made friends easily. Meredith never brought men home. The only people who came to the house were two of her English girlfriends. Meredith said she was not interested in boys, she was here to study.'

Filomena knew that Meredith smoked joints with Giacomo, but said: 'I wouldn't call them junkies or addicts.'

Amanda's behaviour struck others as becoming more erratic.

She didn't like it when she wasn't the centre of attention. One night Meredith and the English girls invited Amanda and Raffaele to the Pizzeria Il Bacio. Meredith felt that if she was more inclusive towards Amanda, relations might warm up. But when the conversation left Amanda in the background, she started singing aloud in protest. The English girls were embarrassed. Later, instead of thanking Meredith for her company, Amanda turned spitefully on her. A grinning Amanda told Meredith: 'I fancy Giacomo as well. He's cute.'

Amanda seemed to know that the quiet and gently submissive English girl would feel threatened. 'Me and Giacomo get on really well,' she bragged. Meredith knew that Amanda went to visit Giacomo late at night, ostensibly to smoke pot and learn guitar. 'But I'll let you have him,' Amanda added in mock generosity. Later Meredith told the story to Amy Frost. Amanda's pals wrote off the English girl's disturbing opinion of their friend as a 'culture clash'.

Amanda continued to smoke pot and chill out to Pink Floyd and Genesis. The Baron visited the house below to watch Formula One of a Sunday. Laura met him too when she went downstairs for dope. Amanda stumbled into work tired.

Patrick Lumumba began to get bored of Amanda's 'people friendly' approach to work.

'She spent more time chatting than serving. I'd tell her I needed her to serve more drinks but she was looking for the tips. We had different mentalities,' Patrick would say later, feeling more confident speaking in French than in English or Italian.

'Every time I looked round she was flirting with a different guy. You know it's hard sometimes to impose discipline. It's not my style anyway. But she wasn't doing her job.' Patrick told how the men would become rowdy when he asked Amanda to go back to work. He was told to mind his own business.

Patrick points to his wife and four-year-old child. 'I'm a faithful man, you know. My wife trusts me, but with Amanda it was different. She felt threatened.' As his faith in Amanda slipped, Lumumba wished that he'd given Meredith the job.

'Meredith, yes, I liked her. We joked about the Polish vodka chewed by bisons. She could make a cocktail with it.' Lumumba points at the shelf of drinks against the wall. 'It's that one, the Zubrowka. Amanda was jealous of the little things like that. Meredith had a sparkly personality.'

His partner Aleksandra thought that Amanda was cold and seemed like a girl determined to get her way. She was in left in no doubt that if Amanda put her claws into Patrick, she wouldn't think twice about pushing her aside.

Patrick Lumumba was not a cruel man. He didn't want to hurt Amanda's feelings by sacking her. As a natural diplomat he was also weary of the negative vibe that could be created amongst his fickle student clientele if he treated Amanda harshly. He decided to put up with her. Even though she'd ask to leave early all the time and got into work late so she could call her American boyfriend. 'They were very much in love or so it looked. He sent her presents and she lit up when she mentioned him.'

Amanda wound Patrick up again by further mixing business with pleasure. She invited Sollecito to drink rum and pear juice while she waited tables. Patrick couldn't believe that she was two-timing her American boyfriend. 'But she flirted all the time, she was on the lookout for men all the time. Even when she was going out with Sollecito, that didn't stop her.'

Meredith and Amanda's relationship had grown cooler but one night at a party he threw in the club for his employees, Meredith popped in and made everyone two rounds of her special mojitos.

'She was sparkly and cheery and lifted everyone's spirits. I bumped into her again in town soon after. I asked her if she wanted to have a spell behind the bar when I next had a female DJ playing, as a kind of ladies' night. She jumped at the chance, although she'd stopped coming into Le Chic, and I heard she wasn't hanging around with Amanda much either. I wasn't surprised. The two couldn't have been more different.'

Amanda, meanwhile, was becoming increasingly erratic. 'She smoked, she drank, she flirted, everything a young woman should do. But she wasn't stable, she would fly into a rage and then apologize. She didn't get a lot of sleep. A bit over the top really. I told her I'd asked Meredith to come and work for me and her face dropped and there was a big silence. Then she said, "Fine", and stropped off. I knew then she was extremely jealous of Meredith. She obviously thought she was invading her territory.'

The situation got worse. One night Patrick spotted Amanda in the middle of his crammed dancefloor. Instead of trying to serve the growing queue for rum cocktails, she was whispering sweet nothings to her latest male partner, her chest pressed against his, their mouths just millimetres apart, seemingly unaware of the chaos ensuing around her. 'I never actually fired her, although I came very close. There was no reason for her doing this to me. I just want to know why, what is it she was hiding. She knows what happened because you simply don't lie if you don't know what's true.'

15

Halloween

Friday, 26 October–Wednesday, 31 October

The Baron liked to think himself as a 'grafter' – a mysterious street hustler who made dollars by using his wits and his shadowy contacts. The students excitedly tried to guess why he was called The Baron. Was he a criminal? A drug dealer? A gangster? The Baron just smiled and kept them guessing. On the street he certainly looked the part, instinctively mixing Italian football terrace chic with a distinctive flash of US hip-hop. Both styles were laddish but with a twist of Italian flair: Italian sportswear, tracksuit tops, designer jeans and spotless Nike trainers. Streetwear designed to subtly communicate that he knew the score.

On 26 October The Baron was pushing his way through the fashionable Friday-night crowds of Milan. Stick-thin, bronzed women sporting plate-sized sunglasses and overlarge leather handbags toppled across the pavement, laughing and gossiping into mobile phones. Footballer lookalikes in £1000 suits and tight shirts, worn with a faint homage to *Miami Vice*, began to fill up the smoked-glass bars. The younger boys buzzed through the side streets on scooters or chatted to students outside the coffee bars. The screensaver on the Baron's computer was a picture of himself taken with his hero, fashion designer Giorgio Armani, at a sleek polished-wood-and-glass bar in Milan. Giorgio was smiling with his arms around The Baron. The Baron, decked out in ghetto-fabulous wear including a jewel-encrusted dollar-sign T-shirt and a black and gold coat, pulled his cool game face. One day, The Baron assured himself and anyone who'd listen, he would be a player. He would have a stick-thin WAG hanging off his arm, quaffing champagne in a designer bar. He was just a few scores away, of that fact he was sure.

He hung around. But he was looking forward to getting back to Perugia, little more than 220 miles away or a four-hour ride on the train. His little out-of-town jaunt, shrouded in mystery, would keep his new student pals guessing. They were boring squares who lived in a bubble. A glimmer of excitement kept him going. Amanda was always curious about his close-to-the-edge lifestyle.

But the reality behind the facade was depressing. For whatever reason The Baron had come to Milan, it hadn't worked out. He was stranded. Most of his wheeling and dealing never seemed to pay off. He was skint, tired and, worse still, he didn't have a bed for the night. His loneliness was exacerbated by the in-crowd glamour of the most stylish city in the world, right in his face.

Humiliated, The Baron lowered himself to take advice from one of the city's more scruffily dressed inhabitants. In the magnificent atrium of Milan's central train station, where style walks side by side with squalor, he tapped a tramp on the shoulder.

'Where can I get my head down for the night?' he inquired.

'There's a dosshouse over there.' The homeless man pointed

vaguely in the direction of a group of buildings. The Baron went inside. The place was deserted but it certainly had the utilitarian feel of a public building. 'Hello, is there anyone here?' The Baron shouted into the empty room. Eerily, there was no reply. The Baron felt uneasy. He found the kitchen, lit only by rays of moonlight streaming through the blinds. He looked up, a full moon. The Baron felt a shiver down his spine. Noisily, panicking slightly, he took a knife from a drawer and put it in his backpack. Just in case, he thought. He curled up on the floor, bright eyes keeping a watchful eye on the door and following the night noises around the building. Soon he was too tired to keep them open.

The following morning The Baron was rudely awoken by a woman screaming at him: 'Who are you? What are you doing here?'

'Sorry, I was told I could sleep here,' replied The Baron, coming around.

'No, it's a kindergarten,' the woman said firmly. 'This is my office. You can't stay here.' As she calmed down she began treating him like one of her nursery clients. Patient but firm.

Maria Antonietta Salvatore called the cops and then pointed to the object in his rucksack. 'What's that?' she asked.

'It's a knife,' The Baron admitted. 'I took it from the kitchen, for self-defence . . . there was no one about.' He handed it over to the woman.

The police turned up.

'Documents!' they ordered

The Baron calmly told the woman and the officers that he had paid 50 euros to a guy to sleep there. The staff said that a few coins had been taken from a wardrobe. The police didn't believe the Baron's story: 'You're under arrest for breaking and entering.'

'What? I was told it was a hostel where I could crash for the night.'

'It's a kindergarten, dummy. And you're nicked.'

At the police station, The Baron was also found to be in possession of a laptop and mobile phone in his backpack, which turned out to have been stolen from a solicitor's office in Perugia. He gave them an explanation for having the computer and phone.

'I bought them legitimately at the train station,' he said somewhat confusedly. After the calls were made he was released without charge. The laptop and mobile phone were confiscated while further investigations were carried out. From this point onwards, The Baron didn't have a mobile. Sheepishly, he made his way back to Perugia. He turned up a few days later in shorts and a basketball vest with a ball under his arm to apologize to the solicitor, claiming he had bought the goods at the station.

He hadn't missed much while he was away. That night Amanda brought her new boyfriend Raffaele back to 7 Pergola for the first time. She'd met him only two days before but keenly introduced him to Meredith. Other than that, the weekend was quiet. Meredith took it easy on the booze, knowing that it would be a full-on week ahead, centred around a string of Halloween parties. She did some studying and spoke to her dad back home in England. The Baron resurfaced on Tuesday at Pergola Road. The foursome headed out into town. Meredith walked in front with Raffaele, whilst Amanda and The Baron lagged behind chatting. A former Perugia University researcher called Fabio, who had just parked up near the Pizzeria Contrappunto, noticed them coming out the farm-like gate in front of the house at around 16:30 to 17:00.

'I know that black guy,' Fabio thought to himself. 'He used to hand out flyers for the Merlin pub in front of the University for

Foreigners.' He was 99 per cent sure. Amanda stood out because she was wearing a red Eighties-style American coat whilst the others wore dark clothes. The group walked towards Grimana Square in the rain.

The tension was building up at work. Amanda was sick of Lumumba glowering at her and mumbling under his breath when she didn't move fast enough. Though she didn't care that much, she could do without the office politics. When she arrived at Le Chic later that night she collected a few glasses to show willing, but when the club filled up, she conveniently lost herself in the crowd and began chatting to boys as usual.

At midnight Patrick did his usual rounds, taking in all three floors of the heaving bar. When he found dirty tables overflowing with empties and ashtrays in every room, his patience finally ran out. He told Amanda she could no longer work in the bar. He was firm but fair. Though he was angry, his nature prevented him from showing it. He was also conscious of Amanda's social power – she was popular and had a certain sway amongst the in-crowd that paid his wages. Patrick tried to soften the blow by telling Amanda that she could carry on handing out club flyers, if she was stuck for money, to tide her over until she found something better. Amanda simply looked at him blankly and walked away.

'The club was busy and I didn't see her again that evening,' he recalled, disappointed and somewhat unnerved. Was Amanda seething inside? Did she feel threatened because he wanted to offer Meredith a job? Lumumba couldn't tell.

University was buzzier than usual the next day. The polished parquet floors glistened under rays of blue, red and yellow light, winter-strong and streaming through the stained-glass windows. Amanda checked herself in the near-perfect reflection of the brass-plated lift doors. She shared her gossip about being sacked from Le Chic and the students discussed plans for their Halloween parties later that night. As the sun set just after 17:00, the lights of the grand chandeliers twinkled above ancient recital rooms and the ornate wooden lecture theatres. A faint echo of tinkling piano keys drifted down the marble staircase. The faces leering out of Vatican frescos distorted in the dancing light, morphing in the shadows. An orgy of angels and demons and saints and sinners. The witching night was here.

After classes Amanda, who seemed to be rapidly losing friends, found herself at a loose end. At 19:00 she texted Meredith to find out what she was doing for Halloween. Was Amanda feeling lonely after not being invited anywhere special? After all, it wasn't only Meredith's English pals who found her hard work. Or was Amanda simply trying to kiss and make up with her flatmate after their recent spat of student arguments? Either way, it didn't really matter because Meredith had plans. Meredith loved Halloween and wasn't going to leave a good night to chance.

Meredith responded to Amanda's text: 'I have to go to a friend's house for dinner.' Amanda persisted, almost desperate to see Meredith: 'What are you doing tonight? Do you want to meet up? Have you got a costume?' Meredith said that she was going to Le Chic and 'maybe we'll see each other'. Amanda was a little miffed – Le Chic might be a bit uncomfortable for her right now after last night's falling out with Patrick.

Meredith and Amanda's Italian flatmates, Filomena and Laura, who were older and had a more settled lifestyle, planned on going out with their boyfriends, Marco and Luca. If Amanda stopped out at Raffaele's, as was becoming more frequent, Meredith would be sleeping alone in the old farmhouse. But for now she wasn't worried. She was excitedly getting ready for potentially the craziest night of term. She rented a vampire outfit from a local toyshop, which had also hired out the same costume to half of the students in the city, and iconic *Scream* masks to the other half. Lucy Rigby, the owner of the Bear's Lair bar, fitted Meredith out and painted on the fake blood dripping from her mouth. Just as Meredith had done with her dad, when she was a kid, except then she had used bin bags for her costume. The English girls giggled.

For the Brits and Americans Halloween is a bit of a laugh, the serious debate restricted to arguments that the celebrations have been over-commercialized in recent years. Or that trick-or-treat is a licence for legalized teenage vandalism. Halloween's origins as a Celtic festival to mark the end of the harvest, and the boundary between the living and the dead, have long been obscured. The colours of black and orange, symbolizing fires, and masks worn to ward or taunt evil spirits remain as decorations largely without meaning.

In Italy, however, Halloween is a much deeper and darker concept. The festival in its modern form was born in the region. In the ninth century the then Pope rebranded the Pagan festival as All Hallows' Day, sometimes known as All Saints' Day. Technically, the festival fell on 1 November but custom soon deemed that it was marked the night before as well, hence the name All Hallows' Eve, later shortened to Halloween.

Prosecutor Giuliano Mignini knew more about occult festivals than perhaps any other magistrate in Italy. More than was probably healthy, he thought, smiling. On his desk, files from the Monster of Florence case lay next to his pipe. The unspeakable horrors within their pages – an unholy alliance of freemasonry, black magic and sacrificial serial murder – hidden by their mundane manila bindings. Mignini shook his head in despair. The Monster of Florence was still haunting his life all these years on. At 19:30 he left his office, a typical 1930s marble-clad municipal building, and walked head first into the blustery wind, leaves and litter swirling around his feet.

Meredith's Halloween gang, including Sophie Purton, Robyn Butterworth, Natalie Hayward and two friends called Monique and Lina, then went to eat at Amy Frost's house before stepping out. Dinner at a restaurant was beyond their budget these days, as funds tightened up towards the latter half of term. Meanwhile, across town, outside the University for Foreigners, students in fancy dress were shivering in the bus queues. The Erasmus coordinators had laid on coaches to the Red Zone nightclub again, this time for a spook-themed party, where they could get wasted on cheap Halloween cocktails that were either blood-red goo or glowed luminous green in the dark. A few yards away in Grimana Square the junkies and drunkards talked amongst themselves. Some of the braver students walked into the shadows of the plane trees to buy some last-minute cannabis or ecstasy. The dealers sat on the edge of the sunken basketball court to avoid the glare of the tall streetlights.

On the bench nearest the glass news kiosk, now closed for the night, ageing 'gentleman of the road' Antonio Curatolo watched the scene with faint bemusement. In silence, as usual. And waiting for the orange buses to pull off and the commotion to stop, so that he could get his head down for a bit, just grateful that it was a dry evening.

Soon enough the ghouls and vampires drew away into the night of witches, while the older Perugians settled in front of their television sets looking forward to the long weekend ahead. The 2nd of November was as much a holiday as the 1st, as it was a Friday. For the Italians, the *Festa dei Morti* is an important event. Loved ones who have passed away are remembered, the earnings of florists at graveyards peak and there is always a good lunch after church and a visit to the cemetery.

As he walked home, Mignini pondered the recent surge in Satanic stories in the press. He'd had to read them during the Monster of Florence investigation. But were they true or just scare stories? Were the so-called Satanists just bored kids who were easily led? Some academics highlighted the religious paradox of modern-day Halloween. The Vatican had rubber-stamped the festival into modern existence, mainly as a ploy to convert pagans in the Middle Ages. But now commentators claimed the church was hypocritically and desperately trying to curb the cult's worst excesses. In 2007, Italian priests joined up with police officers for a war on so-called 'Satanic crime'. An increase in murders linked to devil worship, church desecrations and Black Masses led to clerics being seconded to the police Anti-Sect Squad. Some people at least were taking the devil links seriously.

Critics of the church said they were just trying to grab headlines and scare people into valuing their role. However, the rise of such practices over the past decade has also been treated as a social rather than religious phenomenon. So-called Satanists are often no more than poorly educated and impressionable youths, some experts argued, seduced by exoticism and a desire for mystery rather than a genuine belief in the occult. Others pointed to the influence of youth subcultures such as goths and 'vampyre' fashion, black metal and cyber punk. They characterized devil worshippers as kids who'd simply taken things too far. Even so, they could be violent, they claimed to commit human sacrifice, and the so-called sects preyed on the psychologically frail in the community.

Italy was still reeling from an infamous trial dubbed the Case of the Beast of Satan, in which two 'sect' members were bludgeoned to death amid an orgy of sex, drugs and heavy metal music. Papal experts estimated that Italy was home to 8,000

Satanic sects with more than 600,000 members. Umbria was named as a hotspot.

Mignini could well believe it. He arrived home from the office at 20:00 and after dinner watched the news and read a history book. He looked out of his window into the night, the night when the dark secrets of evil intent in Umbria and Tuscany threatened to break the veil of beauty that kept them in check. He noticed that it had begun to drizzle.

At around midnight Robyn, Amy, Sophie, Natalie and Meredith climbed the cobbled hill to the town square to meet up with a larger group. The girls had decided in favour of a local pub crawl around the old town instead of a coach to the Red Zone. Meredith preferred the intimacy of the old bars and the more relaxed atmosphere of an informal get-together. She could pace her drinking and go home when she wanted.

Meanwhile, across town, Amanda walked into Le Chic as though nothing had happened. Without a care in the world, she knocked back the free red wine and joined in the Halloween party that Patrick had thrown to bring in the punters. He served behind the bar and, as the evening drew on, played his African drums. Slowly the deep African rhythm seeped into the crowd. Condensation ran down the walls. Bodies moved closer and closer. Dancers often said that Patrick's solos were like an organic form of house music, sending his audience mind, body and soul into a trance-like state. Amanda, holed up in a quiet corner, got intimate with two lads she had bumped into. Patrick thought one of them was Sollecito at first, but then realized he was nowhere to be seen. He didn't see Amanda leave.

The Baron rubbed his hands gleefully. He carefully ironed a polo shirt and pulled on a fresh pair of jeans. He'd been invited to a house party by a group of Spanish girls. Cheap booze, free pot and a good chance of sloping off with one of pretty señoritas at the end of the night. A perfect evening for The Baron. He liked their company because the Spanish girls were slightly in awe of him, easily taken in by his tales of derring-do. In addition, the competition was weak. The party was being hosted by a group of Spanish boys who lived at Priory Road. They dug The Baron even more than the girls, simply because of his prowess on the basketball court. He'd met them on the concrete ballpark at Grimana Square, where students liked to come because they could play for free. For all its faults, Perugia was a place where friendship was easy to come by. Young people got to know each other quickly, with doors wide open to strangers and friends alike. The Baron knew he would have been lost without this.

Mignini went to bed. His mind drifted off again to the Monster of Florence case. He couldn't get it out of his head. Staring into the blackness, turning over the details, looking for a fresh angle on a mystery that was almost becoming an obsession. Mignini had been given the case because of the involvement of a local doctor, from Perugia, called Francesco Narducci. Dr Narducci's body was found floating in Lake Trasimeno near the city in 1985. At first investigators suspected suicide but, after a mysterious anonymous phone call in 2003, the police started to treat it as a murder. The life of the deceased Narducci came under close scrutiny. Then there was an astonishing twist in the tale. The police found enough evidence to accuse the dead doctor of carrying out a series of abominable murders and mutilations on nights of the full moon.

The spree of eight double killings took place in Florence from 1974 onwards. The victims were often courting couples who were shot through their car doors whilst romancing in secluded areas. To make matters worse, Perugia's freemasons were accused of covering up Narducci's guilt when he was alive. And switching the body of the drowned man, in a plot straight out of a thriller. The killings stopped in 1985 after Narducci was found dead. But in 2003 the case was reopened with Mignini at the helm. Ominously, he argued that Narducci carried out the murders with the help of a Satanic cult, with the masons covering for both. At first, the authorities believed him. And he was given *carte blanche* to solve the Monster of Florence case once and for all.

At half past midnight Meredith and the gang were in the Merlin pub, where Amy was friendly with the owner, Piero Alessi. After a few drinks they were joined by Pisco, the owner of the House of Delirium, another disco pub that stands behind the cathedral. Sophie was especially enjoying the heady, cosmopolitan atmosphere. She was chatted up by Hicham, a young Arab who worked as a cook in a local restaurant and fancied her like mad. He had met Sophie several times before but was too chivalrous to make a move. Sophie warmed to him after he had saved her from the advances of a man she found intrusive. He had danced with her to fend him off. On another occasion he had taken her home when she was too drunk to walk. Tonight they smooched for the first time.

At 02:00 Amanda switched from Le Chic to the Merlin pub to meet some friends, people she didn't really know. Her night had been restless and patchy, rather than the non-stop fun that she'd expected from the Halloween hype. She felt a bit lonely, so she thought of calling it a night. However, she was also keen to have one last throw of the dice, in particular to catch up with a handsome young Greek called Spiros whom she had set her sights on. Miserably, it didn't work out. Amanda went home to Raffaele's shortly afterwards to sleep off the stress of it all.

The Baron was too cool for fancy dress but had a good time all the same. He enjoyed being 'one of the crowd' and the foreign students he chatted up assumed that he was like them – on a course and from some exotic country. The Baron noticed that the students didn't like to leave their comfort zone, and if he pretended to be one of them they got on better. For a few hours he had an identity and felt a little less insecure. As the night wore on the Spaniards went on to the Merlin pub. The Baron followed. By now he was hammered. At some point in the evening he bumped into a beautiful girl dressed as a vampire. He didn't recognize her at first. Then it clicked. 'So, you've come to drink my blood!' he joked. He remembered that she had supported the England side when they were watching the rugby World Cup in a bar. He thought she looked great. He chatted her up. He recognized Meredith.

When the Merlin closed at 02:30 Meredith and her pals went on to the House of Delirium, where they danced and drank until 05:00. The Baron and a few of the Spanish stragglers followed them down and lost themselves in the crowd.

At 03:00 Patrick Lumumba locked up Le Chic and also headed for the action at the House of Delirium to chill out with a nightcap. He bumped into Meredith and mentioned the idea of her working at Le Chic again.

'She smiled sweetly and said she couldn't wait, and she'd bring all her friends back to my club for me.'

Hell-raising students dressed in *Scream* masks howled into the night. Witches and ghosts made bloodcurdling screeches. Frankenstein and Dracula pretended to attack each other with rubber axes. Patrick finished his drink and shot off back home to his wife and kid. That was the last time he heard of either Meredith or Amanda for three days – until 18:00 on Saturday, 3 November, when a couple of of their friends walked into his club.

Amy, Meredith and Robyn returned home by foot, while Sophie stayed on with Hicham and two of her girlfriends from Holland and the Ukraine. After more dancing and another quick snog with her Arabian beau, Sophie parted company with the hardcore about 06:00.

Mignini woke early as usual. As on most days now, there was a niggling worry in the back of his mind. As a result of his investigation into the Monster of Florence, he'd been charged with a technical infringement of the rules. The Florence Prosecutor's office had accused him of investigating a lead provided by a taped telephone conversation which compromised a high official of the same office in the context of the Monster of Florence case. It was a complicated and confusing issue, not uncommon in politically sensitive cases involving powerful people. But it was one that had to be addressed all the same. Deep down he knew the accusations were formalities of which he would be cleared. He was just trying to get at the truth. However for now, on the night after Halloween, they were haunting his reputation.

16

Murder One: Revisited

Thursday, 1 November

Meredith was tired and giddy when she arrived home in the freezing early-morning hours following her Halloween party. 'Hello, anyone in?' she yelled into the darkness of the interior, after fumbling drunkenly with her keys, not helped by the dodgy front-door lock. No one answered. Amanda must be at her Italian boyfriend's house, Meredith presumed. Amanda had slept out of the house nearly every night since she had met Raffaele exactly one week before on the 24 October. Meredith had met Raffaele only a couple of times since his first visit to the flat on the 26th. She recalled that Filomena and Laura were also spending the night away. She was alone. Sloppily she wiped the vampire make-up off her face and crashed out in bed, her head still spinning.

She slept alone that night. It was cold and she could do with a cuddle. But her new Italian squeeze, Giacomo Silenzi from the downstairs flat, had gone away to spend the vacation holy days at his parents' house at Porto San Giorgio. He hadn't even sent her a text message to ask her how the Halloween parties were going. Italian men! She had been warned.

The house at 7 Pergola settled down for the night. Wooden beams creaked. Doors gently clanked in time with the drafts that streamed through the ancient, ill-fitting surrounds. Meredith pulled her beige quilt up tight – there was no central heating. The excitement of the previous evening was now a fading memory, dissolving as fast as the alcohol in her blood. As Meredith drifted off, she was oblivious to the rain that was beginning to sweep the shutters of her house. And to the rat-like drug dealers who moved around stealthily in the bushes below her flat, fast-moving shadows trying to find their valuable stashes under the faint background light.

In Apple Tree Street, which ran parallel to Pergola Road, more dealers were prying open the iron doors of the gas-meter cupboards to retrieve parcels of cannabis and heroin to sell on to the addicts who appeared at Grimana Square all round the clock. Meredith couldn't remember whom she had spoken to at the Halloween party, or if she had flirted with anybody – it was all a haze and all she wanted now was to get some sleep. As the winter sun rose tentatively at 06:41 Meredith was asleep and the drug dealers had scurried back into their boltholes.

By morning the storm clouds had passed. Bright midday sunshine teased Amanda out of Raffaele's crumpled bed at his flat. That morning he had been using his landline, either on the phone or on the internet. At 12:02 he interrupted his connection, stopping to chat to Amanda. But Amanda didn't want to hang around. Raffaele's was not a typical bachelor pad. He was fastidious in his tidiness. No dirty dishes, no smelly clothes. Amanda arrived home at 7 Pergola at around 13:00 to get herself together again, change clothes, maybe have a decent shower. Raffaele joined her later that afternoon and began preparing some pasta for a late lunch. Meredith emerged from her room, delicate and hungover, while they were pottering around in the kitchen. She looked like death warmed up in more ways than one – the vampire blood from her Halloween costume was still dripping from her mouth. Amanda laughed and then asked her if she wanted some breakfast.

'No thanks,' Meredith declined politely, the thought of pasta making her gag slightly. She went into the bathroom near the utility room, the one where the faeces would be found by the police in less than 24 hours' time.

'I'm going out in a minute,' she explained to Amanda and Raffaele. 'I'm having something to eat at some friends'.' One of them was Sophie Purton. Amanda had never met Sophie, but knew from their banter that Sophie was one of the English girls in Meredith's inner circle. Meredith slipped out of the long bathroom and back into her bedroom and then into the shower room next to her own. Raffaele watched as he poured the pasta into the colander, the steam warming the cold air for a second and misting up the kitchen windows. It was gloomy outside.

Meredith spent around fifteen minutes in the shower, while Raffaele finished off making the sauce and serving the meal. Sitting at the table, at the opposite end of the corridor from Meredith's room and the shower, they heard the bathroom door open and Meredith's door close but couldn't see her.

'Nice jeans,' said Amanda, as Meredith finally emerged to go out.

'Not mine,' said Meredith. 'My boyfriend's . . . my London boyfriend's, that is,' she added, smiling playfully. They all laughed at the in-joke – having a boyfriend at home and another in Perugia was almost standard for the mischievously confident Erasmus girls.

Meredith slung her brown handbag over her shoulder – the one that would be abandoned on her bloody bedsheets in less than twelve hours. She put on her red and white Puma training shoes – the pair that police would find centimetres from her body. She draped a coat over her arm – the arm that would become bruised while fighting off her attacker. 'See you later,' she said as she slid out of the door at 15:00.

After their meal, Raffaele washed up, sat down and built up a joint. Like many young pot-heads he bought into the urban myths that bond smokers together. 'You know,' he said to Amanda, as he carefully passed her the smouldering joint, 'I once met a girl who smoked five or six of these, almost pure, and could still do her exams.' Maybe he felt guilty that he was smoking pot instead of studying.

Amanda smiled as she inhaled, her eyes squinting as the smoke rolled back over her face 'That's nice,' she said, entwining her body over his on the sofa. The joints, fat with skunk grass and popping seeds, went back and forth for the next two hours.

Meredith climbed the hill, past Grimana Square and the basketball court, to Pinturicchio Street, named after a Renaissance artist. She had a choice of going either straight up through the Etruscan gate, a shorter but steeper route, or round the softer slope up to Robyn Butterworth's house at 22 Bontempi Street. In the end, Meredith plumped for the less steep but longer route up to the girls' tiny flat. She arrived there around 16:00. Sophie Purton had arrived half an hour earlier and was already busy making the pizzas.

Raffaele and Amanda left 7 Pergola Road and walked back to Raffaele's flat. Later, under police interrogation, there was an hour's difference in their recollection. Amanda said they left at 17:00. The sun was going down. Raffaele was sure it was 18:00. But both agreed they were stoned. The sun set at 17:04. Like a curtain over a stage, darkness descended quickly that night, of all nights.

One of Raffaele's friends, a Serbian female medical student, remembered that it was nearer 18:00. Jovana Popovic had knocked at Raffaele's flat between 17:30 and 17:45 but no one was in. She wanted to ask Raffaele for a favour, to see if he would run her up to the train station in his Audi to collect some luggage later that night. As she waited around, he arrived but all he said was 'OK'. Popovic thought he was being off and cold, but she didn't realize that he was high as a kite.

Around half an hour later Raffaele turned on his computer and began downloading the movie *Amélie*. A film called *Stardust* also took his fancy. The publicity shot showed a blonde damsel (Sienna Miller) in the arms of a well-dressed, dark-haired young hero (Charlie Cox). Their pose was eerily similar to the embrace Raffaele and Amanda would share in front of the world's cameras outside 7 Pergola in less than 24 hours. The movie ticked all the boxes – action adventure for Raffaele to gawp at while he smoked pot, Harry Potter-esque fantasy romance for Amanda.

Amanda and Raffaele then went for a walk into town. Dusk was the signal for Perugia's unseen army of petty criminals and drug dealers to come out on to the streets. Albanian thief Hekuran Kokomani was in the vicinity of 7 Pergola. At 20:18 Patrick Lumumba sent his text message to Amanda telling her not to come into work. According to Raffaele, he and Amanda returned to his pad between 20:30 and 21:00 to have something to eat and smoke pot. During a second interview with police he said that Amanda left him to go home alone, telling him she was going to Le Chic to meet some friends. But the situation is confused. At 20:40 Raffaele's Serbian pal Jovana Popovic buzzed his intercom to tell him that she no longer needed a lift to the station. Through the intercom she spoke to Amanda, who laughed and said that Raff was there and invited her in, but she declined and got off. At 20:35 Knox replied to Lumumba's text,

'See you later. *Buona serata.*' Her phone was then switched off or at least remained inactive until 12:07 the next day.

The clocks had gone forward the week before in a bid to wring out as much daylight as possible from the winter evenings. The Italian disposition can be especially sensitive to Northern European gloom. But the streets were a velvety black by now, the stars and moon hiding behind ominously low clouds. At around 21:00 Meredith and Sophie stepped out of Robyn's flat into the enveloping gloom. It was time to go home. The girls had opted for an early night after the previous one's excesses. It was faintly foggy but the air was crisp and the sounds sharp.

Glare from the old lamps fell on to the stone walls. Swirls of fast-moving wind jetted up the narrow high-sided street – an architectural wind-tunnel that could unnerve pedestrians caught off-guard. The cold grey walls amplified Meredith's footsteps, even though the soles of her trainers were rubber – the footsteps of her last walk home. The steepness of the hill required concentration. Though the surface was even and smooth, Meredith leaned backwards to compensate for the gradient. A shadow suddenly drew over them – they were walking under one of the five main gates in the Etruscan wall, a lancet arch rebuilt in the Middle Ages. For a moment, caught under its shelter, the air was filled with thousands of years of must creeping out from under the megalithic blocks. The papal coat of arms, engraved with lilies, looked down from the wall.

A sharp increase in gradient took Meredith's breath away momentarily, as the street suddenly gave way to steps, dragging her knees downwards. A faint smell of stagnant water drifted up from the brick drains that ran down each side of the street. Bontempi Street dovetails into Rose Street and then Wolf Street. Sophie Purton peeled off to go home leaving Meredith to complete her final journey home alone. It was 21:05.

The street was deserted but Meredith felt reassured by the familiar sight of the huge red pumpkin lanterns that swayed outside the Chinese restaurant on Pinturicchio Street. She was nearly home – past the barber's and the cramped but stylish black-and-white-tiled hair salon, the telephone shop, the travel agent and the Athena book store where she had browsed spy novels in Italian, forcing herself to brush up her language skills.

She felt slightly uneasy walking past the ghostly, deserted building at number 38, overrun with rats and nettles. Cool, stale air seeps out of the broken windows, and can be smelled all around. At this point on the road, pedestrians are forced to walk around the cars parked on the pavement, and into the middle of the street. They are often taken by surprise by the speeding vehicles that fly around the bend unexpectedly, horns blaring. A risk Meredith would have to take if she was to get home. Ironically, a few metres later, Meredith decided not to take a short cut down a dangerous-looking dark alleyway, a no-go area where addicts from nearby Grimana Square lurked in the shadows. Instead, she carried on walking to the end of the street and at the golden shutters of the Cioccolateria Artigiana, turned right next to Grimana Square and down the steps on to Pergola Road. For a few seconds, she was caught on the grainy, haunting images of a CCTV camera at the entrance to the car park opposite her house. A short while earlier at 20:43 the same CCTV camera had filmed another shadowy figure following the same route, seemingly heading towards Meredith's house. The person was dressed in light-coloured clothing, similar to what the police would later claim Amanda was wearing, and had just got out of a white car. A tall athletic man was also recorded passing by in the same direction.

Meredith arrived home at around 21:10–21:15. From now on, officially at least, she was in the kill zone. According to the autopsy report, she could have been murdered at any time from this point on. She was most probably tired from the previous heavy night and wanted to go to bed.

Before a natural disaster, such as an earthquake or a tsunami, a phenomenon often occurs of a sudden and unexplained increase in activity. Wild animals become noisy and agitated. An increase in movements and events is recorded. During a half-hour period between 22:00 and 22:30 the activity in the dark around the house spiked dramatically.

During this period, when Meredith was most likely dead or in the process of being killed, several strange dramas played out. A car containing a man, woman and child broke down near the entrance to the car park. At the same the Albanian petty criminal Hekuran Kokomani was travelling down the road by 7 Pergola when he found what he thought were two large bin bags in the road. They got up and one of them came at him – a girl brandishing a knife. The other black figure came at him too and Kokomani had to punch him to thwart his advance, causing the assailant's glasses to fall off. Astonishingly, one of the three night-stalkers, he says, was The Baron, whom he knew from when he worked as a gardener in the same country restaurant. An extraordinary cat-fight ensued in which Kokomani threw a mobile phone and some olives at a young woman who was with The Baron. The Albanian said the mystery woman was erratic, violent and threatening him with a knife. She was pretty, sported a blondish bob and spoke with a foreign accent. When order was restored, the Albanian asked why he could hear strange sounds coming from 7 Pergola. The Baron told him there was a birthday party going on. Bizarrely, The Baron then offered the Albanian money to borrow his car. When he refused and drove off, he says he could see a young, white Italian man in his wing mirror, running after him with a knife. Kokomani got away but at the lights he had to reverse his car to allow a breakdown truck to pass by. The truck was on the way to assist the family that had broken down outside the car park.

Kokomani's testimony in court would differ slightly and his credibility was undermined by his declaring that it was raining on the night of 1 November and that he had seen Amanda in July with her uncle. It had not rained on 1 November. However, it had definitely rained the previous night on 31 October. The prosecutor suggested that he had got the nights mixed up and he may have seen them on the 31 October. The defence simply wrote him off as a spoofer. In addition, Amanda hadn't been anywhere near Perugia in July and therefore could not have been spotted by the Albanian at that time.

Around the same time an attractive twenty-something local called Alessandra Formica was walking back to her vehicle in the same car park with her boyfriend. As they came down the steps from Grimana Square into Pergola Road, a young black man wearing a dark puffer jacket bumped into her boyfriend. She turned round and said, 'Excuse me', but the rude pedestrian just kept his head down and walked off in a hurry. Ms Formica also saw the broken-down car with the family in it. The strange vignettes of coincidence swirled around the cottage like litter.

At 23:00 a dark-coloured car was seen parked outside the cottage by the garage mechanic, Gianfranco Lombardi, who was driving the tow truck.

'It was about 11 p.m. on the night of 1 November 2007,' he recalled. 'And I was in the area because I had been called out to fix a broken-down car. When I got to Sant'Antonio road, close to the house where Meredith Kercher was murdered, I saw a dark-coloured car parked outside and I noticed the gate on the drive was open. The car had an old-fashioned number plate. I didn't notice anyone in the car and I didn't notice anyone coming or going during the eight or ten minutes it took me to load the broken-down car on to my tow truck.' Raffaele Sollecito's Audi was dark coloured but according to him he was still safely tucked up in his flat. And it was new. He told police that between 23:00 and 01:00 the next morning he was researching coursework on the internet.

Between 22:30 and 23:00 a bloodcurdling scream cut through the chaos – followed by footsteps running away from the scene. Seemingly no one heard it. But a quirk of fate, similar to that which led Elisabetta Lana to find Meredith's phone the next day, meant that one old woman was at least in a position to. Pensioner Nara Capezzali should have been fast asleep after going to bed early. However, that night she had taken pills that forced her to go to the bathroom more frequently.

When she got up she was startled by a deep, penetrating scream that made her skin crawl. Two minutes later she heard footsteps running in opposite directions – one person ran up the iron steps that led to the roof level of Sant'Antonio car park, which was directly below her flat. The other footsteps were on the gravel on the path of 7 Pergola, which tailed off in the direction of the winding road into the countryside. A young schoolteacher nearby could prove that Mrs Capezzali wasn't going mad – she heard the scream too. Antonella Monacchia also heard two people arguing heatedly.

Like an atomic reaction, the chain of screams, rows and footsteps began to rattle through the half-lit streets and alleyways. Suddenly, in Grimana Square, Antonio Curatolo was jolted from his stupor. Unusually, there wasn't much street life going on. Except deep within the basketball court in front of him, under the trees, he could hear a young couple arguing. They were sitting on the edge of the court wall behaving erratically. One minute they would stop and cuddle. Another they would walk tentatively across the court, jump on to a raised area and look towards 7 Pergola opposite, popping their heads quickly over the edge in a way that made Curatolo think they didn't want to be seen. He said it was it was as though they were scoping 7 Pergola to see if the coast was clear, to see if it was safe to go home. But as it may not have been, with the presence of a broken-down car, a tow truck, a mystery dark vehicle and various pedestrians, the couple simply waited and watched. Later he identified the couple as Amanda Knox and Raffaele Sollecito.

17

Fatal Flashback

2 November, 00:10

The new day was barely ten minutes old when Meredith's father John found himself caught up in a heartbreaking situation. Unknowingly he called his dead daughter on the phone. He waited in silence for the slightly delayed international mobile connection to kick in. Although he was unaware of it, exactly 1308 km (812.5 miles) away his daughter lay dead or dying in a pool of blood. Even if Meredith was suffering a slow, agonizing demise, as the police later suspected, she could not have answered the phone. Both of her mobiles (including the one Filomena had loaned her) had already been deliberately taken away to prevent her from calling for help, and dumped in Elisabetta Lana's garden. John put the phone down and went to bed. He'd wanted to wish his daughter goodnight. Not bid her goodbye. That would happen a few days later when Stephanie Kercher would formally identify the body.

That night someone matching the description of The Baron had been seen acting suspiciously near 7 Pergola by two witnesses. By 02:00 he was out dancing – whilst Meredith's body was still warm, The Baron headed out to the House of Delirium pub. He had a few drinks and then hit the dancefloor. Back at the scene of the crime there were more suspicious goings-on – several people had heard loud voices coming from the house in the early hours. Had someone gone back to check if Meredith was dead yet? Had the couple seen arguing at the Grimana basketball court returned after the coast was clear? Were the murderer or murderers cleaning up the evidence?

Raffaele yawned and shut down his computer, he says, at 03:33. So it couldn't have been him making the noises at 7 Pergola, he states. But he did remember, if somewhat hesitantly, that Amanda was not around at this time. Had she gone back alone? It certainly wasn't The Baron. If The Baron had been involved in Meredith's murder, he wasn't showing it. At 04:30 he was still in the pub. At 06:42 the sun rose, an element of calm fanning out over the chaotic events of the night, cleansing most of the seedy activity off the street.

But not all of it. 'Kill you bitch,' the boy shouted into his mobile phone, his mouth foaming, gesticulating violently with a bloody right hand. Alessia Ceccarelli, the girlfriend of the owner of the glass news kiosk on Grimana Square, watched the mystery boy between 07:00 and 07:30, noting he was wearing a wool cap, a dark jacket and jeans. A few minutes later he was observed washing his wound clean in a fountain. Who was he?

Meanwhile, around one hundred metres away, diagonally across the other side of the square, a young girl with piercing laser-blue eyes and pale alabaster skin was waiting impatiently for the convenience store to open. This shop at the bottom of Raffaele's street. She stomped her feet to keep warm, even though she was wearing a hat and scarf, jeans and a grey-white jacket, similar in lightness to the one worn by the figure caught on CCTV near 7 Pergola ten hours before.

'Good day,' said Marco Quintavalle, the shop's owner, to the girl, as he opened up the shutters. But she didn't reply. Instead she headed straight for the shelves stacked with cleaning products, most significantly including bleach, before paying and heading in the direction of 7 Pergola.

Raffaele said he and Amanda woke up at around 10:00. Around the same time Meredith's Ericsson phone, the one that was registered to Filomena Romanelli, had been found by Elisabetta Lana. And around the same time events leading to the macabre discovery began unfolding. Half an hour later Amanda left to go home to freshen up, carrying a plastic bag, and Elisabetta Lana was at the Postal Police station. At 10:58 Inspector Bartolozzi officially entered Meredith's phone on police records. Two minutes later Amanda says she arrived at 7 Pergola, although the timing may only be a rough estimate. The journey from Raffaele's flat to 7 Pergola would normally take between five and ten minutes.

'Is anybody there?' Amanda had found the door open and called inside, she says. She went into her room, took off her clothes and went to have a shower. She saw blood – but wasn't too alarmed to not carry on with her shower.

By 11:30 Amanda was back at Raffaele's place, according to him, saying she was worried. But not too worried to have breakfast. They both returned to 7 Pergola to investigate their suspicions further. Filomena's room was 'in chaos', Amanda discovered. She later told the court: 'I saw clothes on the floor. I saw the window was broken. I thought we had been robbed. Meredith's door was locked but this didn't alarm me. I was only alarmed when I called and she didn't answer.'

Raffaele made an abortive attempt to break down Meredith's door, he later claimed. At 11:38 Inspector Bartolozzi had identified the phone as Filomena's and got her address. At 12:07 Amanda switched her phone back on – it had been off since

20:35 the previous evening when she texted Lumumba – and called Meredith's Motorola phone with the British SIM, presumably to find out where she was. Or, if she was the murderer, to cover her tracks by making herself look concerned, knowing that the calls would be logged.

Filomena Romanelli received a phone call from Amanda just after midday. She couldn't remember exactly when but records pinpointed 12:08, crucially placing the conversation 26 minutes before the police unexpectedly arrived. Filomena said Amanda 'told me that she had slept at Raffaele's house and that when she had gone back to our house she had found the door open and blood in her bathroom. She told me that she'd had a shower, that she was scared and that she was going to call Raffaele Sollecito. It seemed really strange to me and I asked her to check that the house was in order and to call the police or Carabinieri.'

Amanda and Raffaele ignored her advice and did not call the police. Instead at 12:14 and 12:15 Amanda tried Meredith's Motorola again and the Ericsson with Filomena's SIM in it. A few minutes later Raffaele topped up the credit on his mobile so that he could join the fray, an international telephone drama that would take the police and the media months to unravel.

The police arrived at 12:34. One minute later Amanda's phone rang. Filomena had finally got through to her – she'd tried twice before at 12:12 and 12:20 and Amanda hadn't called her back with an update, leaving the mystery hanging agonizingly in the air. Amanda told Filomena that her window had been broken and that her clothes were all over the room.

Raffaele received a phone call from his dad at 12:40. At 12:45 Amanda and her flatmate shared the third and final phone conversation before Filomena arrived in person. Filomena recalled:

'She told me that the window in my room was broken and that my room was in a mess. At this point I asked her to call the police and she told me that she already had.' The police were already on site.

At 12:46, back at the police station, Inspector Bartolozzi, who was liaising with Inspector Battistelli at the scene, reported that the second mobile phone – Meredith's British Motorola – had been handed in.

'Hello,' said the sleepy voice at the end of the bad line. The next call Amanda had made was to her mum Edda Mellas back in the States at 12:47. The time in Seattle was 04:47, eight hours behind Perugia at that time of year.

'Mom, I'm home and I'm OK,' Amanda told her. Slightly startled, her mother said: 'OK, what's going on?'

Knox replied: 'Well, something strange is going on.'

Amanda told Edda that she had returned to the cottage after spending the night with Sollecito, an early insight into the story that would become her alibi. She said she thought they had been burgled and that she suspected that someone *was still in the house*. Edda told her immediately to call the police. Chris Mellas, her young husband, sat up in bed. 'Tell her to get out of the place and call the cops.'

'We have,' answered Amanda. If the timing of this call is correct, then Amanda failed to tell her mother that the police were already there. However, in general, Amanda's phone calls to her mother throw a much more favourable light on her behaviour in comparison to the awkward conversations she had with Filomena. She spoke openly and with detail, describing how she noticed a few spots of blood in the sink after having her shower. 'Perhaps someone had cut themselves or one of the girls was having a period,' Amanda rationalized. But she couldn't think of any reason why there was unflushed faeces in the other bathroom – this was very odd, Amanda told her mum. Edda said that Amanda was clearly worried but not panicking. Amanda said: 'My mind didn't jump to murder: it's not something that comes into my life experience.'

At 12:50 Raffaele called his sister Vanessa in the Carabinieri to ask for advice. One minute later he called the Carabinieri emergency number for the first time, and successfully again at 12:54, despite the presence of the civil police. He even went so far as to tell them that there had been a break-in but nothing was stolen, while he hadn't even been in the bedroom and Filomena hadn't arrived yet. Was he doing this from the secrecy of Amanda's bedroom, while the police were talking to Marco and Luca?

Marco and Luca, the boyfriends of Filomena and Paola Grande, had arrived shortly before 13:00. Marco said: 'Amanda and Raffaele were in Amanda's room because at a certain point they came out into the corridor and we introduced ourselves.' At 13:00 Filomena and Paola arrived. Amanda and Raffaele eventually emerged from Amanda's bedroom to be introduced to the two young men and the woman they had never met before: Luca, Marco and Paola. They seemed confused and sat in the sitting room/kitchen as Luca began to take charge of the situation.

'What's Meredith's mobile phone number?'

Filomena wrote it down on a yellow post-it note.

'Does she always lock her room?'

'Only when she goes out. Never at home.'

Meanwhile, back at the police station, Inspector Bartolozzi switched on Meredith's British Motorola phone, verifiable later during the investigation because the handset sent a signal to the nearest phone mast – the Strada Borghetto di Prepo cell. According to Raffaele, the Postal Police arrived now at 13:05

instead of 12:34. At around 13:15 Luca broke down Meredith's door.

Shortly afterwards at 13:24 Amanda called Seattle again (US time 05:24). Her mum was sitting up wide awake in bed. Over the noise of shouting in the background Amanda said: 'Oh, my God, they're screaming about a foot near the closet. The cops are screaming. I'm outside the house. I don't know what's going on. I gotta go.' A few minutes later Amanda called her mum for the third time, the agitation in her voice. 'It's not a foot, there's a body near the closet or in the closet. I can't make out which.'

'Who is it?' Edda asked.

Amanda replied: 'I don't know, I haven't seen, but we can't get hold of Meredith. It's Meredith's room. I gotta go. The police want to talk to me.'

If this is correct, then Amanda clearly had details about the position of the body even though she may not have looked at the murder scene for herself. The fact that she had become aware of the position of the body from other witnesses is important. The police and Meredith's suspicious pal later said that they found it odd that Amanda knew where the body was despite not having seen it – the implication being that she must have had access to the room before they had had broken the door down and therefore was in some way involved with the murder or its cover-up. Amanda's phone calls to her mother undermine these suspicions and make Amanda look a lot more credible.

At 13:50 the Ericsson phone, which Battistelli had brought to 7 Pergola, was officially confiscated by him as evidence. Ten minutes later Inspector Bartolozzi entered her British Motorola officially as evidence in the force's log. That night, during their first visit to the police station, Amanda and Raffaele would come under suspicion as a result of their strange behaviour.

Amanda and her mum spoke several times over the weekend, during which Amanda was helping police with their inquiries by going back to the house. Edda has a completely different explanation for her daughter's perceived lack of emotion. Edda said that she was more in shock than in tears. And that she was staying focused to help the police.

'I'm OK, mom. I just need to answer the questions to try to help the police figure out what happened. I can't believe someone would do this. They gotta find them.'

Edda said: 'I'm so proud of you for trying to do this.' But her wishful thinking obscured the portentous signs. A relative from Germany called Edda and said: 'They're talking to her an awful lot – are you sure she's not a suspect?'

Edda replied: 'No, no, no. She was one of the closest people to Meredith. She's just helping them.' Amanda had also insisted on finishing her study-abroad course. If her daughter wouldn't leave, Edda decided to go and get her.

The anomalies triggered a series of police interventions that would lead to Amanda naming Patrick Lumumba three days later in the earliest hours of 6 November. Astonishingly, for Amanda and Raffaele the first day of the week began as business as usual, even while the storm of murder raged around them. Going on as though nothing had happened, Amanda and Raffaele attended their respective lectures on Monday morning. Sitting on an ornate wooden bench, beneath the shabbily elegant flock wallpaper, Amanda drifted off and wrote a letter saying that all she wanted was her mother to take her shopping.

In the afternoon they met up again at Raffaele's. His cleaner, Rosa Fernandez de Calle, came in between 14:00 and 16:00 to vacuum and mop up for the last time. She had been instructed by Raffaele, who could be a bit anal at times, to only use Lysoform disinfectant, a high-quality German brand with a distinctly medical bent that he may have got used to in the doctors' sons' hostel. When Rosa went under the sink to get a bottle, she noticed a bucket full of clear water and wet mop rags. 'There was a leak last night,' Raffaele explained.

At 20:00 flowers were laid at a candlelit vigil, in front of the world's media, around blown-up photos of Meredith and big golden letters spelling out her nickname 'Mez'. Amanda and Raffaele stayed away, preferring to have dinner. Some of Meredith's pals took their absence as rudeness at best, and some thought it suspicious. However, Raffaele's supporters said they had been scared off by the press following publication of the iconic murder-scene 'cuddling' photographs.

As unlikely protagonists, the couple was rapidly being portrayed as a post-modern Myra Hindley and Ian Brady. But Amanda's family saw the pictures differently, after Amanda offered an alternative but equally credible explanation to her sister, Deanna. Deanna said: 'That was for comfort. They're rubbing each other's backs for comfort. They're not French kissing.'

The wicks were still burning at the vigil when Amanda and Raffaele arrived at the police station at 22:15. By 22:30 Raffaele's interrogation was under way. Nine minutes later Amanda phoned Filomena, obliviously asking her if they were still going to live together. Meanwhile, Raffaele was changing his story, and dropping Amanda in it. At 23:00 Amanda was found doing cartwheels in the waiting area, part of a routine to show how flexible she was after an officer had noticed her doing her stretching. At midnight her questioning began informally in the same side room, her official status still that of a witness.

At 01:45 on Tuesday, 6 November, Amanda accused Patrick Lumumba, halting the session and automatically changing her status to suspect. Technically, the one-page statement she had just signed off could not be used against her; in any self-respecting judicial regime, no witness can accuse him- or herself of a crime without a lawyer present. However, there was no law that prevented this 'witness' evidence from being used against others such as Lumumba. Eventually it was decided that the statement could be used against her in her trial for slander, which ran at the same time as her trial for murder. In Italy a suspect can be sued by a wrongly accused person for ruining their reputation. At 03:30 suspect Amanda asked to make a five-page 'spontaneous statement' to Prosecutor Mignini, still with no lawyer present. At 05:45 she was formally put under arrest after effectively admitting to being an accomplice to Lumumba. Both she and Raffaele were detained in custody. At dawn Amanda wrote a two-page note, described by police as a 'memoir', confirming her previous statements but describing some of her lines as a 'vision'. It would seem that Amanda's memory of the night in question was extremely hazy.

18

Day of Reckoning: Reprise

Tuesday, 6 November

The narrow cobbled street where Raffaele Sollecito lived was an ancient puzzle of cryptic signs and secret symbols decipherable only by the ordained. The shadowy societies they represented are now lost in time. Many of the city's prosperous trade guilds had worked out of this winding, gently sloping street but today it's just wealthy students. But the freemasonry codes, though faded in stone, are still as relevant in the twenty-first century as they were 600 years go, despite being veiled in concealment. The Monster of Florence case has proved that. As Marco Chiacchiera opened Raffaele's creaking door he hoped he would be more successful at unlocking the mysteries inside than those that adorned the exterior.

Chiacchiera scanned Raffaele's pad, little more than a 30-square-metre bed-sit with a couple of steps leading up to the sleeping area, a small bathroom and living-room kitchenette. 'What's that smell?' asked Chiacchiera, his heavy-set body moving awkwardly around the tiny space.

'Bleach,' piped up one of the constables, part of a new team of fresh officers specially chosen to search Raffaele's flat. None of them, except the boss, had been involved in the investigation inside Meredith's house, in order to minimize the risk of cross-contamination from one crime scene to a possible other.

In the kitchen drawer, one of the officers found a knife that also reeked of fresh sodium hypochlorite solution, a supermarket-style kitchen blade with a black plastic handle.

'Suspicious – it looks as though it's been scrubbed with bleach,' the officer relayed to Chiacchiera. 'Who cleans a knife with bleach?' Though they were initially told to look for a 10 cm cutting edge, the blade they found was 17.5 cm long with a 16.5 cm handle. However, officers discerned that it was still compatible if only the main, front part of the blade had been used in a partial incision. 'Bag it and tag it,' ordered Chiacchiera. The knife was sealed in a plastic bag and taken to the police station where the evidence to be sent to the Rome laboratory was being prepared. Agent Giubotti placed it in the box that had once held a Renato Balestra designer desk diary, to avoid the blade pricking its carriers. This is where the defence attorneys would claim contamination took place.

Next to Raffaele's bed, they discovered a Manga comic book with a grinning demon pictured on the cover, typical of the cult Japanese picture strips heavily laced with sex, violence and blood. As they left with the evidence bags, Chiacchiera knew they would be back. However, at present he had no time to hang around – he knew that Tuesday, 6 November, would turn out to be one of busiest days of the investigation. From experience, he understood that this would be the day when the police would lose some of their control to external factors. This would be the day when all of the interest groups involved in the case would come into play, the meddlers as well as the genuinely concerned.

Mignini, however, was not going to give up his authority without a fight. Barrister Tiziano Tedeschi walked into the reception at Capanne prison, near the outskirts of Perugia, on the same morning, but to his amazement, the director refused to let him meet his new client.

'Sorry, Mr Tedeschi, Mr Mignini has instructed the prison, under special powers, to keep Raffaele Sollecito in isolation for two days, until the time of the hearing with the GIP [Preliminary Investigation Judge] on Thursday, 8 November.' Despite protestations that the imposition was illegal, the prominent barrister was turned away. Mignini didn't want anyone interfering with his suspects just yet. Not at least until he had some more answers.

Meanwhile, Amanda's ashen-faced mum Edda Mellas had just landed at Zurich en route to Rome. She was suffering from jet lag after a ten-hour flight over the Atlantic, an agonizing and frustrating trip spent worrying about her daughter. The clinical anonymity of the airport exacerbated her feelings of loneliness and disorientation. But what she heard on the phone would send her a whole lot lower. The check call made her blood freeze: her husband Chris Mellas was on the line, telling her that Amanda was one of the three people who had just been arrested for the murder of Meredith Kercher.

Edda was stunned, having been given news that no parent ever wants to hear. She kicked herself for not insisting that Amanda leave Italy before she was interrogated, describing the missed opportunity as the biggest mistake of her life. She put the phone to her side, a giant hollow of fright tumbling in her abdomen, and stared out through the glass roof. The hard winter light pouring in did not soothe her. Her plan to bring her daughter home was now an impossibility. The mass of frenetic airport life – passengers rushing by, red-eyed commuters shoring up the European coffee booths, customers browsing through cameras and sunglasses at the duty-free stall – all were oblivious to her personal tragedy.

Though Raffaele and Amanda had effectively ducked suspicion of wielding the knife against Meredith by naming Patrick Lumumba, technically they were still accomplices. Amanda had admitted being at the scene at the time of the murder. Raffaele's alibi had not been independently verified. On these grounds, Mignini had ordered their arrest minutes after Amanda had named Lumumba in the early hours of Tuesday, 6 November. Both were remanded in custody while police continued their investigations. Nick Pisa on Sky News reported that the pair were being given time to 'reflect' on the differences between their statements.

Edda Mellas just wanted to hug her daughter and take her away from this nightmare. But once again she was thwarted by logistics. She had to wait patiently for a flight out of Switzerland, then a further two hours on a plane to Rome and then a train to Perugia, a terrible ordeal mixed with claustrophobic helplessness and annoyance. Six hours later, an exhausted Edda Mellas walked into the Mayor's office where she found the town's public relations official Daniela Borghesi waiting for her. Coincidentally, the Mayor of Perugia had just been visited by a delegation from Amanda's hometown of Seattle, in Perugia on unrelated business because the two cities are twinned. They had heard about a fellow citizen being arrested and, in the spirit of loyalty and self-help for which Americans abroad are known, had asked the Mayor for advice on how best to help Amanda. He had pointed them in the direction of veteran barrister Luciano Ghirga, a Perugian town councillor. The Americans told Ghirga, a chubby-faced doyen with a shock of white hair, that they felt duty-bound to protect one of their own. When Edda arrived she was introduced to Ghirga and told that his local contacts would prove invaluable. The only problem was that he didn't speak English.

In the meantime, back home in the States, Amanda's stepfather Chris Mellas had been contacted by the American Embassy. Both sides of the family were now doing well – Chris had risen to the position of computer network manager at a property development company based in the Bellevue neighbourhood. The blue-collar heritage of the Knox–Mellas extended family was now firmly in the past. This should have been a time, as both girls were coming of age, when fathers and mothers could really motor on with their careers, as well as enjoy time with their partners. But the children of the most prosperous generation in history, the so-called yo-yo kids, never really left home. It seemed as though they always needed their parents' help, whether they were in trouble or not.

The embassy officials were unaware that Edda had found a local lawyer and had helpfully sent Chris a list of high-powered attorneys who regularly worked for the State Department in Rome. Chris phoned each number but was satisfied that only one spoke good enough English: Carlo Dalla Vedova, a business lawyer with offices in Rome and stateside in Washington, whom Mellas figured would have clout on a strategic level. Dalla Vedova and Ghirga would eventually be contracted to work alongside each other for the defence.

Amanda's biological father, Curt Knox, had also just heard the news and his telephone was ringing incessantly. Curt was now the vice-president and financial director of the Seattle Macy's store. He'd worked extremely hard to get where he was. Prudence and diligence were his watchwords. Now he was staring into the abyss. Nothing could have prepared him for the storm that was about to blow apart his well-ordered existence. While Chris and Edda gained ground on the legal front, Curt felt obliged to protect Amanda's flanks from the media onslaught.

Amanda Knox's Facebook and MySpace sites were, in the words of one journalist, 'raped' overnight. Photographs that Amanda had posted were 'lifted' without authorization and splashed over papers worldwide. In days gone by, reporters often spent days and weeks knocking on doors, trawling relatives and inquiring at school photographic agencies, trying to dig up old photographs of the accused and the victim. Old hands like Nick Pisa were experts at teasing out this these valuable snaps, known as 'collects' in the trade, from greedy or emotional sources under difficult circumstances. Today the internet has rendered the 'death knock' almost obsolete, providing masses of pics and background at the click of a button.

Unsubstantiated reports of Amanda's sexual rapacity, spread by British and Italian media, mixing sexist and nationalist stereotypes, and fed by constant leaks from the police, undoubtedly damaged Amanda's public image beyond repair.

Arty modelling photos on her MySpace site showed Amanda posing in a tasteful but darkly provocative way. Her look was strong, angular 1980s, reminiscent of the iconic Robert Palmer 'Addicted to Love' video – dark-grey eye-shadow, white porcelain make-up and diva-red lipstick. Her lips were overdrawn in glossy lip liner in the shape of a large cupid's bow. She wore an all-black skin-tight outfit, her clingy top slightly see-through, defining her bosom ambiguously under the dark material. Whether she was braless, as in the infamous pop video, was flirtatiously questionable. Amanda was seated side-on on a long antique piano chair; one leg was hitched up, slightly opened, and her high heel dug into the soft, chintzy cushioning. The cloth of her trousers contoured her thighs, visible evidence of her sporty keep-fit regime, the cuffs of her boot-cuts riding up slightly to reveal the black leather straps over bare ankles. Her hair was drawn back fiercely, a few loose tousles left deliberately and fetchingly falling behind her right ear. On the internet, Amanda became a sex object.

Another picture of her posing with a First World War tripod-mounted machine gun in a museum, pretending to fire it, was presented as evidence of her warped and violent nature. The gun contrasted with Knox's plain-Jane-ness in other photos – she looked very square in a pale-yellow shift dress that crime-scene photographs showed was still hanging in her wardrobe at 7 Pergola. The simplicity of the dress painted her in a different light, and accentuated her puppy fat. The many faces of Amanda Knox were beguiling to the media, and adding to her mystery.

Amanda had also, bizarrely, written a short story about the drugging and raping of a young girl and posted it on her web page for all to read. The narrative was badly written and the dialogue hard to follow. But on closer inspection, some commentators suggested that the characters, both of whom were students, mirrored the relationship between Amanda and Raffaele. The plot revolved essentially around a younger, morally bankrupt antagonist who manipulates and controls an older but weaker student.

The younger character, called Kyle, who some say was based on Amanda, denies drugging and raping a girl called Victoria. He justifies his sexual attack as more or less consensual by turning the whole 'no means no' debate on its head, implying that when a girl says 'no' she really means 'yes'.

'What you need to know about chicks is that they don't know what they want,' Kyle says. 'Kyle winked his eye. "You have to show it to them. Trust me."'

Kyle then tries to play down the powers of the drug he used, known as 'hard A', to overpower his Victoria.

'"In any case." He cocked his eyebrows up and one side of his mouth rose into a grin. "I think we both know hard A is hardly a drug."'

Was Amanda writing from personal experience of rape? Or drugs and sex? Or the vulnerability of young women who let go on drinks and drugs? The story concludes when Kyle is attacked by his disapproving older brother called Edgar.

Extracts of the story appeared in most newspapers, playing up the parts when Kyle tastes his own blood dripping from his mouth.

But for the deeper-looking critics it was the character of the older brother Edgar – a violent passive-aggressive filled with rage – and his relationship with his younger sibling that may have been autobiographical. Some commentators suggested that Edgar, like Sollecito although older, was essentially helpless, dominated by Kyle, who looked after his every need and protected him.

> He was both protective and authoritative towards Edgar, even though he was eight years younger. In all other things besides financial, he provided for Edgar persistent counsel. In return, there was a constant quiet respect that Edgar paid his younger brother in his allowance of Kyle's worldly lifestyle. It was because of Edgar that Kyle needn't suffer from rent dues, work responsibilities, and grocery shopping. But Edgar also always questioned Kyle about his daily offences and when he was silent it made Kyle immediately perk up and set aside his calculus homework.

Was it just newspaper speculation or did Amanda have a deeper understanding of classic passive-aggressives like Sollecito? Had she been attracted to Sollecito because she knew of the secret anger that lurked beneath his shy exterior? Commentators suggested that she was a manipulator who was easily able to pierce his thin veneer of socialization and turn him into a raging animal under her spell.

His mouth was drawn tight and creased at the edges, and for a second Edgar thought he was going to say something, but he felt the tightness of his brow ease and he swallowed a large, slippery gulp of the aching, burning rage that pulsated in his forehead, chest, and throat. His fists peeled open and revealed the crescent moon dimples in his palms where his fingernails had dug too deep. His throat was choking on the bile and the question, where was his soul, but instead he asked, 'Did you know her name?'

Curt Knox tried his best to reason with the reporters who'd bothered to contact him. But he couldn't believe the vitriol of the attacks. He called Edda. They had no idea where to turn. Two days later a colleague dropped a card on to Curt's desk: 'Try these. They know how to handle this kind of stuff.' Gogerty, Stark and Marriott – public relations people. For 30 years the Seattle-based firm had specialized in crisis management, everything from crashed airplanes to election campaigns to corporate lobbying.

19

The Beak

First Magistrate's Hearing

8 November

Suddenly the case hung desperately in the balance. A clear and present danger, in the form of Europe's 200-year-old Napoleonic code of law, was threatening to blow the investigation apart even before it got started. Under the justice system that stretches from the Mediterranean to Sweden, the whole file had to reviewed *again* by a separate judging magistrate, *within the first two days* of arrest.

The Preliminary Investigating Judge, Claudia Matteini, a woman in her mid-fifties with a tired face, had to weigh up whether Mignini's evidence was strong enough so that she could decide whether to drop the case and release the prisoners or crack on. Matteini's job was to give the investigators a hard time. She identified holes in procedure.

The girl had confessed without a lawyer being present. On the other hand she also gave Mignini a handwritten statement.

Just as he'd got Amanda to break down crying at the crime scene, Mignini did have one sure-fire trick up his sleeve. He knew that if could throw Amanda and Raffaele into the same cell together, on their own, they would soon talk about the murder. All he would have to do was bug the conversation. The tactic had worked like a dream in a similar case in 2001 involving two teenagers called Erica and Omar, also accused of murder and falsely blaming a third party. The problem was, however, that if Mignini brought Raffaele and Amanda out of isolation now it would open a can of legal worms, not least that he would have to allow access to their lawyers. Mignini bit his lip in frustration and dismissed the thought.

Matteini now ran her sceptical eye over Sollecito's statement.

'So he's not sure Amanda was with him at all at the time of the murder. He's not giving her an alibi,' she noted. 'So the police tricked them into contradicting each other.'

Lumumba deleted the message he sent to Knox saying "See you later". That's suspicious.' Matteini agreed.

However, the bottom line was, at this stage, Mignini simply didn't have all the ammunition he needed – the forensics results had not come back from Rome yet, the autopsy report couldn't say for sure that Meredith had been raped. He found himself falling back on circumstantial evidence about Raffaele's odd character – his love of knives, manga comics and soft drugs. Hardly incontrovertible proof.

Mignini's arguments had been defensive, to say the least. But potentially there was worse to come. At the Preliminary Magistrate's first hearing, if Amanda and Raffaele's lawyers put the boot in, they could well finish him off.

The common rooms and canteens of Capanne prison are spacious, bright and clean, hallmarks of a modern model correctional facility. But it's the surrounding countryside that can drive inmates to despair. The rolling Umbrian hills either taunt them with their beauty or frustrate them due to restrictive vision – cons can barely see the view through their tiny windows.

This was the setting for round one of the court sessions on a chilly morning on 8 November. Claudia Matteini braced herself to hear the lawyers and their wards defending themselves. First up was Raffaele. She opened the dialogue, stating the Prosecutor's case in outline – that 'Raffaele, Amanda and Patrick Lumumba went to the flat in order to introduce Mr Lumumba to Meredith Kercher and then Mr Lumumba attacked and killed Miss Kercher.' Matteini paid particular attention to the footprint evidence against Raffaele.

'The police have collected shoeprints so far that are to do with your shoes, Nike Air Force 1 trainers,' she read from the Interior-Ministry-headed sheets.

Even before Raffaele had a chance to comment, his barrister Tiziano Tedeschi interjected with an immediate attack, complaining about not being able to see his client. Matteini placated him with the paperwork he'd been promised.

But like all lawyers Tedeschi had to have the last word. He went on: 'Furthermore, Mr Sollecito has been the subject of pressure and vilification beyond the bounds of what is acceptable in any investigations, left without shoes for hours, kept in isolation with insufficient clothing and in a cold cell. I demand the immediate release of Mr Sollecito against whom there is not an ounce of evidence.'

When the outburst finished, Sollecito's weak voice broke forth, a disappointment in comparison with his advocate's practised voice.

'I never want to see Amanda again,' was his opening gambit, dramatically distancing himself from his former lover. Gathering confidence, he then told Matteini about his relationship with Amanda, passing it off as short-lived and ephemeral. Moving on to the night of the murder, he gave a surprisingly effective account. Matteini nodded. Tedeschi thought it was definitely looking good for him. Mignini looked down at the functional floor tiles.

'I just remember that a pipe under the sink at my place broke,' Raffaele continued, 'and while I was washing up the kitchen flooded. I tried to dry the floor but Amanda told me to forget it so I did . . .

'That night I received a telephone call from my father, who calls me every night before I go to bed. I don't remember if he called me on the land line or on the cell phone.'

Retelling his story about the day the body was discovered, Raffaele was equally lucid.

Amanda went home in the morning then came back to my house. I remember that she had changed and was wearing a white skirt, while the day before she was wearing jeans . . . She had a mop with her to dry the floor in my kitchen. Amanda told me that at her home she had found the door of her flat open with bloodstains in the bathroom which all seemed strange.

She suggested we go together to her house to see what had happened. I was worried when we got there . . . The bathroom was clean except for the mat and the washbasin which showed bloodstains. She said that someone must have cut themselves or that one of the girls had their period. The only thing I noticed was that the door to Meredith's bedroom was locked and I tried to get into the room from outside.

While I was doing this, Amanda was stretching over the railings on the terrace to see if she could reach the window. She had already knocked and called towards Meredith's bed-

room. I tried to look through the lock but all I could see was
the bag and the open door [of the wardrobe]. I told Amanda
to call her friends. In the meantime I called my sister who
told me to call 112.

We waited outside the house for the Carabinieri to arrive.
The Postal Police arrived who wanted to speak with the
Italian tenant who owned the SIM card.

Matteini seemed satisfied. But before she finished, she grilled
him on the inconsistencies.

'Can you explain why there are shoeprints similar to yours in
the flat? Especially in Meredith's bedroom?' she asked.

An unruffled Raffaele replied: 'I don't understand why my
shoeprints are there, I have never been in that room. I wasn't
wearing those shoes on the 1st of November and on the 2nd.
The person who killed her must have had the same shoes, they
are pretty common.'

Mr Tedeschi, Raffaele's lawyer, butted in to reinforce his
client's innocence.

He said: 'There is no evidence against Mr Sollecito except
for the shoeprints on the floor, which are quite clearly not his.
You have already tested his Air Force 1 shoes and they have no
blood on them, they have not been cleaned, they simply have
no blood on them. I'd like to remind you that Mr Sollecito
was deprived of his shoes and kept without any form of shoe
for hours.'

Matteini accepted it was a touchy subject and moved on.

'Explain why Amanda said that the faeces were there and
then had disappeared.'

Again Raffaele rattled his lines off like a set-piece answer
in an exam: 'As far as the faeces in the lavatory go, I didn't
see them because I was outside the bathroom and only

looked in towards the lavatory bowl. Amanda got scared and jumped up to me saying that the faeces weren't there anymore, and that they had been there when she had gone to dry her hair.'

Matteini: 'There are several points, Mr Sollecito, that differ between your version of today and your version of events as related on the evening of 5 November just three days ago. Can you explain whether you were with Amanda Knox that evening or not?'

Now it was make-or-break time. Matteini had posed the million-dollar question. The one Mignini had been waiting for.

His pay-off was unexpected, effectively an explosive retraction of his initial confession.

'I'm sorry I told you that crap about not being with Amanda. We were together that evening.'

It was a clever move. All the time Raffaele had been politely and skilfully putting space between him and his oddball lover Amanda. But now, on the key point of the night in question, he was sticking to her like glue again. Backing her up.

Rationally he explained:

I lied previously because I was under pressure and very stressed out. I was upset and afraid. I want to make clear that on 5 November I was very upset when the police officers asked me all those questions because I felt the pressure.

I can confirm that I spent the night with Amanda Knox. I don't remember if Amanda Knox went out that evening. We were at my place at 8:30 [p.m.]. I must have mixed things up because I remember that Amanda must have come home with me but I don't remember if she went out. My father calls me every day and it seems strange that he didn't call me on the 1st.

In one fell swoop, by getting onside with Amanda again, Raffaele had significantly lowered the risk of a cut-throat defence, a dreaded legal position in which witnesses start turning on each other in the box, to the benefit of the prosecutors. Defence lawyers have nightmares about the cut-throat defence – against which there is no defence.

Signing his client off, Tedeschi dismissed the evidential question marks somewhat smugly as 'understandable contradictions'. From where he was sitting it looked as if Raffaele was getting a walk out.

Then he took a risky step.

'We would urge you to separate your evaluation of Mr Sollecito's position from Miss Knox's and Mr Lumumba's positions.' Though he wanted Raffaele to stay close to Amanda on the night of the murder, in legal terms he didn't want them jumping back into bed with each other just yet. Amanda was simply too hot to handle right now.

Claudia Matteini took note. She then took a little time out to make up her mind.

The Italian legal system allows for suspects to be held without charge for up to a year while the investigation is carried out. This remains an unusual situation, however, and is applied only where there is a strong likelihood of the suspect fleeing or interfering with the collection of evidence.

When Claudia Matteini met Amanda Knox she was flummoxed. Nothing in Amanda's demeanour indicated that she could have killed anyone. She continued reiterating that she had nothing to do with the crime, that she was at Raffaele's house, but that the evening was a blur. She never spoke a word about Patrick Lumumba.

Later Matteini gave her verdict on Raffaele. The sheer brutality of the murder and the number of contradictions in his story were strong evidence that he was involved in this in some way. His footprints had been found on the murder scene, his telephone was off when he said he received his father's call. There was no evidence of interaction with his computer at the time of the murder. Too many inconsistencies. She believed the knife that killed the victim was one of his flick-knives. She noted that his own Facebook site stated that he was in search of 'new experiences'. He was remanded in custody until such time as the investigation was complete.

For Raffaele, it was a shocker. Both he and his lawyer had convinced themselves that they would be drinking champagne. Either the case would be dropped or at least he would get bail.

But there was more. Matteini put the boot in. 'There are also other contradictions. You telephoned the Carabinieri after the police had arrived, first you say Miss Knox went to le Chic and then you say she came home with you, and that Amanda received a call saying le Chic was closed, not that there wasn't enough clientele to warrant a waitress. Too many, too many.' In a move that shocked Raffaele she refused to grant him bail. In Italy lying to an investigating magistrate and then to a judge is one of the worst crimes: tell the truth and they'll be lenient, lie and be found out, and that's it. The same went for Amanda and Patrick, who blatantly failed to explain the lack of till receipts between the opening time of his pub and 22:30. Since Meredith could have died as early as 22:00, this would have left him enough time to get back to the pub to start making receipts, or so argued the prosecution.

Finally, in a nineteen-page report, the judge added more weight to the sex-attack theory. She summarized that Meredith was killed during an 'extreme' drug-inspired sex game gone wrong, involving at least two men, and that Lumumba wanted to have sex 'with a girl he desired but who refused him'. However, some wily observers noted that the theory was rapidly turning into fact without all the evidence to back it up.

20

Back to the Future

Police Investigation: Old and New Techniques

8–10 November

The press pack had decamped from 7 Pergola Road to Capanne prison, a road train of futuristic blacked-out TV vans and clapped-out reporters' cars racing along the hilly passes. The story was now simply too good to be true. As a small TV city grew outside the main gates, the journalists hoped to get a few words from the defendants' lawyers. The insights behind the soundbites were telling, commentators mused. Amanda's lawyer Luciano Ghirga, accompanied by his tall thin partner, Carlo Dalla Vedova, stopped to talk. Robustly, he stuck to the party line.

Ghirga pronounced: 'Amanda Knox has repeated that she had nothing to do with this murder. She can now receive a visit by her parents.'

Lumumba's lawyer, Carlo Pacelli, was quietly confident, smiling, almost serene in his belief in the inoffensivensss of his client. He referred to Lumumba's utter tranquillity in affirming that he had nothing to do with the murder. The press mêlée pushed against their car windows. Cameramen jostled with heavy kit balancing on their shoulders. Correspondents filed their stories, meandering through the minefield of cables, generators, giant umbrellas and deck chairs that made up the modern media circus. Watching and listening were the only two American journalists to follow the case from beginning to end. The tall, red-headed Andrea Vogt felt a connection to the case because she had been born in America's Pacific Northwest and freelanced for the *Seattle Post-Intelligencer* from her Bologna home. Barbie Nadeau wrote for *Newsweek* and was based in Rome. Both were experienced reporters and fluent in Italian. It looked an open-and-shut case but the cast of characters that the two women were about to encounter while reporting was more flamboyant than in any novel – and at times dangerous.

Fresh from his first courtroom success, tentative though it was, Prosecutor Mignini ordered Flying Squad commissioner Profazio to collect more items of evidence from 7 Pergola and Raffaele's flat. The list included all of the computers, a few articles of clothing and Amanda's Harry Potter book in German. In total, five computers from various addresses were handed over to the Postal Police for electronic analysis.

Their specialist officers were already examining four telephones, two connected to Meredith, one seized from Raffaele and one owned by Patrick Lumumba. Italy's four mobile companies were asked to pull all of their records in relation to the numbers. Broadly speaking, there were two avenues of inquiry. Obviously, the billing information would throw up the times of all calls made, for how long and to whom – the straightforward stuff. In addition, by examining the more complex data from the three mobile-phone cell masts in the area, investigators could find out the exact geographical location of the phones at

all times, thereby proving who was where when. The key com-
ponent of a mobile phone is an electronic switch, invented in
America, that is able to switch seamlessly or 'roam' between the
signals sent from masts. The process leaves a trail, so that the
route of the mobile-phone carrier can be plotted on a map. The
technique had first come to prominence in the UK, in the case
of former Liverpool goalkeeper Bruce Grobbelaar, accused but
later cleared of match-fixing in the mid-1990s. One mast was
close to where the telephones were found at Elisabetta Lana's,
another one to the east of the flat and one in town.

At this stage the computer and phone evidence was particularly important to prove or knock down Raffaele Sollecito's alibi.
He'd said he used his computer until past 03:00 on 2 November
and then gone to bed. He had downloaded a film, watched it,
had sex and then worked on his thesis. He had no other alibi
except Amanda, so it was fundamental that the computer prove
he was at home at the time Meredith was dying in her bedroom.
His father had called him that evening too. Raffaele said, 'He
always calls.' Secondly, the police also wanted to get to the
bottom of Lumumba's deleted suspicious text: 'See you later'.

Meanwhile, a more old-fashioned type of police work was
going on in the background. But the results that were coming
back from the frontline of this inquiry felt like the shockwaves
that warned of an imminent earthquake. Officers asked around
as to what kind of person Lumumba was. University public relations people, the Erasmus staff and business contacts were
straw-polled. Whereas Amanda's character had been almost universally slaughtered, the praise Lumumba got from people such
as Lucy and Esteban at the rival pub the Bear's Lair was standard.

'He couldn't hurt a fly. He's a musician, for God's sake,' Lucy
told the police officers. 'Yes, his pub isn't doing well. We told
him not to open it. We sent Amanda there because we had all

the waitresses we needed.' Murder just did not stack up in his character. The cops on the ground scratched their heads. Alarm bells rang.

However, senior officers at the top of the pyramid weren't picking up the vibes. The senior detective in Rome, Edgardo Giobbi, had recently been hogging the limelight. He reeled off interview after interview boasting about his role in coordinating the investigations. He was convinced Lumumba was the right man. He even put a picture of Amanda being arrested on his vaunted 'Hall of Fame' outside of his office. The photograph hung next to various trophies and awards he'd won, alongside a snap of the notorious Mafia boss Bernardo Provenzano he had taken down a few years before.

Another run-of-the-mill police procedure was also paying off. But in a way that senior police officers were dreading. A publicity drive appealing for witnesses had reached the banks of the Rhine. Winter dark had already set over the orderly streets of Zurich when a conscientious Swiss university professor called Roman Mero received a phone call. The voice at the other end of the line made him jump, even though it was a friend.

'I've just seen the news,' the prof's pal exclaimed. 'The Italian police are looking for you.'

'Are you sure?' exclaimed the professor, slightly panicked. 'What for?'

'A man called Patrick Lumumba,' the pal explained, 'has just been arrested for the murder of Meredith Kercher, the student who was killed in Perugia when you were there. He says he's looking for a Swiss professor who spent some time in his bar with him discussing Congolese politics. That sounds like you, doesn't it?'

'Yes, it was,' the professor recalled with zero hesitation.

'Well, it sounds like you're his alibi then,' the friend added.

Five minutes later, after Googling the phone number for the Perugia police, Professor Mero was talking to a detective. The officer told him he'd have to call back the next day when the case officers were at their desk. But the Swiss professor couldn't wait. Efficient and full of initiative, he called again and told them he was on the way down to Italy to explain in person.

Friday, 9 November, had begun well, with Claudia Matteini officially confirming the arrests. In addition, the forensics squad in Rome had officially announced that they were to start analysing the samples that had been collected – a very important stage in the Italian legal process. But now, as darkness descended on the first full week of the Meredith investigation, a sense of foreboding and despondency was creeping up. If Lumumba was innocent then the Italian police would look foolish in front of the world's media. Worse still, their best officers may have been tricked by Amanda, no more than a slip of a girl in many eyes.

The next day, Saturday, 10 November, the Swiss professor, whom the police did not want to identify, began his statement.

'I was there on an exchange course with my students who were spending a week with students of the Magistrale school,' he said. 'We left Perugia on the 2nd November but had been there since 24 October. That evening I bought a tracksuit in a shop – I was the last customer – and then went to the hotel. I dined in a Pizzeria and decided to go to Le Chic, where I had been before on the 26nd October. It looked closed, but when I pushed the door it opened and Patrick was there all alone. There was no one else there.'

The story went on that Patrick and Professor Mero discussed politics and then two Belgian girls came in. Patrick's neighbour, who'd said that the bar was closed, was clearly mistaken, the professor was sure of it. The professor left the bar at 22:30, the same time as Patrick may have rung up his tab, as per the stamped till receipt.

Chiacchiera and Profazio looked at each other as the alibi took shape. There was no doubting this guy, who was both meticulous and credible. Driven by a sense of justice, he had come all the way from Zurich to do his civic duty.

'Case definitely *not* closed,' mumbled a doubly weary Profazio. 'We'll have to find the Belgians now and more customers from later on that night. More work . . .'

When Mignini heard the news, he could barely disguise his irritation. He had tap-danced so well through the first hearing, defending the police to the last, and now they were telling him that Lumumba could be the wrong man.

He snapped: 'Get out of your office and talk to people. Witnesses – students, teachers, neighbours. Get help from the University. If he's innocent we need to know quickly. And it's not just about Lumumba. There may be other key witnesses we have missed.'

The convenience-store owner had been quizzed but had been asked the wrong questions; the police had failed to ask the A&E ward at the local hospital if they had seen anything on the night; they had not found a key witness who had heard the argument . . . the police's witness policy was an accident waiting to happen. In fact, while the police had been busy with hi-tech gadgets and DNA scientists, *Umbrian Journal* reporters led by Giuseppe Castellini had stolen a march on the boys in blue. They were closing in fast on these 'properties' – trade slang for people with explosive stories – and were poised to heap more embarrassment on the force

Mignini prepared a dossier for Claudia Matteini so that she would be ready to release Lumumba, but the news had already leaked.'

When the press found out about Lumumba, to save face and buy time the police continued to add to the cloud of suspicion around the African bar-owner. Weakly they said that they were still carrying out tests on one of his sweaty T-shirts and on a sample of his hair that they found mixed up with someone else's, possibly Meredith's. Few journalists were buying it. The police storyline was crumbling fast.

Profazio was not looking forward to another wasted weekend written off by worry, if not work, this time. But just as one strand of his probe was going wrong, another came up good. Commissioner Filippo Bartolozzi, the officer who had triggered the case, reported the findings on Raffaele's computer to Profazio: No interactivity with the computer from 21:10 on the evening of the murder to 05:30 the next morning.

'Zero,' underlined Bartolozzi, thereby restoring Profazio's faith in his force's hi-tech forensic work.

'So he switched on his laptop at half past five in the morning?' asked Profazio. 'So he wasn't on the computer until three in the morning then?'

'No,' said Bartolozzi.

'And he got up at the crack of dawn to use the computer?' Profazio asked.

Bartolozzi nodded: 'Exactly 05:32.'

'But Sollecito says he was asleep at 05:32 in the morning,' Profazio said. 'Didn't get up until ten, he said in his statement. How do you know your info is correct?'

Bartolozzi explained: 'The last human interaction with the computer was at 21:10. After a while, as you know, computers go into battery saving and switch off. Well, his was switched on again at 05:32. Simple as that.'

Profazio smiled.

'Anything from Sollecito's telephone?' he asked, not expecting any.

'We're waiting for Vodafone to come up with the logs of telephone calls registered on the three towers, but we have the list of calls made. None between nine in the evening and six in the morning. Phones turned off.'

'Turned off?' Profazio asked, slightly startled.

'And then on again,' Bartozzi said.

'But how do we know that it was turned off and not just that no calls were made or received?'

Bartolozzi said: 'Officially, because we can compare the patterns of telephone calls of the past two months with the night of 1 November. Usually Raffaele uses his phone well into the night. But that night, nothing at all. But there was a telephone connection at six in the morning.' After a pause, Bartolozzi made a cryptical reference to other techniques he was aware of, ways to definitely confirm that Raffaele's phone was off that night. Cautiously he went on: 'Unofficially we have ways of knowing and confirming the status of all the telephones in the land if we so wanted . . .' Bartolozzi did not elaborate. For the investigation techniques were secretive and their legality was questionable in some cases. Often they were only deployed by the intelligence services in the interests of national security.

'OK! Fair enough,' agreed Profazio. 'But who did he call at six then?'

'It was exactly 06:02 to be precise. He picked up his messages. One left by his father the night before at 11:00,' Bartolozzi replied.

'OK, write it all down, but I'll tell Mignini,' ordered Profazio.

'We're working on the cell towers,' Bartolozzi said. 'When we get that information we can tell where all the telephones were when they were operating.'

Finally Profazio spelled out his remaining wish list: 'We need to find out what time Meredith's telephone reached Elisabetta Lana's at Sperandio Road. And where Amanda was when she received the call from Lumumba. It's a priority.'

Matteini had officially remanded all of the suspects in jail, rubber-stamping her court decision of the day before. The fear that one or more might flee, or interfere with evidence on the outside, was used as justification to keep them locked up. But the unspoken reason was simply: pressure. Mignini hoped that the effect of discomfort or confinement on their soft natures might be enough to induce further confessions. In addition, all three now received regular visits from lawyers, a situation that could be beneficial to the police. Collaborating with the police brought discounts and privileges. He hoped one or more might be tempted to take the bait, if prompted by a knowing lawyer.

However, before the day was out, the only news was more bad news, and embarrassing news to boot. The question over the message that Lumumba had deleted suspiciously from his phone was cleared up within seconds. And it hadn't taken a genius to work it out. One quick-thinking officer had simply scrolled down to the menu of the seized phone and gone into the settings option. He then realized that the phone was on a default option that automatically deleted outgoing messages, or at least didn't save them. 'Doh!' one of the officers teased. Patrick Diya had not deleted 'See you later' after all. Neither had he made any other strange calls.

21

DNA Shock

Before DNA boffin Patrizia Stefanoni could begin analysing the DNA, there was a mountain of tedious administration, preparation and planning to take care of. Hurdles designed to induce best practice or get evidence thrown out on technicalities, depending on how you looked at it. Stefanoni had spent the week of 5–11 November cataloguing and re-photographing all 480 items of material she had brought back to the Rome lab from Perugia.

After reading the autopsy report she prioritized Raffaele's kitchen knife and Meredith's bra for DNA testing. She reasoned that if the bra had been removed after Meredith had been killed, evidenced by the lack of blood on her breasts, then the killer's DNA must be on the fibre. But even before she had touched a single test tube, there was a devastating setback. The bra clasp had been lost. Stefanoni seemed to remember the torn clasp being under a pillow or a towel. Gioia Brocci had come across it in the early hours when she was busy and tired. Stefanoni ordered a thorough search of the evidence bags after the bra clasp was not found. 'Damn,' she said. 'We'll have to go back to Meredith's room.' But not quite yet – the crime scene had been wound down and there was simply too much lab work to plough through. In addition there was now bureaucracy to contend with: the police couldn't go back without all the lawyers and the prosecutor agreeing, now that there were official defendants to deal with.

Friday, 9 November, had been the big paperwork day. Under Clause 360 of the Italian penal code, Stefanoni had to solemnly invite all three sets of defence lawyers to Rome to witness the DNA tests being carried out in person, if they so wished. It was tediously time-consuming, but open and fair. This inflexible law, which acts as a favourable insurance policy for defendants, applies to samples of blood or tissue that are so small that Stefanoni would have only one crack at them. Such DNA samples are likely be consumed by the chemicals of the analytical process itself and therefore cannot be repeated in the future. In addition, under the slow-moving bureaucratic system, Stefanoni even had to ask for special permission from Mignini to carry out the tests in her own lab. This 'consulting contract' is supposed to guarantee 'Chinese walls' between the sample collectors and the analysts to reduce corruption or contamination. The checks are an attempt to stop defence lawyers getting evidence thrown out by the supreme court in the future. Later during the trial the presiding judge would reject a call for a retrial because the defending attorneys had had the opportunity to verify the procedure *in situ*.

The legal observers met near the police labs in Rome's Tuscolana Road, not far from Cinecittà, the heart of Italy's film industry, after the weekend. To keep the pressure on Stefanoni, each defence lawyer appointed a forensic scientist as their specialist *consigliere*. Amanda's lawyer Luciano Ghirga had found

Italy's most famous independent expert outside the police, the flamboyant Carlo Torre. The TV-friendly face of Torre, his craggy authority softened by round glasses and long curly hair, was famous in Italy. To bolster the team further, Torre had hired his personal DNA specialist Sara Gino.

The Sollecitos' lawyer, Luca Maori, the chubby *bon viveur* of Perugia's law courts, had roped in equally eminent university professors Vincenzo Pascali and Valter Patumi; he would later hire a DNA expert, Adriano Tagliabracci. A young curly-haired lawyer in smart clothes stood alongside another middle-aged woman with short hair. He was Francesco Maresca, the Florentine lawyer the Kercher family had elected to represent them in the whole legal process. His expert was Francesca Torricelli of Florence's genetics institute. Although all the scientists had been invited, only Patumi and Torricelli were present.

The laboratory buzzed with political energy as much as the electrical equipment that whirred in the background. Reputations and egos jostled for position. The elegant and self-possessed Patrizia Stefanoni welcomed them with charm and determination, her Neapolitan accent disguised by the clarity of professional jargon. She began by sombrely underlying the importance of the event, and in a way, its unrepeatable finality.

'I'd like to remind you, ladies and gentlemen,' Stefanoni opened, 'that this is an institutional moment. We are obliged to allow you to participate and I would encourage you to make any remarks during the report, or for ever hold your peace.' She knew they wouldn't.

'This is an official event, and constitutes part of the justice process. The documents that come out of this series of tests will be official documents which all of you will be required to sign as proof that you were present and agreed to the processes adopted.

Any complaints or differences you may have with the approach adopted must be recorded and if not recorded cannot be raised again. Is that clear?'

It was. They had done this many times before. But she had to say it.

Stefanoni then gave the non-scientists a quick idiot's guide to the principles of DNA testing.

'Ladies and gentlemen,' she began.

For those of you who are present but are not geneticists, deoxyribonucleic acid is the long molecule that gives each individual his or her special characteristics. The building blocks of DNA are four protein molecules called adenine, thymine, guanine and cytosine. Every person has a different, specific combination of these blocks, known as a sequence, running up the DNA chain. Most of all human DNA is the same but there are sixteen molecules or combinations of the building blocks that are repeated a different number of times in each individual. These are called loci. It's a DNA profiler's job to identify this bar code for a person under suspicion and then match it to the bar code found in a sample at a crime scene.

Stefanoni then went into more detail. 'For example,' she said,

one individual might have ten repeats of a specific locus while another thirteen. But they may have the same number or repeats of a different locus. Out of the sixteen loci we test for, no one will have the same number of repeats for every locus. It is a highly discriminating test.

DNA investigators therefore look for the quantities of each of these sixteen repeat sequences in order to establish the identity of a donor. Remember that there are two of each loci we are looking for because we all get one half chromosome from our mothers and one from our fathers.

DNA sampling process involves several specific steps: isolating the DNA from the rest of the cell content; diluting this extract in a solution containing enzymes that break the DNA coil into segments or repeat sequences that correspond to individual loci; amplifying the signal, during which the repeat sequences are 'photocopied' using what is called a polymerase chain reaction or PCR. These sequences are given a fluorescent 'tail' using a primer so that we can evaluate the quantity of material we are measuring.

The polymerase chain reaction causes the sequences to bind to other molecules in the enzyme solution in a mirror-like fashion, thereby replicating each sequence hundreds of times. Although the loci are amplified hundreds of times over, the repeat sequences remain in the same proportion to the original sample. This makes the search for each individual repeat sequence easier.

This solution of enzymes containing molecules or loci is then passed through a capillary tube and subjected to a technique called electrophoresis which gives the molecules an electric charge. The heavier molecules move more slowly, the lighter ones faster. The machine then measures the amount of each of these molecules along a grid and creates graphs with peaks, the height of which for each individual locus – there are sixteen, remember – reflects the quantity of material we are working with. These are called relative fluorescence units or RFUs. Next to each peak we also find the number of repeats existing in that sample of that locus which is the distinguishing value we are looking for.

So we have two values: the height of the peak, which is the

quantity of material, and, at the base of each peak, the number of repeats, which is the individual characteristic we are looking for. Obviously the greater the quantity of material, so the higher the peak, the more reliable the reading is. The graph we create is called an electropherogram.

There is another technique that saves time: a specific genetic test for a Y chromosome, left only by males. Men have a Y chromosome, so called because of one of its legs being shorter.

Putting the theory into practice straightaway, Stefanoni began the analysis of the knife taken from Raffaele's flat. She removed the knife from its plastic bag and placed it on a throwaway sterilized cotton cloth and put the blade under a binocular microscope.

'Look,' her running commentary revealed. 'I have identified a portion of the blade where there are small scratches.' Stefanoni was convinced the grooves had come from intense scrubbing, possibly with bleach after the fact. Effortlessly and without lifting her head off the eyepiece, she clicked up a fully labelled catalogue picture of the knife on a big screen in the laboratory. 'I have identified the area with the letter B. You will also see that I have identified three other areas on the knife where there could be material of interest. A is the area of the handle close to the blade, while C is on the other side and D is on the very tip of the blade.'

Stefanoni carefully swabbed the area A using a small cotton bud. The fiddly process took time. The experts looked on. Stefanoni hoped to begin with a preliminary test for blood. She explained: 'Before we proceed on to the DNA, however, it would be preferable to establish whether the substance we are testing for is blood or some other type of tissue such as skin cells or saliva. This is the TMB test. It is extremely sensitive. Since this tests for red cells and we derive our DNA from white cells (which are far fewer than red cells) it does not destroy our sample.' But unfortunately the cotton bud with the magic substance on it remained white: negative. No blood in any of the samples.

Then she moved on to the DNA test proper. First of all she extracted the DNA from the cells' nucleus using a salt solution. Sometimes a mixture of chloroform and phenol can be used.

The next stage involved growing the small sample from the cell nucleus into a big sample capable of being tested – the polymerase chain reaction. The sample was diluted in an enzyme solution. In the background, the sound of the lab was layered. A soft, heavy silence melded perfectly with the whirr and hum of the space-age machines that sat perfectly dampened on the pristine worktops. The murder of Meredith Kercher was not the only crime being investigated that day.

The experts watched as the solution was then inserted into a test tube and shaken. Stefanoni continued her commentary.

A DNA molecule looks like a bit like a ladder that has been twisted into a spiral, or helix, as scientists call it. First of all we need to split the ladder down the 'rungs' by heating it. Both sides of the ladder consist of a strip of the bar code like repeat sequences. When the DNA cools, the enzyme rebuilds the missing sides of each half ladder, so that you're left with two new strands of DNA. By heating, reacting and cooling again you get four new strands from the two, then eight and sixteen and so on.

The bar codes are effectively 'photocopied' using the polymerase chain reaction. The system causes the sequences to bind to other molecules in the enzyme solution in a mirror-like fashion, thereby replicating the exact sequence hundreds of times. The result is that the whole sample is amplified hundreds of times over, but the repeat sequences remain in the same proportion to the original sample. This makes the search for each individual repeat sequence easier given the mass of material created.

The defence forensic experts weren't interested in a blow-by-blow account. As Stefanoni proceeded, they scoured the lab, on the lookout for contamination. Then they watched her carefully to see if her methods contravened the ISO 90001 international quality standard, which, though the Italian government had not officially adopted yet, the police still used as best practice. The defence had already tripped up her team by watching the CSI video from the first day of their investigation. The eagle-eyed Torre had pointed out areas of concern including errors in collection of the evidence and sloppiness in moving objects, but they could see none of that in the laboratory.

'Every human inherits twenty-three half chromosomes from the mother and the same number again from the father,' Stefanoni explained. 'The only chromosome to specify the male sex of a child is the Y chromosome. In rape cases investigators use a special test for that Y chromosome as they can be sure that the likelihood of a male being involved is high, and that the DNA extracted from that male-only chromosome is almost certain to be able to identify the culprit . . .'

The evening of 12 November was showtime. The lawyers would now find out if their clients' genetic fingerprint would expose them as the murderers of Meredith Kercher. But some of them were flagging, their brains frazzled by science. Patrizia Stefanoni unveiled the graph produced by the DNA electropherogram – four horizontal lines, each line with four peaks. The peaks

Giuliano Mignini, Chief Prosecutor, in reflective mood. (© Andrea Vogt)

Monica Napoleoni, head of the Perugia Police Murder Squad, in 2007. (© Giancarlo Belfiore)

Dignified in grief. John and Arline Kercher with their daughter, Stephanie, attend a press conference in Perugia on 6 November 2007.

Perugia Scientific Police Team, 2 November 2007. Agatino Giunta, fingerprint expert, in centre.

Knox and Sollecito at court hearing
26 September 2008. (© Reuters)

Patrick Lumumba, the
Congolese bar owner
wrongly accused by Amanda
Knox of murdering
Meredith. This totally
innocent man had a cast-
iron alibi. (© Andrea Vogt)

Patrizia Stefanoni, head of
the Biology department of
the Polizia Scientifica, makes
her case. (© Giancarlo Belfiore)

Domenico Profazio, head
of the Perugia Flying
Squad, in 2007.
(© Giancarlo Belfiore)

Meredith Kercher, 21 years old and full of life. She posted this picture of herself on Facebook.
(© Rex Features)

The kid from Seattle. Amanda Knox, young, free and on the road.

Meredith always stayed in touch with her family and friends.

Party on, dude. Amanda, in happier times.

The scene of the crime – 7 Pergola in Perugia, where Meredith and Amanda lived and where Meredith was murdered.

(© Paul Russell)

The news stand in Grimana square. Witness Antonio Curatolo sits on the bench to the right, covering his face with a newspaper. (© Paul Russell)

The houses and hills of Perugia with locations. (© Paul Russell)

Filomena Romanelli's room showing staged break-in. The stone landed in the black bag.

Kitchen at 7 Pergola looking towards Laura Mezzetti's room. Long bathroom on the right.

Above: Murder scene. Photo taken shortly after discovery. Meredith's body is under the duvet.

Right: Arc of blood. Is this a handprint or blood which has spurted from a severed artery?

Images of Amanda and Raffaele kissing, shortly after Meredith's body was found, brought the attention of the world's media upon the young couple.

Meredith at a Halloween party 31 October 2007 – within 24 hours she would be dead.
(© Rex Features)

Candlelit vigil for Meredith in Perugia Cathedral.
(© Rex Features)

Curt Knox and Edda Mellas, Amanda's parents.
(© Rex Features)

Rudy Hermann Guede is arrested when returning to Italy after a long train journey. (© Getty Images)

Rudy Guede, aged 5.

Guede was sentenced to 30 years in jail after a fast-track trial in 2008.

In the dock – Amanda Knox looks pensive before entering court. She was found guilty on 4 December 2009 and sentenced to 26 years in jail. (© Andrea Vogt)

God help him. Raffaele Sollecito. was sentenced to 25 years in jail on 4 December 2009.
(© Andrea Vogt)

corresponded to four loci, or sequences of molecules. The peaks also indicated the quantity of each of these molecules, whether it was weak or strong. The graph was then superimposed with the DNA profiles of Amanda, Raffaele and Lumumba, originated from saliva swabs.

Gasps of shock reverberated around the room. Both Amanda's and Meredith's DNA were on the knife. Or so it seemed at first instance. Amanda's DNA was at sample A, on the handle close to the blade. Meredith's came from sample B, three quarters up to the tip of the blade. How else could both Amanda's DNA and Meredith's DNA be on the same blade unless they had been involved in a violent fight and this was the murder weapon? That was at least Stefanoni's reductive argument.

Sollecito's expert asked for a re-run. But there wasn't enough of the sample to test again. That was the whole point of them being there under the penal code. So they could see that it had been done right first time, only time. And then to have faith in the result. The Real Time PCR read-out on sample B was 'Too Low' – less than ten micrograms of DNA substance. Of course the test could be carried out all the same – and it was – and if they read the electropherogram properly they could see that there was next to no substance, but Stefanoni had gone beyond normal practice and re-concentrated the sample. Unorthodox as it might be, the result was there.

While the strength of the sample showing Amanda's DNA was strong, in the hundreds, the machine had analysed fewer than five cells belonging to Meredith. However, this is perfectly possible if the picture is clear, Stefanoni argued. One cell can be analysed if necessary.

The lawyers had another ace up their sleeve. The samples might not be blood, meaning that the tissue could have been skin cells or saliva or mucus or any bodily material. So that means the knife may not be a murder weapon. There may be a perfectly plausible reason why Amanda's and Meredith's DNA might be on the blade together.

Faced with no chance of repetition, Luciano Ghirga turned to Carlo Torre, his old friend, Professor of Forensic Pathology in Turin and wily consultant in many a criminal case, and Sara Gino. He needed a get-out, an argument to undermine Stefanoni's results. Carlo Torre gave him one. Raising doubt about DNA is like boxing: the lawyer knew that he had to land several blows on Stefanoni's box of tricks in quick succession, to knock the evidence out of court, once and for all. And he had to do it early on in the fight. The technicalities were too close to allow it go to a points decision.

Like a trainer, Torre demonstrated a combination to Ghirga. Torre said: 'The low strength of the DNA signal tells me that we are talking of four or five cells in all,' he said. 'A good DNA sample has twice as many. Use that on them, and you might see them off.'

Then he showed him another punch. Torre said:

The fact that Meredith's DNA is on the blade could simply be from contamination in the laboratory or from the box the knife was in or from Raffaele's house. We need to find out if the same cops went to Amanda's house and to Raffaele's to see if they could have brought Meredith's DNA with them. But I think it is most likely that the contamination happened in the laboratory.

Also, if they haven't tested for blood, there is no way they can say it is blood. Of course they say the sample was too small, but unless they can prove it is blood, then they can't say it is the murder weapon. If the TMB test is negative it simply is not blood.

Of course Amanda's DNA is there because she used the knife in Raffaele's house, but if this is the murder weapon the investigators are going to say that the murder was premeditated, that Raffaele brought the knife with him. He needs to be briefed about what to say.

If you look at the crime scene you can see hundreds of ways they could have picked up Meredith's DNA and carried it to Raffaele's place. It's a total mess. Don't worry about the knife.

Ghirga felt emboldened by Torre's barrage of decisive jabs. Now all he had to do was try them out on Stefanoni and then Mignini.

When it came to the bra, there was an even bigger shock. None of the samples matched any of the suspects. Only Meredith's DNA was present, plus the DNA of another unknown male. Stefanoni was puzzled. Who was the mystery man who'd handled Meredith's bra?

Further tests were carried out on the vaginal swab. Again, neither Raffaele nor Lumumba was present. Their lawyers breathed a collective sigh of relief. But again an unknown mystery male popped up. Stefanoni found the Y chromosome of an unknown male, but not sperm, possibly from skin tissue. This was turning into a free-for-all. Patrizia Stefanoni continued ploughing through the evidence, but failed to keep a proper log of her procedures, which would come to haunt her later: she would not be able to explain in detail how she obtained the clean DNA read-out for Meredith on the knife blade, despite an extremely low copy number.

All in all, the first day of forensics went well for the defence. Nothing strong had come out to pin anything on the three suspects. In fact, the weakness of the DNA findings sparked an all-out offensive. The lawyers immediately lodged an appeal against the incarceration to a special panel of re-examination judges. The panel's job was to ensure fair play in the very early stages of the investigation. The lawyers celebrated when the appeal was granted without question. A hearing was pencilled in for 5 December. They now had Mignini on the ropes.

22

Prints of Darkness

The case was now going to take a dramatic turn because of two types of prints – fingerprints and shoeprints. Every new revelation brought a chance for the top brass to shine. As the camera flashes grew more intense, Rome-based police director Edgardo Giobbi had started to edge into the limelight. He pulled rank on his provincial Perugian detectives Profazio and Chiacchiera, glory-hunting the success of the investigation on TV and in the papers. But when he heard that the Swiss professor was shaking his castle, like the skilled political animal he was he subtly backed into the protection of the corridors of powers again. Now, despite the defence lawyers' criticisms, the police were talking up the DNA on the knife, asserting it to be the murder weapon. Before he claimed the credit, Giobbi got a full report off Stefanoni, just to make sure he was on safe ground.

She told him confidently, her opinion diametrically opposed to the defence experts, that although the strength of the Meredith sample only reached 48 RFUs it produced an almost complete profile of her her. DNA was not an elemental science. Nothing was ever black and white.

At first the fingerprints didn't look as good as the DNA results. Of the 108 traces found to be readable as fingerprints from 7 Pergola and other evidence, only forty-seven were identified: seventeen belonged to Meredith Kercher, fifteen to Laura Mezzetti, five to Raffaele Sollecito, five to Filomena Romanelli, four to Giacomo Silenzi and only one to Amanda, on a water glass. The shortfall of fourteen were unidentified people. Four unidentified fingerprints were found in Meredith's bedroom, none of which corresponded to Amanda's.

Amanda's single print looked suspiciously low. 'Had she assiduously wiped hers from the crime scene?' officers asked.

However, there were more rational explanations based on technical knowledge. Many of the prints found were only partial or smudged. In TV cop shows impeccable fingerprints can be found almost everywhere at a crime scene. But the real world was like a fingerprint graveyard. First of all, most touching leaves little trace. Just the right amount of pressure needs to be exerted to leave what's called a latent print. Then, to complicate matters, fatty fluid or sweat at the right temperature and on the right surface is required for a fingerprint to be left. Drinking glasses and window handles are notoriously good sources because they need to be gripped. Tables, chairs and computers are frustratingly useless. And doors – hence Giunta had been forced to use superglue heating on Meredith's wardrobe to get anything at all.

Amanda's fingerprints may have also evaporated. Most prints, left by the humidity on the hand, disappear within 24 hours. Fatty fingerprints, caused by a person touching sebaceous areas such as the forehead before touching a surface, remain much longer.

Even if all the conditions are perfect, the final hurdle faced by the detectives is even harder – the print has to match loops and whorls and other patterns in at least sixteen different places for it to be counted as a positive identification. Despairingly Giunta put the fourteen unidentified fingerprints through the national database. A long shot – but it just might work, as they say in TV cop shows.

The Sollecitos were riding high. No DNA evidence and now a measly five fingerprints of his at the murder scene which could be easily explained away. After all, Sollecito had visited the 7 Pergola flat more than three times, benignly, as Amanda's boyfriend. He could have touched any number of surfaces while he was cooking pasta, for instance. As far as they were concerned, there was only one more piece of evidence that hung over Raffaele – the trainer shoeprints. If that could be kicked into touch, it would be three strikes and out of jail, for sure, Luca Maori reasoned.

Determinedly, the Sollecitos turned private eye. Being bright, middle-class and organized, they soon excelled in the gumshoe game as they did in most things they turned their hands to. In a bid to prove that the print was not Raffaele's, his sister Vanessa did her own search for another type of running shoe that had a concentric ring pattern on its sole. There were thousands. The dining-room table became the repository of paperwork centimetres high. Friends and family trawled sports shops and internet sites. The team quickly discovered that all types of Nike Air Force One trainers, those worn by Raffaele, had eleven concentric rings and not nine as in the blood print. Encouraging news, but not enough to take to Mignini just yet. They would have to find the actual shoe with nine circles before Mignini would even let them in his office.

Then the family spread out, searching shoe shops in Bari and

Perugia. Uncle Giuseppe, a 51-year-old business manager, spent the day counting rings. In Bari he picked up a display model of Nike Outbreak in a sports shop. Eureka! The sole had nine rings. Excitedly he bought them. He would never wear them. 'God exists!' exclaimed Raffaele's dad, as he proudly handed them over to his lawyers later on.

Raffaele's lawyer Luca Maori had high hopes that his client would get a walkover based on the footprint elimination. But devastatingly Mignini remained unimpressed by their DIY detective work. The shoes had now become irrelevant, Mignini intimated. Now he had the knife as a murder weapon, the print didn't matter, in his humble opinion, of course.

'Murder weapon!' exclaimed Maori, 'That's a joke. There was no trace of my client on it. Plus, the traces of Meredith are too small to be conclusive.'

Mignini: 'We disagree. And the bottom line is this – the murder weapon was found in Raffaele's flat, so in our eyes he's a suspect. Still.'

Raffaele was staying put. He was despondent. Mignini was, however, careful not to reveal his hand completely. He didn't want the defence lawyers knowing how much they valued the knife just yet.

But the subtle game of legal politicking was about to be blown apart. A news story, based on an authorized leak revealing that Meredith's DNA was on the knife found in Raffaele's house, broke in the Italian press. The story heavily spun against Raffaele, characterizing him as the likely accomplice of the killer because the knife was his. An image that would be hard to shift from this point on. And one that would be damning to their re-examination committee appeal, which they had just submitted. Raffaele's family jumped up in their seats when the

TV news came on at 20:00 on 16 November. They blamed the authorities for the leak, shouting that they were trying to smear and fit up their son. But the truth was that Mignini also disliked the publicity – and the leak breached the law on confidential information. The damage was done, however, and there was nothing he or Raffaele's dad could do about it.

The incident sounded the end of the honourable accord that had held between all sides so far. The first salvo in a PR war had just been fired. Raffaele's dad swore revenge. In Seattle, Amanda's PR guru David Marriott sharpened his sword in preparation for the battle. The question was: who would they attack first?

The lawyers were despondent. Their arguments about a weak 50-picogramme DNA sample seemed fiddly and hard to understand in the wake of the damning news story, and the press took no notice. The defence lawyers had also had high hopes because Lumumba's situation was looking better. If the Lumumba thesis broke down, then so would the rest, they argued. That evening Raffaele Sollecito saw the news too on his prison TV set. He wrote a letter to his father which was promptly intercepted.

In the text he stated: 'I remember I was cooking fish at the girls' flat one night and pricked Meredith in the hand by accident. She said it was OK and we laughed about it.' That was his explanation for Meredith's DNA being on the blade. A copy of the letter went into the investigation documents and Giuliano Mignini made a mental note to ask Filomena Romanelli and Laura Mezzetti if Raffaele had ever cooked fish at their flat. By making that statement he felt that Raffaele was falling into his own trap: why did he have to explain it if the knife had nothing to do with the murder? He also checked the photographs of the crime scene. Did the knife fit the bloody outline on the bed? Another question for Giobbi and Stefanoni.

The first skirmishes in the PR war flared up in the Italian press soon afterwards. But they were blunt and reactionary. Italian journalists Fiorenza Sarzanini of *Corriere della Sera* and Meo Ponte of *Repubblica* split their readers like crowds at a gladiatorial contest. Those who thought the three suspects were either innocent or guilty were encouraged by various lawyers sounding off, for and against. Meanwhile, Team Amanda was planning a more sophisticated black operations campaign, to take the war to a different level altogether. The US PR execs, schooled in the dark arts of preemptive spin and aggressive rebuttal that are common in the rough-and-tumble world of corporate America, were not afraid to criticize the police, the prosecutors and the justice system. The Italians were taken aback by the gung-ho attacks. They were used to a more reverential and circumspect approach.

By a stroke of luck, Luciano Ghirga and Carlo Torre had worked on the Monster of Florence case together, the same case that Mignini was still investigating and being investigated for. They understood the cause could be used to seriously damage the prosecutor's credibility. No matter if the charges against Mignini were trumped up or not, he was *de facto* under internal investigation – a fact that would look bad in the headlines, if not in the detail that followed.

But did they have the will to go below the belt? After all, they were fellow Italians and legal professionals. Luciano Ghirga was against mixing the two cases, which were entirely unrelated. The lawyers took a step backwards, distancing themselves from the PR. A group of media-savvy lawyers and PR reps that defined itself as 'the Friends of Amanda' initiated a number of underhand character attacks. While the Italian lawyers resisted the temptation to attack Mignini in person, PR boss David Marriott had no such qualms. After all, that was his job. In addition, he had just stumbled upon a fortunate coincidence. One of the journalists whom Mignini had allegedly harassed during his Monster of Florence case was an American author called Doug Preston. Preston had written a book called *The Monster of Florence* that had grown into an international bestseller. Preston had maligned Mignini in dozens of interviews and clearly had an axe to grind. His co-author was Mario Spezi, the Italian-based jounalist whose conversations Mignini had allegedly tapped. Preston was in talks with Tom Cruise to sell him the movie rights to *The Monster of Florence.* If Marriott and the Friends of Amanda, including filmmaker Tom Wright, whose daughter had been at school with Amanda, could persuade a big gun like Preston to come on board and attack Mignini it would be PR gold. The plotting and scheming got under way with a vengeance.

While the main players allowed themselves to be mired in the dark arts, it took a no-nonsense cop to shine a light on the way forward. Fingerprint guru Giunta had some explosive news. He phoned his boss Edgardo Giobbi at once. It was 16 November and the last fortnight had been intense.

'We have a positive identification on one of fourteen mystery fingerprints found at the crime scene,' Giunta revealed.

Giobbi gulped in anticipation: 'Who is it?' Either of three suspects would be a result, he wished. He looked up to the heavens and held his breath.

Giunta held the suspense: 'It's from the person who made the bloody handprint on the pillow we found under Meredith's body.'

Giobbi: 'Well, who then? Come on . . . tell me.'

Giunta: 'And guess what? It's someone we have never come across before.'

Stunned silence.

Giobbi finally responded: 'What? Do you mean a new, fourth suspect?'

Giunta served him up: 'Yes. His name is Rudy Hermann Guede.'

A.k.a. The Baron.

23

Guede: The Baron's Getaway

16 November

All hell broke loose.

'Who the hell is Rudy Hermann Guede?' Giobbi cried, incredulous.

'He lives in Perugia at 12 Little Dog Street,' replied Giunta. 'He's a gardener. That's what's on his papers anyway – he's got a resident's permit.'

Giobbi: 'A what?'

Giunta: 'A resident's permit. He's originally from Africa.'

Giobbi was stunned once more into submission. Another African, like Lumumba? This is mad, he thought.

Giunta carried on: 'And that's how we got him, to be fair. The only reason we have his fingerprints on the national database is that they were taken when he applied for his resident's permit.'

Giobbi: 'I just can't believe it . . .' Thinking of how bad it looked.

Giunta: 'I know, we're very lucky' – he was thinking of how good his team were – 'to have got a usable print from the bloody hand on the pillow. And then to have spun it successfully through the computer. It was a million-to-one chance.'

Giobbi wasn't in the mood for celebration. Indeed, the find was a great piece of detective work, no one could disagree. But he knew the fact wouldn't play out that way in the circus that had now enveloped the case, an incendiary cocktail of ruthless police politicking and media hype.

Mobile phones vibrated on the polished desks of police chiefs and prosecutors from Rome to Perugia. Bleeps and texts resonated in the pockets of expensive Italian business suits. Giobbi drove all the way to Perugia to tell Mignini and caught him as he was leaving Sollecito's flat.

'Are you telling me that we've found the fourth man?' Mignini asked.

'That's right,' said Giobbi, trying to maintain a sense of normality.

'And it's taken us two weeks to find out?' said Mignini, his irascibility unyielding.

'That's the time it takes, Dr Mignini,' said Giobbi defensively. 'There's a lot of work going on down there in Rome. That's just police work. That's murder. It's never straightforward.'

Mignini puffed out grey smoke from his pipe. He didn't need a copper's sob story right now. Wait till the papers get hold of this one, he reflected. This was becoming a mess. He ordered the Lumumba dossier to be sent to Matteini. She already knew that Lumumba was about to exit the scene while Guede became the 'New Entry'. Lumumba remained a suspect but was released on bail. Mignini opened a new dossier on the leaks.

Mignini burned the midnight oil. Soon, emails from the social services, the office for foreign residents and from police records filled up his in-box with background on the man known as The Baron.

'Rudy Hermann Guede,' Mignini mumbled, a halo of blue computer light glowing around his desk. 'Twenty years old. Ivory Coast citizen. Fostered with the Caporali family, a prominent industrial dynasty in Perugia who made world-famous coffee machines. No criminal record . . .' But his eyes lit up when he read about the knife incident at the Milan kindergarten just a few days before Meredith's murder. There could be something in the knives thing, he thought.

'Get me the full report and here's an arrest warrant for him,' he instructed Chiacchiera. 'Go to his house and see what you can find. This time call the forensics squad straight away. I don't want any cock-ups.'

Commissioner Chiacchiera opened the door to Guede's bedsit and peered into the black silence. He sniffed. The air was still and stale. Guede was long gone, he just knew. Call it a copper's nose, instinct, whatever. Guede was on his toes, for sure, long ago. Chiacchiera didn't even have to switch the lights on to know that.

Exactly 992 km (616 miles) away in the German city of Düsseldorf, Rudy Guede sat on the cold stone steps of a night shelter for the homeless, a huddle of poor and desperate immigrants around him. He shivered because he didn't have appropriate clothes. He'd given away his Nike trainers to a bum worse off than himself, or so he said.

Some of the Africans laughed and joked about the bizarre situations they found themselves in every day, as 'unpeople' on the streets of a Western city without status or money. Humour was a cheap way of cheering each other up, boosting morale. Another way involved talking of their dreams, of getting a job and moving on to France and Britain, where the police were less on top and prospects were better because most spoke English.

Guede wasn't laughing, though, his confidence smashed by the meteor-like disaster of the past two weeks. His conscience ate away every living moment, awake and asleep. His eyes constantly darting around the street looking for the blue lights. That he knew would come soon enough. This was the life of the fugitive – cold, hunger and worry.

He ate his last chunk of chocolate before going back to his room. He pulled the scratchy institutional blankets over his head to block out the German winter. To block out the groans and shouts of dispossessed down the corridor. To block out the memories. But one nightmare wouldn't go away. The one tinted in red. Drenched sepia-like in a sea of horror and haemoglobin. That flowed rivers of blood. With Meredith writhing on her knees in terror. With Meredith squirming on the floor in agony. With Meredith pointing to the gaping hole in her neck. Begging him to help. Begging him to call an ambulance. Begging him not to leave her to die alone. Slowly building up to the most lurid, depraved scene of all. And to him, this was *a scene*. The whole episode was just like a film. A scary movie. It was that unreal. The final take of him standing there helpless. Over Meredith's choking body, next to her wardrobe. No mobile. No first aid. No courage. Holding blood-soaked towels in one hand. After vainly trying to stop the flow. The fingers on his other other hand just like Meredith's – coated perfectly in her blood as though they had just been dipped into a can of paint.

Guede tossed and turned. He hadn't slept whilst being on the run. The nightmares. The guilt. The waiting. For the standard-issue kicking-in of his door. If this was freedom, it didn't seem worth it, trapped in a prison of his own sordid making. He'd thought about handing himself in. But his escape from Italy had been hard-won. A million-to-one escapade. Like a prisoner of war, he'd crossed two borders, passed through the Alps and evaded the police in three countries. He couldn't give it up that easily. Plus, he knew that if he did no one would believe his story. No one would want to hear the truth. After all he was black. He was a flake who couldn't be trusted. Rudy cast his mind back to the fateful night sixteen days before on 1 November. The sound of Meredith's pleas, gurgling blood and drowning, ringing in his ears.

His getaway from 7 Pergola Road had begun with a sprint. Rudy had sweated heavily as he ran up the hill to his own bolt-hole at 12 Little Dog Street. Had he gone past the steps where a black man had bumped into the restaurant goers going back to their car or in the other direction, up the hill, towards Mrs Elisabetta Lana's house, where Meredith's two mobile phones had been thrown away?

Guede was covered in blood. He had no telephone. He slipped the key into his lock silently, hoping his Spanish party pals from upstairs didn't hear him. Overwhelmed by anger and fear, pumped up on stress-inducing noradrenalin, he ripped off his jeans and shirt and stared at himself in the mirror. What now?

Human reaction to stress is one of the greatest mysteries of the mind. Everyone reacts differently. Should he fight or flight? Front it out or flee the scene? Paralysed by confusion, he did neither. He did what he knew best. Out of habit Rudy Hermann Guede partied on. He got another pair of jeans on and another shirt, put his blood-drenched clothes in a plastic bag and took it out of the bedsit with him, pulling the door quietly shut behind him. The witching hour had just passed, the town clock chiming in the distance. Guede needed company.

A few hundred yards down the road he knocked on his mate Alex Crudo's door. As the crowd inside laughed and joked, Guede milled about in a daze. Did he dare tell them? No – that would be suicide. He kept shtum. But his body wouldn't – sweat was still rolling down his back and chest like tears, hours after he had left the scene and Meredith to die.

'Are you all right?' one of them asked. He nodded. He followed them on automatic pilot as the group filed out of the flat and ambled down to the House of Delirium where they bopped for an hour or so. Guede began to smell. He tired soon and stumbled back to his flat. It was Friday morning, and he was out of a job. So he slept in.

When news of the murder hit his TV screen on the afternoon of 2 November, Guede remained detached. Like many people involved in a murder, a macabre curiosity drew him to back the crime. He walked into the main square to watch the two minutes' silence in memory of Meredith at her vigil that evening at around 20:00. Then, to drown out the cries, he partied on throughout that evening too – in pubs and discos just a few minutes away from where Meredith's body lay in the mortuary. Guede knew it was a matter of time before he was identified. After all, he had left every possible clue there. He knew it – he'd watched scores of CSI shows on the TV.

On the morning of Saturday, 3 November, his nerve broke. He took his last 50 euros and bought a train ticket for Bologna, 171 km (106 miles) northwest of Perugia straight through the middle of Italy. He intended to stay on the train until Milan, about the same distance again further, hoping that there would be fewer ticket collectors over the holiday weekend. Guede knew the route by heart from when he had been to stay with his aunt in Lecco on the Lake far to the north-west. That's where he was aiming, but if the heat was turned up, it was a convenient jumping-off point to the northern borders with Switzerland and Austria.

Guede clocked the conductor getting on at Bologna, slowly making his way through the carriage. He decided to take his chances. Italian collectors are generally laid back, and don't call the police.

'This ticket's valid up to Bologna,' the collector explained.

'Oh, really!' Guede feigned surprise. 'We've passed Bologna, have we?'

'Yes, really,' said the conductor, shaking his head in mock annoyance.

'Just get off the train in Modena,' the conductor ordered him finally, 'if you don't want to get a fine.'

'OK, thank you,' said Guede, breathing a sigh of relief. As an African immigrant, he had learned to be extra polite to people in uniforms. A virtue that was especially important in his current position.

He hopped on the next train going towards Milan in the same direction, but it was late and he missed the connection to Lecco. The next one was at five in the morning from Milan's main rail hub. With the few coins he had left, Guede chilled out in the Sol to Sol pub. After last orders he walked over to Milan's grand Central Station.

From a distance Guede scoped the building's massive profile, on the lookout for cops. He had a clear view – the facade looms over a vast open space as though it were an imperial palace, not a temple to steam. The coast was clear, so he went inside. Guede was always overawed by the concourse's opulence, a majestic monument to the industrial age, celebrated with colossal statues, glass archways and ornate decor. Did he catch the eye of a gargoyle, leering down from the shadows, reminding him of Perugia? Of the evil deeds that he was running from? The gnawing of his conscience was never far away. As the alcohol wore off in the cold, so did its very temporary powers of soothing. Suddenly, he was snapped out of his stupor. He began to notice hundreds of drug addicts, homeless and destitute, who lurched across the marble floors like zombies, wrapping themselves in rags in the dark recesses. The station was haunted by poverty at night.

Guede knew that the homeless attracted relentless police patrols, so he had only a few minutes to make a decision. He knew they'd allow him to spend the night on the hard seats in the waiting room, but even that semi-authorized limbo was also a risk. He had already been copped for going to the kindergarten rather than spending the night in the station just a few days before. They might ask him for papers or, worse still, recognize him as a troublemaker.

As he turned to make a quick exit, his worst-case scenario came true – a couple of police officers stopped him wandering along a platform.

'Papers!' they demanded.

Guede took out his identity card.

'Resident's permit!' They demanded more.

That was being renewed, Guede explained. He didn't have it.

The cops stared into his bloodshot eyes.

'Come with us, will you,' one of the cops said, as he grabbed Guede's elbow.

That was it. The end. Thirty years in jail.

Guede then took a risk. An unusual one for him, with figures of authority.

'No! Leave me alone,' he yelled. He pushed them away. 'I'm waiting for a train to Lecco. Just leave me alone.'

The cops looked at each other, not knowing what to do. Guede upped the brinksmanship and began to walk off.

'If we find you here in an hour's time,' the cop said, saying goodbye to a certain commendation, a possible promotion if they had been the ones to catch the prime suspect, 'you're coming down with us.' They told him to beat it.

Rudy carried on, his nerves allowing him the weakest of smiles. There were people boarding a train and he joined them. The train rumbled on into the night. He found himself a seat in a dark second-class carriage and fell asleep. A lost soul on a journey to nowhere. His mind raced back to the Ivory Coast shanty town where he had once found himself lost as a child, and to his mother who had found him and taken him home. How he wanted to be back there now. Snow had begun to whiten the tops of the Dolomite Mountains. Woken by the cold and the discomfort of the seats, the lights halfway up the dark sky told him he was going through a mountain chain with villages perched at intervals along the narrow roads to the peaks. Dotted here and there were floodlit castles and churches.

The glaring lights of the station at Bolzano woke him for real. He'd overshot Lecco and was now at the frontier with Austria. He'd passed through Verona, then Trento, up the Adige valley. Guede left the train again at the frontier. Despite the Schengen treaty, the Austrian and Italian frontier police still patrol the trains – looking out for people like Rudy. He had his Italian ID card with him but not his resident's permit. He'd been resident in Italy for fifteen years, but was still not an Italian subject.

For the third time in two days, he was challenged by another ticket collector and more cops. Now Guede was becoming more confident. He blagged them and they let him pass. On the morning of Sunday, 4 November, while the cops were still poring over the murder scene and as Meredith's body was being dissected on the slab, Rudy Guede boarded a train to Germany.

More than a fortnight later, on 17 November, back in Perugia, Profazio and his colleague had no idea that this was how their new prime suspect had given them the slip. The detectives looked tired when they walked into Mignini's office. They had been up half the night searching Guede's empty house, coordinating forensics' tests and knocking on neighbours' doors. Their boss Edgardo Giobbi was much fresher, even though he'd driven up from Rome. The trio had to report to Mignini that the case was not closed. 'It's a very funny thing. Guede's flat and Sollecito's flat are close to each other,' Profazio said. 'Less than a hundred metres, maybe. And do you know what is even more interesting? There's a little pathway, almost a secret, that starts near to both flats, goes through a little gate in the city walls, and on to a grass verge next to the hill pass. You know which part of the hill pass this secret passage leads on to?'

'What?' said Mignini.

'Sperandio Road,' Profazio said. 'The villa where the phones were found is just there, just below the little gate. The little gate is about ten metres from Guede's flat and fifty metres from Sollecito's.'

'Aha!' said Mignini. 'So that means either Guede or Sollecito could have run up the hill from 7 Pergola. Come to the passage and the gate in the wall. And decide to lash the phones there. Most convenient.'

'And do you know what we found at Guede's?' Chiacchiera intervened. 'A shoebox. A Nike shoebox for a pair of Outbreak. Nine rings. Like the bloody shoeprints.'

Sollecito's uncle's amateur sleuthing had finally come in handy after all.

24

Train to Nowhere

17 November

The day after Rudy Guede had been exposed Giuliano Mignini received a call from the *Umbrian Journal*s editor-in-chief Giuseppe Castellini. His team of resourceful hacks were now making more breakthroughs on the case than the police, so went the mischievous gossip of the press corps. Chasing up tips and leads about witnesses that had not yet come forward, or been overlooked by bungling coppers, would soon land the local paper several spectacular scoops. The consequence was red faces all round at police HQ. In the meantime, the cigar-chomping Castellini had a morsel to throw the senior prosecutor that would keep him in his good books.

'I've got a tip for you,' Castellini proffered, in a bizarre case of role reversal. 'It may help the police track down the new suspect Rudy Guede.'

'Any assistance would be greatly appreciated,' Mignini replied. He was old school and had none of the fear of the press that younger lawmakers and coppers had. They would talk to the papers only through official channels, suffocatingly controlled by an army of over-protective press officers.

'We've had a ring in about this Rudy Guede,' Castellini revealed. A ring-in was industry jargon for a tip-off, usually anonymous, from one of the paper's punters. The caller had claimed that he was a close friend of Guede and that he knew where the elusive Baron was hiding out – but he wouldn't give an exact location.

'OK, so who made this call to you?' Mignini wanted to know.

'Well, we don't know, because the caller didn't tell us his name,' Castellini said. 'We told him we couldn't offer any money for his story and he never called back.'

'OK. So what do you think it means then?' Mignini asked.

'It's significant,' Castellini said, 'because it means that Guede is watching the news, that he is in touch with friends. So if you can find his pals, you might be able to reel him in.'

Though the information was sparse, Castellini's proposal wasn't as far-fetched as might be expected. Putting Guede's mates under surveillance and tapping their phones might lead them to the prize. However, the problem was finding these close confidantes. Without them, Mignini knew that finding the prime suspect would be a needle in a haystack. He reasoned that Guede could have fled to Africa or Alaska or Australia by now, based on the assumption that he'd had two weeks' flying time to make use of. Just in case they couldn't find a friend, Mignini ordered his detectives to check the passenger rosters for flights out of Italy on the days after the murder, including Sunday, 4 November.

By choosing the train to take him to freedom, Guede had gone under the radar. The train was cheap, anonymous and didn't require a passport – at least, not a European one or one with a visa. On Sunday, 4 November, Guede took off his Nike Outbreak trainers and kicked back, relaxing in his compartment.

He was woken up by the door sliding open. An African man

came in and sat down opposite him in the compartment. They looked into each other's eyes. Through the international language of the streets, they didn't have to tell each other that they were on the run. One from poverty or oppression. One from the police. Their eyes told their back story. In the netherworld of immigrants, it was all the same.

'Where are you going?' the African traveller inquired.

'Don't know,' replied Guede.

'Come with me. I'm going to Munich,' the African said. 'To the Caritas place. It's a Catholic charity and at least they will feed you there.'

The offer was an ideal opportunity – by posing as a new arrival to Europe, a clandestine immigrant, Guede could get lost in the raggle-taggle, chaotic world of false names, expedient papers and fabricated life stories.

As the train hurtled towards Germany, Rudy felt confident enough to tell his new friend the real story of why he was on his toes – or at least parts of it. A story that he would repeat in parts to several drifters he encountered on the road. He began working out in his head what he was going to say when the authorities finally caught up with him, what he remembered. His mind went back to when he met Amanda. They were at Le Chic, Patrick's bar. Later he would write it all down.

I remember very well that Amanda came to me with a big smile on her face and she wanted to talk to me. 'How are you?' she said. 'And where are you from?' Then she said she was from Seattle. I said I also had friends in Seattle and asked if she knew him because he was studying at the University of Washington. She said yes, she knew him and asked if he was Chinese but I told her Victor is a Russian and I understood we were talking about two different people.

We were speaking and I asked her if in this bar they played hip-hop and rap because this evening they were playing Latin American music, which I don't like very much. She said they usually did salsa and African music. I then left the bar and went to meet other people. That was also the first time I met Amanda then I met her many other times but only to say '*ciao*' and to go on. I did not have any relationship with her or her group of friends and for this reason I was not attached to her at all.

Even one evening, when it was Owen's birthday and we went out together, myself, Alex, Philip, Ernest, Owen, Ben, we all went out to celebrate. Owen got drunk and we had to take him to sleep at Alex's house. I spent the rest of the evening at the Shamrock. There were two Italian boys I knew from basketball and I remained with them.

I knew them and I decided to approach a girl and began to chat her up. I asked where she came from and she said she was called Amanda and was from Seattle. I had not recognized her and told her I had met a girl from Seattle before and she said I was the same boy that she had already met.

He remembered how he had been invited round to the flat of the boys who lived under Amanda's.

I don't remember that evening precisely except that I didn't ask her to go to bed although I felt that was possible. One of the boys began to roll a joint and I asked if I had to pay him and he said, 'No, of course not.' One of the boys said, 'Let's imagine all of us in bed with Amanda alone' because we were all males and felt at home and we were debating about whether to have her or not.

Then we heard a knock at the door and who was it? Amanda, and we all laughed. Then Amanda sat and began to smoke the cigarette because she smoked a lot. The boys told me they saw in my eyes that by comparison with them smoking, I was just a beginner.

That evening my eyes and Amanda's crossed a lot and we exchanged that smile, of the kind that says, 'I know that you like me.' But nothing else happened after that. I remember asking the boys who lived above. They said two Italians, Amanda and an English girl. I said they were lucky because where I lived there were two Italians and two Spanish girls.

Later there was another knock at the door and another girl came in and it was Meredith and I saw that she was beautiful and knew she must have been the English girl because of her Italian. The first thing I said to her was 'You don't look English at all.' I was speaking in English and, if I remember correctly she said her mother was from India or somewhere from those areas.

I looked at the two girls and saw that she was very beautiful and that was the first time I had met Meredith. Maybe I had met her somewhere else, but I had never taken any notice. That night, speaking at length, I can say that we spoke about everything until we were tired. Then we went to sleep.

Outside, the cold bit into the darkening countryside. Austria turned into Germany between one mountain and the next. Rudy kept going over the story in his head. In Munich he slipped through another police check, a pair of officers weakly warning him to get back on the next train to Italy. In the confusion, he had lost his travel mate but he soon came across other

African immigrants who pointed him in the right direction to the Caritas hostel.

A fortnight later in Perugia, neither the police nor the prosecutors knew any of this. The police were still trying to piece together Guede's relationship with Amanda and Meredith the hard way. As yet, his flat hadn't thrown up any significant clues over and above the shoebox, but the forensics people were able to get DNA samples from his toothbrush and clothes.

However, on 18 November, a significant breakthrough did occur. Chiacchiera had tracked down Guede's former foster family called the Mancinis. Excitedly the detective told Mignini the good news.

'Their real son is called Gabriele Mancini and it turns out that he is one of Guede's best friends in Perugia.'

'Bring him in for a statement, will you?' Mignini ordered.

'We've also found an old school friend called Giacomo Benedetti.'

Mignini wondered whether he had found the bait that they were looking for to snare Guede. Maybe Castellini's idea had not been as far-fetched as he first thought.

25

A Tainted Tryst – Guede and Meredith

At first, Gabriele Mancini and Giacomo Benedetti just wanted to help Guede by acting as character witnesses. Gabriele, who was like a brother to Guede, painted a picture of him as a helpless loser who continually let himself down but would never hurt others.

'I think he must have got into a depression during the summer just gone,' Gabriele told the police. 'I heard that he hadn't been to work for more than three weeks. I have never seen him drunk but I don't think he used drugs. However, he was living in the centre of town and there's a lot going on down there; he used to go out with students. But he had no money. Around September, October-ish we noticed that he was down on his luck and would ask him out. He had no other friends, his dad was non-existent, he had no mum. Then I heard nothing of him since 31 October. I called him several times but got no reply. I heard nothing from him until the 16th. The news hadn't broken about Rudy being involved on the 16th yet.'

The police officers nodded and listened patiently.

*

Twelve days before, in Munich, the poor and desperate, mostly with dark skin, milled around in the Caritas centre. What to do next was pressing on Guede's mind. He had been there more than twenty-four hours. Tuesday, 6 November, was only his fourth day as a fugitive, but he was cold and unclean and the incredible journey felt more like four weeks or four months. He needed to move on. Just as he had drifted in and out of discothèques in Perugia on the 1st and 2nd, now he drifted in and out of conversations with other guests of the Caritas hostel in the hope of finding his next move.

'I'm going to Augsburg,' said another immigrant. 'Come along with me if you want.'

His new associate seemed more streetwise than the immigrants he'd met so far. An old hand. Instinctively, Guede knew he had a choice. He could either stop running now, or follow his new associate ever deeper into the murky world of statelessness and non-persons. A world he knew he could disappear into more or less for ever, if he so decided. Guede weighed up his options. If he gave himself up one of the main problems was credibility. Would anyone believe that he was not capable of hurting Meredith? His defence was that he was seemingly falling for Meredith, or at least wanted to win her affection, as opposed to someone who would attack her. Guede went over the details of how he got to know Meredith. An account he would later write down. A story which he hoped he could find witnesses to back up.

We continued not to see each other until the day when the final match between South Africa and England happened, when I saw Meredith again, for the whole match. During the match I turned around often because she was very beautiful. When the match was over some English people, in a joking way, decided to go to the Domus. But since Alex and I had quarrelled with a bouncer and didn't like the place we decided to go somewhere else. So we all went into the centre and we all went home from there.

Since then, whenever I met Amanda and the boys, or Amanda was in the street, we would say '*ciao*' to each other but we did not stop and never got close to one another.

I only went there to speak to her, I don't hide the fact that she had attracted me, she was fascinating and sweet, like many good girls. We met the night before at the Halloween evening at the house of a few girls. That evening I went to the house of a few Spanish friends who were friends of the two Spanish girls who live above me.

There we watched the football match and then we went to this party where I met a lot of people including Meredith. I didn't recognize her at first because she was dressed as a vampire and I was dressed normally and it was her who recognized me. And when I recognized her I asked her if she wanted to suck my blood because they [England] had lost the cup and she laughed . . . It was because the night before England had lost to South Africa.

England had lost to South Africa in the rugby final. We were together all evening and we exchanged a lot of quips. That day I was with Alex, Alex's cousin and a friend Philip. With us was a group of English, including Meredith. That evening we had a good time, it was an evening I had a chance to speak to her in a deeper way, we flirted together.

I asked her if we could meet because I wanted to speak to her again and she accepted. After that all the people went out to the Domus club but Meredith didn't come and I didn't see her at the Domus club.

I often saw Meredith at the Merlin where we spoke, even on the evening of the 31st when there was a Halloween party, even if it was not in a deep manner. We talked about rugby and that evening we had something to talk about. I flirted with her and we kissed once and that's all. That's why I wanted to see her the next day and she gave me a date and a place for the appointment that evening. That's why I was happy and left my house early that evening, around 7:30.

So Guede's story was becoming clearer, essentially that he had a number of bar-room trysts with Meredith. They had got on well, so much so that she invited him around to her place on the night of the murder.

In Perugia, the police were completely in the dark. Even though Mancini and Benedetti were warming up, the childhood pals could not fill them in on Guede's links with Meredith. So far, they had no evidence that Meredith and The Baron even knew each other. Officers were dispatched to interview Meredith's friends, her flatmates, the boys downstairs and other witnesses. Still, the feedback they got was tenuous, to say the least. The police were desperate to talk to Guede. If they could prove that Meredith and Guede knew each other, it would be a huge step in the right direction. To prove that Guede was the murderer.

26

First Cough

18 November

The police wanted more than general background out of Gabriele Mancini and Giacomo Benedetti. Soon they got it. Officers nearly fell off their seats when Giacomo revealed that he had had an internet phone conversation with Guede over Skype in the last few days. *While Guede was on the run.*

'At that point I didn't know of his connection to the murder. I just thought he was running away from his life because he was down. I told him he was running away again,' Giacomo relayed to the police. 'Running away from his friends, like he did when he went to Lecco. I told him I couldn't understand. All he could say was that he couldn't come back. That I knew why . . .'

'Did he mention anything about the murder?' the officers asked impatiently.

After a short stay at the Caritas centre in Munich, Guede decided that he must go on running. He was convinced that no one would believe his story – and that his colour would go against him. He shook hands with his latest acquaintance at the

Caritas centre, a fixer who helped immigrants get political asylum. From now on they would be partners, that was the deal. Later, they took a train from Munich's Hauptbahnhof, the old station that had once received the Empress of Austria Sissy and later Hitler when they had visited this merry German city. Rudy was in no mood for sightseeing. Such was the hollow feeling inside him that the outside world looked like various shades of white. One big impenetrable blank. The train dashed across the neat German countryside. Augsburg was a picturesque medieval city.

'I'll take you to the McDonald's, but you've got to tell me what you're running from,' the fixer asked. 'I can't help you unless I know what you've done.' His friend had some cash. He had none. Over a burger, Guede began telling him about the Meredith case. Astonishingly, the fixer was the first person to get a glimpse of what had actually happened inside Meredith's room on the night of the murder. Guede didn't name the killer – but he did refer to the appearance of a mystery man at the scene. Incredibly, Guede said this man turned on him with a knife. It all became part of his handwritten statement.

OK. I was in this house where a murder happened. I didn't call the ambulance, I just split. I just split, I didn't do anything, I tried to stop her bleeding but I'm black, they would have thought I did it . . .

Only once before have I seen so much blood and that was because I lived at that time with my father and he broke a stick on my head and I saw everything red, blood coming out of my head and I fell on the floor but it does not compare with what I saw there. He hit me on the hand with something sharp, it seemed like a scalpel but it gave me a deep wound.

He tried to attack me but Thank God he left the house. She was crying and complaining and trying to speak but I went close to her and she kept on saying, 'Af, Af', and I was looking for a piece of paper and the only thing I could hear were those two words. Her mouth was full of blood and her neck was bleeding and that was why she couldn't say any more.

I tried to find a cloth, a towel but it was quickly, within a minute, full of blood and I saw everything was red, it was everywhere. And if I had not been in the bathroom maybe I would have protected her and nothing would have happened . . . Oh my God, I would have preferred this to have happened to me.

I didn't see him well because the house was not lit well and maybe for this reason they accused Patrick first. I didn't go out often with Amanda and Meredith, in fact we didn't really go out at all. So maybe the person who saw me thought I was Patrick. They had to blame somebody and since I'm black that was not a problem, because I was black . . .

I always respected everything that had to do with heroes that saved the world and I dreamed often of saving the whole world. And yet I was unable to even call 118 emergency service on the telephone which was so easy. I am ashamed of myself and I would have wanted to have been in her place because she would have done the same for me. She would have done for me what I had not done for her . . .

Instead of shopping Guede to the police, the fixer agreed to help him disappear. They got on another train to Stuttgart. 'Papers!' demanded the the ticket collector, almost routine to Guede now. He examined the Ivory Coast passport which Guede had dug out from his bag and now had the confidence to use, and handed him back a fine for no ticket.

In Stuttgart Rudy and his new companion walked together along the modern streets of the city that was home to Mercedes and Porsche. The fixer took Rudy to a place he said was his home. They ate a snack and slept. The next day, 7 November, they went down to the asylum seekers' centre.

In Perugia, Amanda and Raffaele were already in gaol, and if he could have read German, Guede might have been able to catch the latest update in the local papers. But for now he was determined to focus on creating a new ID and getting political asylum. His new friend, who was expert at playing the system, guided him.

'As soon as you register at the hostel they'll get the police on to you, so you mustn't have anything that can identify you as being from Italy. Think of a new name and pretend you've just fled from Africa.' Immigrant solidarity went beyond the realms of the credible, but Guede had nothing to lose.

'Give me your papers and your rucksack,' the fixer said, 'and come and see me after you've registered.' His friend pointed at a low door with an anti-panic handle on the inside. 'Go into there and tell them you want political asylum.'

Guede gave his name to the receptionist as Roger Wheid, from Abidjan, in Ivory Coast, and claimed that he was fleeing civil war. The police turned up a few minutes later and took him down to the station. They gave him a train ticket to a centre in nearby Karlsruhe. Before he left the following day he picked up his rucksack from his amateur immigration adviser but left behind the Italian documents he had spent a lifetime earning as a new resident in Italy.

The train rolled into Karlsruhe on the morning of 8 November. As Amanda, Raffaele and Patrick Lumumba were facing the Preliminary Investigation judge inside Capanne, Guede checked into his next hostel and his new life under a new identity. He was now virtually home and dry. No one would ever find him, he was confident of that – unless of course he wanted to be caught. The will to fail ran strong in Guede – it had defined much of his life. Who knows what he would do?

On 11 November the hostel manager sent him to a more permanent residence in Düsseldorf. The Siesta hotel was a boat moored on the river. He showered, got fed well and after a few days felt like the new man he had become. Far from being chased by the police, he was now being actively helped by the authorities. On 16 November he felt confident enough to check his emails. He borrowed a euro and connected to his Hotmail account. Giacomo was waiting and gave him an appointment to speak over Skype. Guede desperately needed to talk to someone. Giacomo had asked him what he was fleeing from – not knowing he was in Germany.

'You know,' Guede answered hesitantly. But Giacomo hadn't yet put two and two together. Giacomo had wrongly assumed that Guede was being his usual self, running away from his responsibilities in life, and told him so. Guede simply clammed up further.

'Don't be like this,' Giacomo said. 'What's happened to you? Where are you?' But Guede wouldn't say. Deep down he was bursting to tell Giacomo about Meredith. How he would never have hurt her and how in fact they had been friends who had a drink together on Halloween. Instead he said nothing and rang off.

Back in Perugia two days later on 18 November Giacomo relayed all he knew about the Skype conversation to the police. But neither Gabriele or Giacomo could tell them about Guede's relationship with Amanda and Meredith, or crucially what had happened on the night of the murder. They were still in the dark about that. Guede had chosen to confide in an anonymous immigrant rather than his mates back in Perugia. If the police were to have any chance of catching up with the story or catching Guede then they would have to act fast.

27

Skype Trap

18 November

Giacomo and Gabriele found themselves sitting at police HQ, the latest witnesses to be drawn into the investigation. They simply intended to act as character witnesses for Guede.

'He could be dumb, but Rudy was no murderer,' they repeated over and over to the officers. But Giobbi had different ideas. He wanted Guede at all costs. He didn't want to listen to hard luck stories about Guede just yet. Leave that to the social services and the probation officers, he thought.

'Skype!' announced Giobbi to Gabriele and Giacomo. 'You've got to get him on Skype again and persuade him to come back to Italy.' Giobbi knew that no one ever wanted to grass up their friends but he persuaded the pair that it was actually in Guede's interest.

'If you can talk him into coming back on his own volition, it will look better for him. The courts will take that into consideration.' That much was true. But what Giobbi didn't say was that if the police had to extradite Guede from Germany the process would take weeks. He wanted to get the boys to lure

Guede back over the border into Italy under his own steam to save time and paperwork. The boys agreed to set the trap. They would talk to him on Skype but not tell him that the police were listening in.

Duly Giacomo sent Rudy a Skype message with a time and day to talk. Then all of a sudden, there he was. Guede appeared on the line. He told them where he was. Then after a while he opened up. He agreed to tell them what had happened when he went to see Meredith on the night she was murdered.

Meredith had invited him around to her flat that night, Guede insisted. Not a formal appointment, just one of those studenty arrangements whereby you drop in to see how it's going, Guede explained. He began by talking about what he done in the couple of hours before going around to 7 Pergola.

I went first to the house of Alex [a friend] but he did not open the door immediately but I waited a bit because I saw the light in the house and he was working. I had not seen Alex for a little time; he had been in Greece or Corsica and so we talked for a time and when I left I said we would see each other later on. I told Alex I was going to eat and come back later.

Then seeing it was early for the appointment with Meredith I went around to see where I could eat and I went to the kebab place in front of the Bear's Lair and ordered something to eat. Then I waited in front then I ate and met Philip. I spoke to him at length and then we agreed we would meet later on at Alex's house. Philip said he was going to meet somebody and I said I was also and joking he asked me if it was a boy or girl. I said it was a girl. Then I went to Meredith's house.

I went around and I waited until approximately 8:30

because that was the time we were supposed to meet and I wanted to be punctual at her house. I went to the front of the house and I noticed a white car with a druggie pusher who was often seen in the area but I didn't pay attention. I went into the courtyard and knocked at the door but nobody answered.

I went downstairs to the boys' flat but there too there was no one in. So I waited in the courtyard. A little afterwards, here comes Meredith, smiling. She asked me how long had I been waiting and I told her it was about a minute. She smiled and took the keys from her bag, opened the door and we went in.

There was nobody in and it was all dark and in the kitchen/sitting room. She shouted, 'Is there anybody in?' as if to say she had come back. And there was no answer from the other rooms and I thought for a minute she had bought something at the kebab, even something to drink. I needed something to drink because what I had eaten was very spicy and I asked for something to drink. She told me to make myself at home. I opened the fridge and I drank an apricot juice then some water.

She saw me drinking from the bottle, so she didn't worry where the glasses were. Then I sat down. I don't know what problems she had with Amanda but she was complaining. At her anger I got up and went towards her. I saw she was furious and she said, 'That whore of a drug addict'. They were words that were very strange for two friends.

I asked why and she said she could not find her money any more and she showed me a little box next to the bed where she kept underwear. Maybe it was a thief, I said, but there was no indication from the inside or the outside there had been a break-in and she complained about Amanda but not about the other girls that lived with her.

Then she went into Amanda's bedroom to see if there were

any breakages in her bedroom, but there was nothing and she opened a drawer and I saw that her money was not there. Meredith knew where Amanda kept the money and she was very suspicious. She went into the others' rooms but everything was tidy.

I tried to speak to her to calm her, saying a beautiful girl like her should not get angry because it would give her wrinkles. She started to laugh and I said she should laugh because everything would work itself out and she needed to speak to Amanda and with the other girls to see what happened.

Then we spoke about other things, me and her and how we were both similar and she had secrets and these had conditioned her. We spoke about how we were similar and how her parents were separated and how this had conditioned her adolescence. She was more or less like me even though I was different to her and I'd had a disturbed adolescence, I told her.

She asked about my life and my parents and I told her I'd had many mothers and many fathers and many brothers but none of them had ever been mine for ever and I'd been in many families but never had real families. She told me it was better to have bad ones than none. Then I told her I needed to go to the bathroom urgently because the kebab had given me stomach ache. She told me to go to the bathroom, next to the fridge and I went in there.

When I was in the bathroom, I heard the sound of the bell, I am sure of this because it rang more than once. Then I put my headphones on and listened to music on my iPod for the time I was in the bathroom. I listened to the first three pieces. At the end of the last piece I heard a shout and although I kept the volume of the music high I could still hear the shout.

I had not finished doing my dos but I tried to hurry as quick as I could and go and see what was happening. I opened the door of the bathroom but in the sitting room/kitchen there was nobody so I went to Meredith's bedroom and there was this person who had his back to me and he was inside the bedroom. I said, 'Hey, what's going on?' I saw immediately the body of Meredith on the ground and saw the blood.

I said, 'What the fuck have you done?' I shouted and this guy turned round and it was a man and he was Italian because he insulted me and he had no accent. He had a knife in his hand and he tried to strike me but I defended myself with my hand but it was very sharp and by just touching me it made small wounds, it was like a scalpel.

I didn't have my trousers well done up with my belt and while moving backwards I fell and he tried to attack and I took a chair to protect myself. Because I was stronger than him and had a chair he ran out, saying, 'A black man found is a black man condemned.'

I was covered in blood. I adjusted up my trousers and went into Meredith's room and it was all covered in blood and she had a neck that seemed like a river. She was asking for help and I kneeled next to her and I tried to close the wounds. I have never seen so much blood before and so I went into the bathroom to look for a towel that I put on her neck. But in a very little time it was all drenched. I put another one on but nothing could stop that blood.

I could not see the wound and I asked her what happened. She kept repeating:' Af . . . Af . . . Af . . .' I tried to write this somewhere and since I didn't have paper and my hands were covered in blood I wrote on the wall. It was the fastest way, I thought.

Giacomo asked him if he had seen Amanda there. '*Amanda non c'entra*' – 'Forget about Amanda'.

So there it was: Guede's confession. In his own words. And on tape. With the police listening in. Guede had admitted being at the scene – but, incredibly, on the toilet at the point at which Meredith had been murdered. Crucially, Guede had also introduced the possibility of a new motive for the murder. He wasn't saying that it was a sex game gone wrong, but implying that money was at the centre of the row. Was Meredith's murder a botched robbery that had descended into violence? Guede also implied that the break-in or staged break-in had, or at least parts of it had, been carried out before he got there. And even before Amanda and Raffaele, or their mystery look-a-likes, had arrived at 7 Pergola. Did the 'break-in' and the murder occur at separate times? Did Guede have a role in this alleged robbery? These were important and detailed questions. But for now the police were only interested in strategic objectives. The first goal was to get Guede home. Then perhaps he could start filling in the minutiae.

The tale went on. Giacomo interrupted. 'Come home, Rudy. The police know all this, they'll understand. Come home.'

'OK, I'll get on a train tomorrow,' he agreed.

28

Confession in Blood

Commissioner Domenico Profazio turned to Monica Napoleoni.

'Get to the frontier,' he urged. 'Get Guede as soon he crosses. Don't miss him, for God's sake!'

It was a nail-biting time for the Meredith murder team – a thousand things could go wrong before Guede got to the border and the Italian police had little or no control over the situation. If Guede changed his mind and ran, he might end up being more difficult to find; the element of surprise would be ruined and he would have the resourceful paranoia of a hunted man. The police were putting their trust in a flaky drifter, who'd been accused of being deceptive before and had proved to be unreliable even to those he cared for.

However, proving them wrong, Guede stuck to his word and got on the train. The tension was all too much. What would he say to the police? Was he railroading himself into a thirty-year sentence? If he was innocent, was he being a mug?

Between Düsseldorf and Koblenz another ticket collector appeared at the side of his seat. Rudy wasn't bothered. He'd blagged so many times, it was second nature now. He didn't even have any documents now to wing it with. Unbelievably, he was nicked. After surviving over ten official stops on various legs of his escape, how ironic that he would be arrested after volunteering to go home. After a quick Interpol search, the German police identified him as the fourth Meredith suspect. A despondent Guede, tired and frightened, didn't even pass GO – he was sent straight to prison.

When he heard, Giobbi looked to the heavens in frustration. At the border, Napoleoni rubbed her brow. Profazio stared at his desk.

From Perugia to Berlin, mobile phones lit up. The wheels of the full extradition process started to turn.

Meanwhile in his cell at Schifferstadt Prison, Guede didn't panic. He followed an old saying, a stalwart of streetwise lags the world over: 'Make the time work for you.' He started to write down his story. The story, which he claimed, he had repeated to several people along the way. And one that he would stick to throughout. One that he said was The Truth.

This is a handwritten account of what happened. It was like an explosive mix for me, I can't take it any longer and I can't sleep and I can't close my eyes. I see everything red. I have never been able to overcome all that blood, it was so strong, it was like a film and I tried to help her but my hands were not a strong enough and she kept saying 'don't leave me alone,' and I told her not to worry. I said to her to 'not worry', if only I only had a cell-phone with me I might have saved her . . .

She was holding my hand and would not let me go. She didn't want to die but I wasn't able to save Meredith, I didn't have a phone. Immediately after those words I was frightened, I was covered in blood and she told me not to leave her alone and I understood because she was complaining with her hands raised towards me.

But I was shocked . . . all that blood I'd only seen in television and in horror films. This has never happened to me before; still today I can't close my eyes without seeing that sweet face full of blood and I ask myself why did this happen to her.

If only I had been a real man I would have saved her. But I am not and I am ashamed of it. I would like to be in her place and for her to be alive still. I would have wanted to save the world and I was never able to lift up a single person, I was selfish and was thinking only of myself and for this reason I don't deserve to live.

It is not right that I have lived and a sweet and perfumed flower like Meredith be cut off, I am breathing this air but she should be breathing it. I hope that up there she will forgive me because up there I will never go because of my cowardice. She is a new star, a splendid angel call Meredith.

I ask myself only how Amanda could sleep with all that mess and have had a shower with all that blood in the bathroom and the corridor? Why Patrick? Who was that person? Raffaele? And then 'Af . . . Af' it could be for his name. If there had been thieves as Amanda has said how is it possible that she said nothing about money missing and who was in the house below when I ran away?

What has happened between Amanda and Meredith? What are you hiding, Amanda? Please tell me why you have accused Patrick? Why have you accused Patrick? Why did that person say, 'A black man found is a black man condemned . . .'? Did you think that I was Patrick? Are you already thinking who to blame?

I am sure Meredith would still be alive if you say you slept at the house; why didn't you call an ambulance. How can you sleep quietly. Why do you say that she had been raped? That evening Meredith and I talked, that's all. What the fuck happened? Tell the truth, what are you hiding?

Who was it that night? One of your many drugged lovers that you brought to the house? Was it someone from the Merlin or the Domus? Were you the ones downstairs? Many people have described me as a 'new Patrick' but I have done nothing.

I tried to save that sweet angel but I was afraid. I would never have been a witness to something of this kind and I can't think of anything but Meredith. I could have saved her, if not myself. I went to Alex's house and it was about mid-night.

What else has changed between you and your friend so much as to kill her? God help you if this is true.

As far as I'm concerned I don't deserve to live. I too should have died that night I didn't even manage to save one life and what happened has shocked me.

It is not a valid excuse and I realize that and maybe now I don't and shouldn't deserve to have a good life. But life is made of this and if you fall it is important to get up. But I don't know how to fall and I don't know how to get myself up, it has always been the others who have saved me.

I did nothing to save a divinely sweet creature. This story comes on top of the pain that suffocates me and makes my life impossible to live. It's bigger than me and I'm not able to take this weight any longer. As far as my life is concerned I say only that I don't care how it went. I would have liked to have had a family of my own but when I think about it I have been lucky because I have had lots of families and there are people who have not had any at all.

I don't accuse my real father of anything other than he could have been better as a parent in his duties and I could also have been a better son. My mother, I hope she is alright and God is protecting her. To all my friends and all those who have believed in me and all those with whom I have grown from the primary school to the middle school and the secondary school, thank you for having given me protection and warmth.

I ask forgiveness from all my friends, to forgive me for what has happened. I have not helped them by my behaviour. If this story has hurt you, publicly I'm sorry and I ask forgiveness for everything that has happened before and you'll understand what I'm talking about.

Guede felt alone. But on the outside he wasn't. One of the first phones to light up was owned by a community worker representative on Perugia's local council. Italian authorities have a common policy of inviting representatives of the immigrant populations, known as 'New Italians', to observe their workings. Without prompting, the community worker called Frank Gosse took it upon himself to find a lawyer for the young Guede. The larger-than-life figure of Nicodemo Gentile, a young solicitor born in the deep south of Italy, agreed at once.

Another phone lit up. This time on the crisp white tablecloth of a posh dinner table, amid sparkling cutlery and gleaming bone china. Valter Biscotti was one of Italy's top lawyers. Coincidentally, on the day Guede was sent to prison in Germany, Biscotti was in Africa, dining with the Ivory Coast ambassador to Italy. Fortunately for Guede, Biscotti also specialized in human rights and defending the underdog. The ambassador raised the case with Biscotti. Slight of build, eagle-eyed and astute, he listened and agreed that something wasn't quite right. Guede needed help. He agreed to take the job for free or 'pro bono' as it is known in legal circles.

The day he returned to Perugia from Africa he made contact with Nicodemo Gentile and Guede's biological but absentee dad, Roger. They went to visit him in Germany. A pane of glass separated him from his father and lawyers. Roger wept.

'I'll get you out of this, boy,' his father promised, 'don't worry.' The German prison guard watched every movement of the three. Guede agreed to be extradited.

'Once you are, you need to be ready for the full array of press tricks,' Biscotti warned. 'They'll ask you stupid questions, they'll shout at you. They just want a reaction, a picture, a story. OK?'

Guede showed them a rapidly healing cut right across his right hand to back up what he had said over Skype and in his statement. To prove that he'd been slashed by the man who killed Meredith, who looked suspiciously like Raffaele Sollecito.

'Now listen, Rudy,' Biscotti added. 'I will be there at the airport in Italy to collect you. I will be there at the questioning by police and the Public Prosecutor. Nicodemo and I are here to defend you. You have to trust us. Speak to no one unless we are there. Is that clear?'

'Don't change your story and tell us the truth,' Nicodemo Gentile warned.

Before they left, Guede gave a wad of papers to the guard to hand over to his lawyers.

'It's all written in there. The truth,' he said.

PART THREE

Justice

29

Grown Ups

Winter descended quickly on Perugia, silencing the wildlife in the fields and hushing the boisterous clamour of the students. The city, high and exposed, bedded down against the cold as it had done for three millennia. The coffee bars, steamy and warm, became crowded, offering respite from the freezing downpours. Powdery frost settled across the hills. Cloaked figures, braced against the swirling winds, cut through the mountain mists at a pace. The ancient cast-iron radiators at the university clanked and bubbled. The new intake sweated off their early-term hangovers and caught up on their assignments.

Meanwhile, the activity level of the case remained at peak noise. But one aspect remained almost unnoticed. The Kercher family had stayed out of the limelight since the death of Meredith had blown their world apart. Their mourning, in deliberate and dignified silence, was almost drowned by the shock headlines about Amanda Knox and the thriller plot turns that seemed to erupt from the case every few days.

With implacable courage the family went through the heart-breaking process of identifying the body and making arrangements for Meredith to be flown home. They navigated their way through the bureaucracy that accompanies the complications of a crime committed abroad, without ever showing frustration or anger. Now and again they appeared in public, when it was necessary, to see to official business. But whilst others loudly attacked the police for bungling parts of the investigation, or criticized the justice system because it was different from what they were used to, the Kerchers remained serene. In fact, they found it within themselves to show support for the officers who were trying to find out who killed their daughter, thereby expressing their faith in Italian justice.

On 6 November John and Arline had flown to Italy for the first time. They lit candles at a vigil. Arline looked frail, John tired and grief-stricken. Stephanie was smart and dignified and looked very much like her sister – striking, youthful, well-groomed. She steeled Arline and they stood looking in utter despair across the mortuary. Over the next few weeks it seemed as though Stephanie's strength was the only thing keeping her parents going.

John Kercher seemed to wear the agony of his ordeal in his face, the impact amplified by his shock of shoulder-length grey hair. He couldn't face going into the morgue, preferring to remember his lively daughter from her last visit to the UK, the final time he had seen her. Meredith had flown home briefly in mid-October to fetch her winter clothes, showing off some fashionable winter boots she had just bought.

The unconfirmed news that his daughter might have been killed had reached John at 17:00 on 2 November. Arline had called to tell him of TV reports that a British student had been killed in Perugia. Just over twenty-four hours earlier John had spoken to Meredith for the last time. She phoned him while he was at the counter in the bank, an unusual time for her to ring, but she was enjoying a class-free public holiday. It was around 15:15 in Italy and Meredith, recovering from her Halloween hangover, was heading out for a meal with Amy and Robyn and the girls.

The following day he began to panic when he tried to call her at least a dozen times and her mobile was switched off. It was only switched back on later by the police, who had taken custody of it. The first thing the phone did was sound a double beep. The message that John had left the night before at around midnight, when she was dead or dying, became available for retrieval. Finally, John got the bad news from the *Daily Mirror* foreign desk, which reluctantly confirmed the dead girl's first name to him.

John later wrote in the *Daily Mirror*, a paper for which he had freelanced for many years: 'I drop the phone. I don't believe it and think there must be a mistake. But I know it's probably true. I can't cry. I'm numb with shock.'

As the night rolled on, he described the unfolding events: 'At 9 p.m., Meredith's photo comes on the news. The room falls silent. We all hug.' The account was the hardest story he'd ever have to write. No journalist, no matter how many tragedies they've covered in their career, no matter how many death knocks they have reluctantly undertaken, ever wants to write about the death of his own daughter.

The next day the family was touched when more than seventy of Meredith's old schoolfriends laid flowers at the Old Palace School. A few days later in Italy, Arline and Stephanie officially identified Meredith at the morgue while John stayed outside.

Six weeks later on 13 December, following the arrest of the

final suspect, Rudy Guede, Meredith was laid to rest. The hearse carried a wreath of yellow flowers spelling the word 'Mez'. The funeral service was held at St John the Baptist, Croydon's parish church, just a few yards from her old classrooms. More than 500 people attended, some from as far away as Canada, Europe and Japan. A moving service was conducted by the Reverend Colin Boswell, the town's vicar and school chaplain, and Stephanie read a poem she'd written. Tears flowed when Meredith's favourite song, 'With or Without You' by U2, echoed around the Norman-style arches.

John signed off the hardest story he'd ever written with the following words: 'As Arline puts it, Meredith leaves a void that can never be filled but wonderful memories of her live on in our hearts. All of us who knew her know what we lost. Meredith is not only a terrible loss to her family and friends, she is also a huge loss to the world.'

The funeral had thrown up some happy memories, however, and mourners laughed at some of the stories told by her brother Lyle. Meredith had lived an exciting and fun-filled life right up to the day she died. Just before she had left the UK for Perugia, she had starred in a pop video for a ballad called 'Some Say' by Kristian Leontiou, which later sold 150,000 copies and reached the Top Ten. In the video she plays the part of an exotic love interest and looks more like a model than a student. She wears a sleeveless black dress and has flower petals in her hair. She gazes hauntingly into the camera. Eerily, the backdrop is an old church. Flowers fall from the grey stone arches on to the altar in front of which she stands.

However, despite the haunting romance of the image, Meredith wasn't a girly girl all of the time. She also had a secret side. Meredith Kercher was a karate expert. She had taken up the martial art as a teenager and had become a strong and proficient self-defence fighter. She wasn't a pushover. She knew how to handle herself. This little-known but important fact would become crucial to explaining her and her killer's movements in the final moments of her life.

Meredith had enjoyed making the pop video with her University of Leeds friends, but Amanda's summer job, before travelling around Europe and going to Perugia, had not been so successful. A politically well-connected uncle in Hamburg had got her an internship to die for – a job working for a German MP at the Bundestag. Kindly Uncle Uwe also set Amanda up with a flat on the outskirts of Berlin. Astonishingly, two days later, his seemingly ungrateful niece walked out on the job without telling anyone, moaning that she had nothing to do and she wasn't sure if she was getting paid. Again, money was a big feature in her thoughts. She'd spent most of the time reading Harry Potter and showed no curiosity about how the parliament or the high-powered people in there worked. She ignored conversations about its history and architecture. After walking out, she spent her time drinking wine in the local bars and reading more Harry Potter. Two days later she left Berlin for Hamburg, where her uncle was waiting for her. He was furious – she had let him down.

It seems Amanda craved excitement on her terms, usually based on getting drunk and goofing around. Her friends said she simply feared boredom like any young girl. She showed a healthy streak of youthful carelessness, they said, no worse or better than anyone else. A video posted on YouTube showed her drunkenly giggling in a friend's kitchen after downing shots. On campus, back in the US, Amanda had been fined for being drunk and disorderly at a party held in a fellow student's house. During the incident she had also insulted the police. However, her defenders gave another version, portraying a magnanimous

Amanda. They said that in fact she was courageously fronting up for her underage friends, who were in no state to talk to the police; she was the only one sober enough to handle the situation. A big plus in her character assessment, they said, possibly displaying a sense of chivalry that would later get her into deeper trouble in Perugia.

Despite her college party lifestyle, there was no denying that Amanda was clever and that she could compartmentalize her life. She made the Dean's List, an elite commendation of the University of Washington reserved for the institution's brightest students, and an honour that would ultimately qualify her for a prestigious and sought-after place on the study-abroad exchange programme. If Amanda wanted something, she would go all out to get it, no messing around.

Raffaele Sollecito's later years were quite different: he seemed to laze around and evade responsibility. He posted pictures of himself on the internet wrapped in blood-covered bandages, brandishing a meat cleaver, and wrote a weird story to go with the images. In a blog he expressed satisfaction at once being lodged in the same hostel as the infamous 'Monster of Foligno', a murderer who slaughtered two youths in the 1990s. And yet his new-found fascination with gory horror and violent comics would have surprised the friends he left behind at Liceo Scientifico Einstein secondary school at Molfetta. They said Raffaele suffered from excessive softness – his kickboxing instructor recalled that he even hesitated when kicking out, for fear of hurting the hardened expert.

Newspapers tried to rationalize these complex and untidy lives into patterns that neatly fitted the profile of a murder suspect. However, the recent arrest of Rudy Guede distracted them from the often unrewarding task of trying to find more dirt on Knox and Sollecito. Unlike Amanda and Raffaele, the background of

Rudy Hermann Guede seemed to inspire a degree of sympathy in readers and viewers. At least once the undercurrents of reactionary racism had run its course and readers were able to identify with Guede the individual.

Guede had been dragged up a virtual orphan. He seemed to be luckless, directionless, prone to following others into trouble, his carers said. He'd never had a paternal figure to look up to or guide him. That, and the fact that once he'd been caught he seemed to be at least trying to tell the truth about his involvement with Meredith, gave him a certain credibility. He was often given a fair hearing in the papers for not trying to evade guilt by changing his story. Editors and readers seemed to appreciate that he had not relied on high-powered family connections to duck out of one of the most tragic cases that had ever come before them.

Guede came to Italy in 1992, when he was five years old. His father Roger had emigrated from the Ivory Coast a few years before at a time when the Italian economy needed new manpower to fuel the country's post-industrial boom. The idea that eventually one tenth of the population of the big cities would be from outside the European Union, many from sub-Saharan Africa, would have shocked Italians at the time.

Roger Guede had trained as a teacher in the former capital city of the Ivory Coast, Abidjan, where his wife still lived with little Rudy, but in Italy he found work as a bricklayer. Life was hard because of exploitation, denial of workers' basic rights and rampant illegal labour. After five years he was granted a regular resident's permit and returned to Abidjan to his wife, to see if he could take the young Rudy back to Italy with him. She agreed that in Italy he would have a chance of a better life.

Roger and Rudy found a flat in the shabby low-lying suburb of Perugia called Ponte San Giovanni. The neighbourhood was not at the top of the hill, with its wide vistas, ancient buildings and air of academia. Roger's life had no room for aspiration or fanciful gap-year adventures. He settled for a seedy new-build on the valley floor near the railway station. An unhealthy stream meandered through the projects like a sewer. Still, it was better than the shanty town where Rudy's mother was eking out a bare existence.

New to immigration, Italy's attitude to race relations has often been schizophrenic. Far-right extremists have been known to whip up dissension. But in Perugia, a small community like many that made up the backbone of Italian society, Roger and his son were welcomed. His presence stimulated the lively curiosity of Italians, not their hostility. The kindness of his neighbours and the willingness of social services to offer him childcare were proof of that, and he was free to hit the road to find building-site work. During these absences Rudy was fostered by local families. One of his first full-time carers was a Mrs Mancini, who had been his maths teacher at school. She never lost interest in him and was to be like a second mother. Rudy also struck up a lifelong friendship with her son Gabriele and another schoolmate, Giacomo Benedetti. The fabric of a close-knit Italian working-class community felt like a protective cloak and Rudy thrived.

His teachers and foster families all say that he was a quiet child, well behaved and responsible. He had moments of day-dreaming stupidity, but no more than other kids. He was good at basketball – tall, athletic and serious. The local professional basketball team was sponsored by one of Italy's most successful companies, Liomatic, who manufactured coffee dispensers – a link that would later change the course of his life.

One day, Rudy's dad went home to Abidjan to renew his passport, but civil war broke out when he was in the country and instead of spending two weeks away from his son he was trapped for six months, as strife raged in the Ivory Coast. Back in Italy, the social services stepped in with a view to formalizing Rudy's foster status and finding a long-term home for him. Rudy was unhappy but he coped with the loneliness and uncertainty with admirable courage. He didn't complain. And he was soon rewarded. Astonishingly, he was catapulted into the heart of one of Italy's richest families. His change of fortune was like something out of the plot of the musical *Annie*. Rudy had met one of the Caporali sons at basketball. Now the family wanted to officially take him in as one of their own. He never lived with Roger again.

The change wasn't smooth. Rudy found it difficult to adapt. When he moved out of Ponte San Giovanni, he lost touch with many of his old friends, which he found particularly hard. They had been the bedrock in what had so far been a rather unstable family life. He soon missed the informality, the lack of pressure to succeed and the maternal bonds that Italian families are famous for. It wasn't long before his new father figure, Paolo Caporali, was calling Rudy 'an inveterate liar'. He skipped school and spent his time in front of the television or on PlayStation. Caporali's wife and kids were much kinder in their view: Rudy was introverted and shy. He lied to protect himself, but not maliciously to hurt others or gain personal advantage.

The move from a poor area to the home of the super-rich Caporali family had confused Rudy and, to some degree, had embarrassed him. His basketball trainer Roberto Segolini said Rudy was friends with everyone and never missed a training session. Where he could prove his worth and show success to his new high-status family, Rudy thrived.

With such a chequered school career, Rudy would find it hard to find a job that suited him once he left school. But at the age of nineteen he went to stay with an aunt in Lecco and landed a job as a waiter in Pavia. Finally, he had found his way. He was ecstatic. He was now going to prove that he could knuckle down and stand on his own two feet. He thought about learning the trade and one day opening a restaurant. But as soon as he settled in, the rug was pulled from under him – his employer was arrested and the business folded. To someone with a fragile view of himself, this chance setback took on a great and doom-laden significance. Rudy blamed himself and worried about how he would explain his bad luck to the Caporalis. Confidence shattered, he fled back to Perugia in shame. It was July 2007 and the beginning of the long summer that would end in tragedy.

The Caporalis were desperate to bolster his self-esteem. In August they found him a gardener's job at a restaurant they owned out of town. He stayed with the Mancinis, where the father and mother made sure he got up early to catch the bus. But the rot had set in; he wanted to live where the excitement was. He was distracted by the scallywag antics of the lads in Perugia, who never seemed to work but always had money, and by the beautiful students from all over the world who were descending on the University to find digs and party. Amanda and Meredith would be among them. Once he failed to go to work for a whole week, claiming he had flu and snivelling unconvincingly over the phone. He was sacked. He lived off his savings until 2 November, when the murder and his doomed getaway would end any hopes he had of turning his life around.

A few months before, in February 2007, Rudy had posted a video on YouTube entitled 'boy in da house'. He pulled back his eyelids and slurred his speech to parody a zombie horror flick. His bloody eyelids and crazy-eyed stare had the desired effect. He said he was a vampire. 'I drink blood,' he roared.

30

Jail House Confession

Extradited from Germany, Rudy Guede arrived at Milan's Linate airport on 6 December. The Y-chromosome DNA that had been found on Meredith's vaginal wall had been identified as his, though the scientists concluded that it wasn't necessarily from semen or blood – it could have come from a skin cell from his finger, for example. Guede's DNA was also found on the bra, as well as on the brown bag the police had found on Meredith's bed. The important question now was whether those shoeprints with the nine concentric rings could be connected to him as well.

The police breathed a sigh of relief as soon as Guede reaffirmed his desire to collaborate. Maybe he'd admit to the shoeprint without a fuss. Encouragingly, he began to retell his story in accordance with his handwritten statement – but this time replete with show-stopping detail. For much of Guede's statement the police officers held back, simply going over the new information in their minds – processing, comparing, checking. As time went on, judges Mignini and Matteini, who were present during the questioning, turned up the heat. The face-to-face attacks were designed to test his version of events to destruction – and, hopefully, get him to crack, if he wasn't telling the whole truth.

'On the 1st November I left home about 7:30 p.m. and went to Meredith's place,' Guede said. 'There was a white car parked in front of the gate with two people in it.'

'Who was in the white car?' the interrogators quizzed. Was it local drug dealers? Was it Knox and Sollecito?

Guede told the story as he saw it and wouldn't be put off by interruptions just yet. He carried on: 'I went past it and up to the front door. I knocked but there was no reply.' Guede's lawyer Valter Biscotti could not find a reference to the white car in the earlier handwritten statement. Guede revealed that when he came back later to knock on the door again, the white car had gone. Most of the story followed the previous statement – he repeated the sequence about the money. But after he was shown the CSI photographs he specified that the bed was made and the room tidy when he was there.

'Then I managed to calm her down [after the money flare-up] and we begin to flirt,' Guede said coyly. 'I began my approach and we began to touch each other but then she asked if I had a condom and I didn't, so I decided it was time to stop. And I had gone too far.' He added that whilst caressing her he had touched her bra, thus validating the DNA found on its back strap.

The bathroom sequence followed exactly what he had written to his lawyers. Moving on, he then spoke of the white man who was standing in the doorway of Meredith's bedroom.

When I went to the bathroom the light was on, and when I came out it was off. He had a white headwarmer with a red stripe on it and light brown hair protruding from underneath it. This person tried to strike at my right hand with a knife and he wounded me. He had a black tightly fitting Napapijri jacket. I don't know what he was wearing underneath. I was wearing a yellow tracksuit and under that a British T-shirt with dollar signs on it [the one he had worn in the photo with Giorgio Armani], and light-coloured jeans with white stripes on the pockets.

Guede's clothes did not match the description of the black man in a dark puffa jacket who had bumped into a restaurant-goer later.

Seemingly unaware of the significance of what he saying, Guede then revealed: 'I was wearing Adidas shoes. I wear size 45–46 . . .'

'Adidas!' The interrogator's attention clicked into red-flag mode. 'Adidas! But we thought the nine rings were from Nike Outbreak.' The police officers checked their notes and swapped glances. Guede ignored the look of concern on their faces and continued.

I didn't see him clearly in the face. Meredith was lying on the floor next to the bedside table with blood pouring from the left side of her neck. She was dressed. She was wearing jeans and a woollen vest. I defended myself from this person and as I stepped backwards, I fell between the fridge and the table. We were in front of each other. I had nothing in my hand while he had a knife. When I fell, this person tried to attack me but I took a chair and I pushed it towards him and then threw it. The man ran towards the door and I heard him say, 'Black man found, culprit found.' He spoke Italian. I didn't see anyone else but I did hear the footsteps of another person. In Meredith's bedroom the drawer was open, but it wasn't untidy.

The police thought about this. Had the attacker rifled through her belongings looking for money or valuables? If so, maybe there was a robbery motive.

Guede continued.

She was lying diagonally on the floor. I was frightened by what I saw and by what had happened. There was so much blood near Meredith. Blood flowed down to her shoulders. I went to the bathroom and found a small towel and tried to stem the flow, but it got drenched, and then I went to the bathroom again and got a larger towel. I kneeled next to her body and she said a number of things but I only understood 'Af'. I tried to write these letters on the wall. I have never seen so much blood, ever . . .

Guede couldn't nail the time of the events, only stating that he later arrived at his pal Alex's house at 23:30 or 23:45. He said that he didn't see Meredith use her telephone and couldn't explain the contact made to Meredith's London telephone banking at around 22:00. Shamefacedly, he said that he didn't have a telephone so couldn't call an ambulance, and he had been too scared and confused to go out to get someone to help; his hands and feet were covered in blood and he had touched nearly everything.

'When I tried to help Meredith,' he added, 'she was dressed. She had her woollen vest on. Meredith was wearing this T-shirt, but she wasn't in that position. She held my hand as if to ask me not to leave her, but I was afraid.' Like many dying people, Meredith did not want to die alone. She was reaching out for any human contact.

Referring to the fingerprints that led to his capture, Guede told the police: 'I don't remember how I could have touched the pillow. I don't understand how I could have left my palm marks there. The bed was covered with a red quilt which covered the whole bed and the pillow was outside the quilt.'

The police officers checked the pictures and their evidence logs. No red quilt had been recovered. Had the murderers tried to wrap the body in it later? Who had disposed of the mysterious red blanket?

Rudy was shown the pictures of the crime scene, just to make sure. He recognized items, he described the quilt again, how the body was more parallel to the bedside table, and how he had got the towels from the bathroom to soak up the blood from her wounds. Jolted by the photographs, he reeled off admissions and explanations as the memories came flooding back.

'I went into this [Filomena's] bedroom,' he said. 'And the windows were wide open with the blinds down but the outside shutters open. The body was parallel to the bedside table. Her head was more diagonal compared with the table.

'These are my prints. I was kneeling on my left knee near the bedside table and I tried to write on the wall. When I left the room it wasn't like this, it was tidy. The wardrobe was closed. Only the drawer was open.'

The story became more confusing when Guede began to explain how he had met and kissed Meredith on Halloween night. Several statements from partygoers seemed to contradict Guede's account. There was some confusion too over the exact location of the flat Guede had gone to before the party to have some food with his Spanish pals. But he was adamant that the vampire-clad Meredith had approached him, and that they had kissed and arranged to meet the following evening at 20:30.

'Oh, I forgot,' exclaimed the interrogator. 'Have you ever met Raffaele Sollecito?'

'No, never,' Guede replied.

'You never met him with Amanda?' the officer asked. 'You didn't know that Amanda was going out with him?'

'No.'

'You never saw him even in the first-floor flat?'

'No.'

Guede returned to the events of the night of the murder, repeating again and again what he had heard while he was in the toilet.

'Did you see anyone else?' the officer asked. 'Did you look through the window?' The police were keen to know whether he had glimpsed Amanda.

But the response was a clear negative. 'No,' said Guede.

The judges were determined to go deeper.

'When you went to the bathroom what did Meredith do?' Mignini asked.

'She went to her bedroom or the bathroom,' Guede replied. 'Why?'

'To wash, I think.' Guede knew where it was going, but he became embarrassed. Several of the police officers found it hard to believe that a young man who thought he was on to a good thing would get up and ruin the moment by going to defecate – even if it was in the flat's second, more distant toilet. No girl wants to think or hear about that, do they? the officers thought.

'So, you had got that far with your flirting?' Mignini resumed.

Valter Biscotti interrupted so they could get to the point quickly. He turned to Guede. 'Pretend you're telling a male friend,' Biscotti advised him, 'about a sexual encounter.'

Guede began to describe the sexual detail. 'Yes, we had begun fingering each other and after ten or fifteen minutes, she asked me in English if I had a condom, and I said no . . .'

'You only touched her with your hands?' Mignini asked.

'Yes,' Guede answered quickly.

'Tell me about what you did afterwards.'

Rudy recounted the whole story again about the vampire party. Mignini put the pressure on. He said: 'I have to tell you that Meredith's English friends say they and her spent the evening somewhere else. Do you know any of these: Amy Frost, Sophie Purton, Robyn Butterworth?'

They meant nothing to Rudy. But he didn't flinch. 'But someone took photographs at the party. She must be in there . . .'

'Describe the house in detail,' Mignini asked.

Rudy did.

'Look at these photographs. They are of Meredith at her party. It's not anywhere like the place you describe. None of them would lie about something as important.'

'All I know is that she was there,' Guede retorted, as though he was telling the truth.

Mignini and Guede locked horns over the location of the party and the various timings. But it seemed to go around in circles.

Mignini: 'Now Marta Fernandez Nieto says that she met you around 10:30 of the Halloween night at the flat inhabited by Adriane Minues Omodina, another Spanish girl, who lives in Battlefield Street. Then she says about thirty of you went to another Spanish boy's house in Piazza Italia and then around 1 a.m. you went to the House of Delirium pub, she says. None of this stacks up with what you've just told me.'

'But we all went together,' Guede said.

Mignini: 'But Piazza Italia is the other side of town compared to the place you've just described!'

Guede: 'The place I went to was not in Piazza Italia.'

Mignini: 'But even if she made a mistake, the timing's all wrong.'

Guede: 'She knew what time it was. I didn't. I don't have a watch.'

Mignini: 'And why do the English girls say they were at the Merlin at half past twelve?'

Guede: 'But I saw her there.'

Mignini: 'At least tell me the names of the Spanish kids you went out with.'

Guede: 'Carlos and Thomas, I don't know the names of the others – they lived in the second flat . . .'

The clashes went on and on, neither side giving way. Then the judge disagreed that Guede could have written 'A' and 'F' on the wall while kneeling beside Meredith. It was physically impossible, he declared, to stretch that far across and upwards to write the letters at that height. The hours were dragging on and Rudy was becoming less and less lucid, but he explained that at that point Meredith was lying in a different position from the one in which her body was finally found. Her feet were close to the bed, he said, close enough to the wall for him to stay kneeling and write on the wall. Mignini didn't believe it but moved on to open up on another flank. 'How could you press towels to her throat and write on the wall and hold her hand?' The Prosecutor asked him to kneel in the same way. Could he reach that high on the wall? No.

Judge Matteini then took up the lead. She wanted to know who had called Meredith's bank that night. The police officers hoped that this was a backdoor way of asking Guede who else was in the house with him. To come clean if he was protecting anyone. To name Amanda if possible.

'We know the telephone was in the house at that time because the radio tower that picked it up was the one that covers Pergola 7,' stated Claudia Matteini. 'How do you explain that? Who made the telephone call?'

'I don't know,' Guede said. 'I certainly made no call.'

'So, now tell us who else was in that house with you!'

'I swear that if I had had a telephone I would have called an ambulance, ma'am.'

'I don't believe you. Do you understand that your story doesn't work?'

'I'm sure it's not working in my favour, but I sent no message.'

'So who did?'

Judge Matteini turned up the heat. 'You were awake enough to wash and change your clothes, and then you went to the House of Delirium pub and the Velvet.' He had been all too calm for her liking

Guede: 'I was shocked. I have never been in anything like this before. My friends asked me if I was all right and I simply said yes.'

Biscotti intervened. 'He didn't actually go dancing; he was just following his friends around.'

'Well, he's got a special gift for behaving normally. Most people wouldn't have gone out after seeing someone die in their arms.'

'Did you hear anyone else?' Matteini asked again.

Finally Guede introduced the possibility of a third accomplice: 'No, I heard two people on the gravel outside. And if the man said, "A black man found, a culprit found," he must have been talking to someone else.'

Apart from this extra snippet of information, he had largely stuck to his story. At last they were getting somewhere.

31

The Hook

DNA boffin Patrizia Stefanoni was desperate to reopen 7 Pergola to carry out more tests. Firstly, she wanted to find the missing bra clasp. Secondly, she wanted to do more experiments on the mixed blood samples in the bathroom. Finally, she wanted to carry out a special test that revealed blood patterns that were too small or weak to be seen by the naked eye. This procedure – the Luminol test – could only be carried out at the end of the investigation, because the chemicals tended to contaminate all the other biological evidence present, such as fingerprints and saliva residues. It was crucial, then, that before the Luminol was applied all the defence lawyers had to be sure they didn't want to re-collect any of the original samples. So, in a way, it was good that the application to reopen the crime scene came six weeks after the murder.

The problem was that Stefanoni couldn't simply breeze back into the house of her own accord and quietly get on with it. She would first have to convince the Prosecutor that it was just and beneficial; and, if permission was granted, she would have to

take the whole circus along with her, including the defendants'
lawyers and their experts, a team that had now grown to the size
of a small army, albeit a very well-dressed and well-paid one.
Reopening a crime scene was always a bit of a palaver.

On the day of the application, Stefanoni summed up her reasoning to the Prosecutor. She said that she had identified a large
blob of Amanda's blood on the tap, and their blood was mixed in
the basin, bidet and on the cotton bud box. This meant Meredith
and Amanda must have been bleeding at the same time. The
implication was that Amanda had cut herself in the violence of
the murder struggle. Stefanoni wanted to confirm this.

'Excuse my ignorance, sorry to interrupt,' Mignini said. 'Can
you explain to me how you know the sample contains blood
from both the victim and Knox? Couldn't it just be the victim's
blood and say, other biological substance, saliva for example, from
Knox?' Stefanoni explained she knew both samples were blood
because white corpuscles provide an immense quantity of DNA
compared with other substances, and this sample contained a
lot of Amanda's DNA. 'This in itself proves that it is blood,' said
Stefanoni, and added: 'Actually, in some cases we see more of
Amanda's DNA than Meredith's, such as here in the basin. This
means that there is a lot of Amanda's blood, not a smudge.'

'You want to do a Luminol test? Could you explain what
Luminol is, please?'

'Yes, it's more Agatino's field,' Stefanoni admitted, 'but
Luminol is a chemical substance that binds with the haemoglobin in blood and turns it fluorescent. Since it only binds with
haemoglobin in blood it does not interfere with the white cells
that provide us with the DNA. It allows us to work on traces
and to identify DNA of any blood we find. So if it throws up
any more mixed blood samples in the bathroom, I can DNA-
test them.'

Luminol tests are often shown on CSI shows on TV. Near-microscopic particles of blood become visible because they glow an eerie light green or sometimes light blue in the dark. The disadvantage is that Luminol also binds with common household cleaning substances and grass, and traces of these also fluoresce, confusing the forensics officers. However, experienced officers like Stefanoni can often sift the wheat from the chaff with a simple back-up test. If a pattern glows, the tetramethylbenzidine (TMB) test is used to verify that they are seeing blood and not something like kitchen cleanser. In addition, the sheer intensity of the glow from the concentrated iron content is often enough to distinguish between blood and other substances, at least to the trained observer.

Permission was granted and, on 18 December, exactly forty-six days after the body had been discovered, a procession of cars turned into Pergola Road and number 7's gravel driveway, where a police van was already in place. In order to avoid further contamination, Stefanoni had set up a remote video camera, which fed live pictures back to a monitor in the van so the lawyers could remain outside rather than stand in the cramped flat. The lawyers agreed that was sensible.

The observers watched as the seal was taken off the door and the forensics squad moved in. The room was dark as the three people in white suits moved around. One of them held a bright light in his hand and shone it on the floor obliquely. The cameras could not relay to the people outside, huddled in and around the van, the oppressive and unnatural atmosphere – the smell of damp, the sense of claustrophobia, an unnerving feeling that time had stood still. The crime scene was still caked in blood, and the marks of murder were no less horrifying when dulled by the passage of time.

The search for the missing evidence got under way. The

officers picked up the blue carpet they had left in Meredith's room. And there it was – the missing bra clasp, revealed as if by magic, or perhaps providence. A collective sigh of relief rose from the prosecution side. One–nil to them. The collective defence hid their disappointment.

Patrizia Stefanoni picked it up and showed it to the man holding the camera. That was what they were looking for, at last. She passed it to the man carrying the plastic bags, who put it into the standard container. They were all wearing gloves.

The next step was to recover a blue tracksuit top that had been left there along with some socks. Photographs were taken before the evidence was taken away. Then they moved into Amanda's room and began working around there too, picking up a second tracksuit top and also a second sample of socks. Other items were taken, just in case – they didn't want to come back for a third time.

They photographed Meredith's room again. This time they took pictures of the wardrobe doors from the front, using a plumb line. The vertical reference would help establish the angle of impact of the bloodstains on it. Blood pattern analysis can reveal where the blood came from and possibly where the killer was standing when the blows were struck. That was the key to understanding the dynamic of the murder: who made what stabs, where and when. Who was holding Meredith down, if at all. What kind of punches subdued her. And whether she fought back.

The spray of blood on the wardrobe consisted of dozens of small droplets, later examined and found to contain air bubbles. Meredith had coughed blood in the last minutes of her life. They were similar to the globules that were found on her chest. The globules were coughed on to her breast and cleavage later when her T-shirt was pulled up, during the alleged 'staged' rape.

Next came the Luminol. The chemical compound was decanted into a spray container and set on maximum nebulization to ensure that the thinnest, least contaminating coat was dispersed. The forensics officers proceeded, again in anti-clockwise fashion, to examine the surfaces of the house. The bloodstains they had already identified shone brightly in the bathroom. They sprayed the walls and picked up more little marks that had been too pale to see in the weak light of November as it filtered through the bathroom skylight.

They moved into the corridor. Walls and floor were sprayed. Amazingly, prints of two right feet appeared from nowhere like a ghostly apparition, shining in the dark and pointing in the direction of Meredith's bedroom. The thick blobs of Luminol glowed brightly enough to indicate to the experienced Stefanoni that this was blood. Good, very good, she thought.

Buoyed by that success, they moved into Meredith's room and once more turned their attention to the wardrobe. Sure enough, the Luminol revealed more stains they had initially not seen. With renewed confidence, they were now on the lookout for traces that would confirm mixed blood samples.

In Amanda's room, another previously invisible footprint appeared. Stefanoni had been right to push for a second CSI. They were making good progress. They moved into Filomena's room, where the window had been broken. Another goal: a huge patch of Luminol glowed on the floor, but this time the pattern was not a clear footprint, more a patchwork of shapeless blobs – but blood all the same. Then another foot, a larger one, appeared further down the corridor.

The team got to work collecting the DNA samples from the newly highlighted bloodstains while the experts outside looked on. Like Native Americans scenting a track, Stefanoni and her assistant concentrated on finding more footprints. They had already found a visible footprint on the bathmat in the previous November CSI. The ones now highlighted by Luminol were what are called latent footprints, created when the blood content is too small to be visible to the human eye. Latent prints occur when the original heavier stain has been rubbed off the floor during a post-crime clean by the perpetrators, or because they didn't realize there was any blood on their feet in the first place. Latent prints can also occur without blood when a pattern is made like a fingerprint from sweat or fat residues on the skin.

The officers could already measure the size of the footprints in the corridor – size 37 or 38, so most likely a woman's. They were the same in Amanda's bedroom. Hearts sank on the defence side, especially in Amanda's camp. But their experts were quick to offer them comfort: size 37 or 38? How many footprints had the police collected that had clear outlines and could be measured with accuracy? The problem with Luminol, if it is not vaporized on to the bloodstain, is that the footprints are little more than a collection of blobs that become more diffuse at the edges of the foot. Only a delicate application brings out all the details of the foot. Often, too, the outline can be drawn in a number of different ways. They were footprints, the defence experts said, but they weren't clear enough to be 100 per cent identifiable. They could still be contested.

One defence expert said: 'There's also other counter-arguments – for instance, we know that Luminol binds with some household cleaning products including bleach, so what's to say these aren't bleach stains?' They were words of comfort, especially for Amanda's lawyers Luciano Ghirga and Carlo Dalla Vedova, who had just seen the first serious evidence against Amanda emerge before their eyes – the first piece of evidence they would have trouble combating. Less worrying, in their opinion, was the mixed blood in the washbasin and on the light switch. They could explain this because Amanda had recently pierced her ears. They could extend that argument to the bidet, explaining that she had had her period.

With the new evidence tagged, bagged and photographed, the police officers returned to their Subaru Forester and left. The Postal Police technicians took down the video equipment in the van and the lawyers moved back to their cars. Prosecutor Mignini stopped to talk to one of the legal guys whom he hadn't seen as much as the others, a man of middle height, good-looking, with curly hair and blue eyes – the youngest in appearance of them all. Francesco Maresca was the Kercher family's lawyer. He was there to see, to understand and report back to the bereaved family that the investigation was being carried out properly and that eventually justice would be done. He was based in Florence and felt slightly out of touch with the Perugian scene. Mignini reassured him in the cold outside the cottage: 'We're building a good case.'

As soon as she got back to the lab, Stefanoni logged the best finds of the day that would go forward for the next batch of tests: the bra clasp and the light-blue Adidas tracksuit; the best Luminol-highlighted footprints, including three small ones and another long one similar to the original visible trace on the blue bathmat; the messy trace in Filomena's room. She then asked the lawyers when she could proceed to another set of unrepeatable tests. A date was pencilled in for all the experts to be there again in Rome: 22 December.

Three days before Christmas, the streets of Rome glistened with fairy lights. Freshly cut pines from the Alps draped in baubles added extra sparkle to the city's already beautiful piazzas. Carol music drifted out of expensive department stores as stylish Romans shopped for that last-minute extra-special gift. Inside police HQ only the stark white microscope lights and the omnipresent buzz of the centrifuges adorned Stefanoni's world. The gifts of the day include a mangled bra clasp that might hold the key to one of Italy's most brutal murders. She took swabs from two places: the cloth of the bra clasp and the bent hook. The hooks were so twisted they were almost horizontal, indicating the violence with which they were pulled before the cloth they were attached to was slit, freeing Meredith's breasts from the constraints of elastic and cotton.

The polymerase chain reaction ramped up the DNA content that had been extracted. The machines whirred and the experts looked on. Again the tests were treated as a part of the trial, a guarantee of the independence of the result, squeaky clean. Five hours later the electropherogram was plotted – four coloured lines of peaks and troughs. Yes, there was a lot of DNA there. Each locus has a name, an acronym. The graphs were laid out on the table with the four known DNA sources of the suspects laid out alongside them.

Two different graphs had been drawn from the material extracted from the bra clasp, one for the cloth and one for the bent hook. The cloth clearly indicated Meredith, and only Meredith. But the hook showed at least three peaks for every locus. Each peak had a little number by it, which indicated the number of repeats in the sample of that particular molecule. The numbers indicated the distinguishing features of the individual who had touched the bra clasp. The numbers rang out.

Stefanoni spelled it out: 'Locus D8S1179, 13, 10, 5 – yes, this works for Sollecito, Meredith and Amanda. Locus D21S11 – yes, this works for Sollecito, Meredith and Amanda. Locus D18S51, D19S433, TH01, FGA – Sollecito and Meredith plus an unknown person.' The police scientist called out all sixteen loci and after each the numbers set next to the peaks. They fitted perfectly with Raffaele Sollecito and partially with

Amanda Knox – DNA from both of them was on the bra clasp. End of story, they felt.

Stefanoni was pleased. This was the first strong evidence they had against Raffaele Sollecito. The presence of Amanda was a very reassuring bonus. Now the print people could work on the Luminol marks and match them to sizes and prints from the suspects. And she could work on identifying whose blood it was that someone had walked in, to make the print in the first place. As she worked on, Stefanoni contemplated the result of the bra clasp. While the knife had worried her because of the low number of cells she was working with, the bra clasp was strong. The only disappointment was the fact that it had been examined forty-six days after their original crime scene analysis. The defence might claim that there could have been contamination. But in her opinion that wasn't decisively negative. As specialists say, 'DNA can't fly': genetic material cannot cross a room by itself.

The results from the swabs taken from the Luminol-highlighted bloodstains in the bathroom were now ready. An array of DNA tests had come back, but four appeared particularly damning of Amanda. The multicoloured peaks and troughs showed Amanda's blood mixed with Meredith's in one of the footmarks and in the confused bloodstain in Filomena's room. This could now be added to the mixed blood in the washbasin, the bidet and on the cotton-bud box, and to Amanda's blood only on the tap. Stefanoni's conclusion was simple: Amanda and Meredith were definitely bleeding together, at the same time. How else could their blood have mixed in five places? They had to have been involved in a violent struggle.

Lorenzo Rinaldi's report from the print department landed on her desk. The Luminol prints, although they were not perfect and the green blobs were not as clear as he would have liked, corresponded in many places to Amanda's footprints. The larger prints were Raffaele's. He would have liked to have been able to see the ridges on the print pattern, but the Luminol technique used hadn't been refined enough.

The blood was Meredith's or a mixture of Meredith's and Amanda's. That meant Amanda had stepped in Meredith's blood and walked it through the house. Therefore, at least in the view of the prosecution, she must have been at the murder scene.

Taking an overview of the main evidence gathered from the first and second CSI visits, Stefanoni was quietly pleased with their progress. There was Raffaele's footprint on the bathmat, and a new trace indicating that he too had walked in Meredith's blood. A welcome further discovery was the presence of Guede's DNA on the blue Adidas tracksuit top they had collected during the second visit. That supported his story that he was there that night and had been in close contact with Meredith. The pieces were falling into place neatly: all the suspects had been present.

32

The Sex Diaries

Nelson Mandela and Oscar Wilde both kept journals of their prison experiences. Amanda Knox might not have had anything very deep to say in her diary, but when it was leaked to the press the story made headlines around the world. Not since the disgraced former Tory minister Jeffrey Archer's account of life in a cell had a prison diary caused such universal outrage and fascination.

Disappointingly for the police, there was little reference in the diary to the murder. 'I still couldn't remember what I had been doing at my boyfriend's house,' she wrote in the first days of captivity at Capanne. 'This was the great mystery I had to answer and couldn't.'

Amanda looked to God for inspiration. She prayed that divine intervention might fill in the blanks concerning the fateful night. The diary continued:

A guard on the second day brought a sister to my door to talk to me and give me courage. I'm not religious, but I was eager to talk to her and she told me that all I had to do was to have patience and God would provide an answer. I nodded along but as she left I remembered what I had done when I was with Raffaele in his apartment and wrote it all down. Hense [*sic*] the beginning verse: 'And in my hour of darkness she is standing right in front of me, speaking words of wisdom, Let it be.'

Amanda had compared her awakening at the hands of a nun to the lyrics of the famous Beatles ballad 'Let It Be'. Yet, curiously, in light of these memories, that she had spent the fateful night at Raffaele's, she never thought to mention that, by extension, Patrick Lumumba was innocent. Over the next few months she would embrace the words of the Fab Four with almost messianic zeal. She repetitively strummed their tunes on her guitar, to the annoyance of the other inmates, some newspapers claimed. On Valentine's Day 2008 she wore a T-shirt with 'All You Need Is Love' emblazoned on the front. Some said the words were a secret message to Raffaele to keep him on her side. Others said she was clinging to the universal hope that Beatles songs often inspire in the melancholic. Either way, journalists were nearly falling over themselves in their rush to file copy.

In a 14 November diary entry Amanda complained that Raffaele had been telling the papers that he never wanted to see her again. But she will be kind to him when all this is over, she says magnanimously. She had high hopes that the appeal, due on 5 December, would open the prison doors for her. 'I want for the police to search through all the evidence,' she wrote. 'My lawyer says there were boxes and boxes of evidence that were seized, so I'm hoping to be free by mid-December.'

She described how a guard asked her questions about her sex life, and insulted her with unpleasant comments. She was worried and angered by the attack, but continued to be confident that within the next two weeks she would be freed, at least to live under house arrest. She will be able to see her family, she wrote, play the guitar and do what she likes.

The bombshell arrived on 22 November when the prison doctor told her that she might have the HIV virus, although it might be a false positive test. Amanda was understandably shell-shocked.

'I don't want to die,' she pleaded in longhand. 'I want to get married and have children. I want to create something good. I want to get old. I want my time. I want my life. I can't believe this. Why why why?' On top of her incarceration, the possibility of death looming pushed her close to the edge. Desperately, she looked into her past for answers. She said: 'I don't know where I could have got HIV from. Here is a list of the people I've had sex with in Italy [Italy is crossed out] in general.' The list follows, with a comment about why she can't have got HIV from any of them. With an unusual, almost philosophical, rationale she thinks through her dilemma. Then she decides not to freak out. Finally, the next test shows she is clean.

Raffaele also struggled to come to terms with his new situation in prison. He tried to make the time work for him, diverting his attention to finishing his thesis and working on his case. But his efforts were unconvincing and he didn't have the focus or strength to truly make an impact. He tried to explain away the seemingly unexplainable – why Meredith's blood was on one of his knives, and the presence of his shoeprints. Like Amanda he turned to God. Both of them became convinced that once the 'fourth man' (Guede) had been caught they would be freed.

Amanda's diaries were seized by the authorities on 29 November. Guede had already been caught. It made no difference. The hearing of 5 December went against them.

Even without the new DNA and footprint evidence that would come later, the obstacles were still there – the contradictions of Amanda and Raffaele, the inactivity of computer and telephones that appeared to knock down their stories, never mind the knife. The case made by Judge Matteini seemed damning. Raffaele had lied and changed his story; he had gone back to supporting Amanda, and that was bad enough, inasmuch as it made the police's work more difficult. But it was the judges' description of Amanda that shocked the world. The report described her as 'being capable of satisfying her every whim, even if they were to turn to violence'. In short, Claudia Matteini asked for her to be kept in prison because, in her opinion, Amanda was capable of repeating the crime. She was totally without inhibiting instincts.

Raffaele was little better, said the panel of three judges. His lies and contradictions made him a prime suspect, and his decision to return to his original assertion that he was with Amanda all the time made matters worse for him. He was admitting to being with Amanda and, by extension, to having been part of the crime. The judges did not think Amanda actually committed the crime, but organized the encounter to satisfy the desire Raffaele had expressed in his Facebook site for 'something other than the usual sex'.

Matteini ended with a character assassination of Amanda that would have undoubtedly secured her a place on the gallows, had the murder taken place a century or so earlier. Amanda was prone to histrionics, Matteini concluded, with a multifaceted character that demonstrated cunning and guile, though not without some naiveté. The appeal judges agreed. The pair was simply not to be trusted with house arrest.

The British tabloid press went into overdrive. They picked up the unsavoury nature of Amanda's sexual appetite. Her supposedly unnatural lust was reported as truth, uncritically accepted. Her AIDS scare and diarized list of lovers characterized her as a slut, a familiar form of demonization in cases where young women are suspected of murder. The articles mentioned her tendency to want to dominate men. The *Mail on Sunday* ran a story in which Amanda's desire to escape her mother's sexual shadow was explained as one of the causes of her sexual promiscuity. Edda's relationship with Chris Mellas was identified as something particularly hard for Amanda to accept, and a driving force in her own sexuality. There was a suggestion that Amanda might have held Meredith down as she was stabbed. For Amanda and her family, the picture that began to emerge could not be more appalling.

The onslaught was a turning point in the PR campaign on Amanda's behalf. In Seattle they redoubled their efforts to change the picture the world had of the young Ms Knox. Prominent members of the Seattle legal fraternity were roped in under the title 'Friends of Amanda' to help 'turn the super-tanker of disinformation around'. Journalists who were onside were rewarded with access to the Knox family and fed good exclusives. The family image itself was rearranged for public consumption. Edda Mellas was seen together with Amanda's natural father, a partnership that was promoted, while Chris Mellas took a back seat. Big legal guns fired back at Amanda's critics. In January 2008 the renowned New York Italian-American lawyer Joe Tacopina arrived in Italy to throw his weight behind the case. He appeared on an ABC documentary, where his statements were partisan and loaded: 'There is not a single piece of evidence against Amanda.' He fingered Rudy as the sole perpetrator of the murder and supported the 'lone wolf' theory with selective evidence.

Paul Ciolino, a private investigator from Chicago, visited Perugia, claimed to have spoken to the authorities, and came to the conclusion that there was nothing that implicated Amanda in the murder. The claims were later denied by Prosecutor and police. Critics claimed that instead of trying to woo the American audience back home – and potential donors to Amanda's cash-strapped cause – they should have focused on convincing an Italian jury.

Some American journalists remained impartial. Barbie Nadeau and Andrea Vogt were the only two Americans on the case from the beginning. One had been brought up on a ranch and the other in a logging community. The mixture of outdoor American know-how and dogged female determination won them a reputation from the earliest days for unbiased attention to detail. Andrea was patient. She had spent hours waiting in the driving snow just to speak in person to Luciano Ghirga. The waiting paid off. She got in, got a statement and scooped an exclusive. Their unbending desire for fact as opposed to opinion earned them a bad name with some fiercely pro-Knox supporters. Some reporters complained that Amanda's PR machine had unfairly divided the world into two parties – for and against Amanda.

The waters were muddied further by the looming squabble between the pro-Amanda author Doug Preston and Prosecutor Mignini. It may have been a cold case, but the Monster of Florence cast a dark and haunting shadow over the Meredith affair, like a curse. Preston spoke about how he was questioned by Mignini and threatened with arrest as he was writing his book about the Monster of Florence. American newspapers reported errors of fact; vociferous attacks upon the Prosecutor and, by extension, Italian justice followed apace. The implication was that Mignini had bungled one big murder problem and could not be allowed to lead another, especially one that involved an American. Amanda's supporters protested that if this was the US, Mignini would be removed from office and forbidden to practise. Mignini was clearly shaken. The nub of the dispute was a 'visit' made by Preston, his Italian co-author Mario Spezi and a third accomplice to a Tuscan villa where they were alleged to have planted evidence. Their conversations were legally tapped by the police and Preston was called in for questioning.

Much was made of Mignini's 'obsession with Satanism', an idea that derived from the thesis that the Monster of Florence was in fact a group of people motivated by Satanic belief. The image fit the Meredith Kercher case well because of the closeness of the murder to Halloween, and Sollecito's collection of violent mangas.

Wisely, Amanda's Italian lawyers kept quiet. The PR campaign was controlled from Seattle; all they were asked to do was to protect their client in the courts. Unlike Valter Biscotti, who threatened to sue anyone pointing a finger at Guede before the trial, Carlo Dalla Vedova and Luciano Ghirga let the gossip run. Guede's lawyers even threatened to silence the pro-Amanda gumshoe Joe Tacopina if he peddled his 'lone wolf' theory too far.

The US networks ABC and CBS attempted to cover the story in great depth. Some of the coverage was criticized by media mogul Rupert Murdoch, who owns US rival Fox and UK news channel Sky, for being over-protective of the American interest – meaning Amanda. Amanda's parents learned to handle having cameras in their faces, delivering concise statements dispassionately but credibly. Impact was the name of the game. Fearsome encounters with photographers and cameramen during the first weeks of the trial rapidly become part of their routine. Schedules and resources were well honed. Edda and Curt Knox decided to take it in turns to spend a couple of weeks in Italy to be close to Amanda. To be seen as a normal family by the Italian media, which was slightly less hostile than the British press, helped their cause.

The case also created a new phenomenon: several dedicated blogs sprang up on the internet. Never before, at least in Europe, had single-issue websites played such an important role in the coverage of an event outside politics or global issues. Often the blogs were run by amateurs, but much of their copy was accurate and balanced, or at least rigorously argued. Their non-traditional approach to unedited use of pictures, TV streams and rolling but well-indexed copy pointed to the future. Though criticized by newspapers, the sites were praised by others for being exciting and user-friendly. Citizen journalism and fragmented news sites could hold the attention of readers. The bloggers had proved it. However, the blogs could not make money, so were unable to send reporters to cover the story on the ground – a major flaw.

Candace Dempsey, a blogger on the *Seattle Post-Intelligencer* website, began a pro-Amanda blog, exchanging information and even video footage with a home-spun blogger from Perugia called Francesco Sforza. His blog 'Perugia Shock' was set up the day after the body was found. The Knox family initially relied on Sforza's local intelligence. His blog was described as heavily pro-Amanda. A more independent, unbiased blog was formed in Seattle by a woman called Peggy Ganong. One of the most successful and enduring sites was True Justice For Meredith Kercher. Run by the British ex-UN official Peter Quennell, the blog was praised for in-depth story collation and analysis. However, pro-Amanda supporters wrote it off as being too biased against her.

The blogs clocked up tens of thousands of hits every day. One of their strong points was the analysis of Amanda and

Raffaele's phone and computer records in comparison to the timings of their alibi. They were successful because dozens of people in chatrooms could interpret and swap notes on complex data at once, double-checking times and picking holes in the suspects' various explanations – a resource that traditional newspapers could not fund the manpower or put aside time for. When the blogs began poring over the forensic material in the same way, an explosive mixture of fact and supposition rocked the case. However, no matter how hard the bloggers tried, they could only get an overview; they could reconstruct the build-up, murder and getaway, but only for the first twenty-four to forty-eight hours with any hope of accuracy and only in steps of minutes and hours. They could not give a blow-by-blow account of the murder, a second-by-second account of Meredith's final moments. The only people who could do that were the police.

33

Murder Reconstruction

The hairs on Stefanoni's neck prickled. The anticipation of this meeting had left her mouth dry. She poured a glass of warmish still water and replaced the government-issue carafe on a featureless pine table in front of her. Today, in this bland office setting, the best brains on the case would try to reconstruct the most horrific and senseless murder in recent Italian history. Using the latest results, they would try to work out where Meredith was positioned when she was attacked, where the stabs came from, what blows rained down on her body and what she did to defend herself. Using their experience, they would have to imagine the scene in front of them like a hologram. The white walls and cheap carpet would be a blank screen splattered with blood, trodden with footprints; the dead or dying body surrounded by animated killers or accomplices. It was like trying to choreograph a dance to fit the footprints, bloodstains and DNA traces, markers that hinted at but did not reveal the whole story. The difficulty lay in filling in the gaps to make the dance seamless and credible. How did her arms flail when that blood spurt happened?

Did she fall backwards or forwards? Did the killer walk away to the bathroom, Filomena's room or Amanda's room? This was the meeting when the police officers ascended from being mere technocrats and took up the mantle of the true detective. If they could. If they were made of the right stuff.

Mignini, Giobbi, Intini and Giunta pulled up their seats. Stefanoni took centre stage. She set the scene with generalities.

'Overall we agree that the break-in was staged,' she began. 'And that the victim was undressed after she died. However, if we look at the autopsy, we see that the droplets she was breathing out when she died are on her chest but not under her bra. That tells us that when she was bleeding her bra was on but the vest pulled up. So her stomach was exposed but she was wearing the rest of her clothes.'

Conclusion: the bra was taken off when she was dead or nearly dead – proving that the murderer or accomplices tried to make it look like a rape after the fact.

'There are bruises on the back of her head, on her right forearm near the elbow, cuts on her right hand,' Stefanoni continued. 'We have Guede's DNA on the left wrist of the tracksuit and on the bra close to the cup, and of course his Y chromosome in her vagina. We have Sollecito's DNA on the bra clasp, as well as Amanda's and Meredith's.'

Conclusion: Guede tried to feel her breasts and touched inside her vagina, in line with a normal sexual encounter. He may have helped her undress a little during foreplay. Or at least that fitted Guede's version. The other detectives nodded. For now she let Guede hang in the air. She wasn't quite finished with him yet. On the other hand, Sollecito's and Amanda's DNA on the bra strap suggested they might have tried to cut it off and remove it after she was dead.

'We have a lot of blood in the victim's room,' Stefanoni went on.

There are two main areas of blood loss: in the corner of the room between the outer wall (north) and the wardrobe and between the wardrobe and the bedside table. There are obviously also swipes or smears of blood on the floor, indicating that the body was moved, pulled along the floor, from where the wound was inflicted to where she died. But what's interesting are the small droplets on the wardrobe doors and on the victim's chest. This is blood mixed with air, blood breathed out of the victim's mouth. This tells us she was looking at the wardrobe when she was knifed. She was coughing blood on to the wardrobe and continued as she was turned over on to her back.

Conclusion: the killer knife-thrust happened in the far right-hand corner of her room, near the wardrobe, but furthest from the door.

However, that's only part of the story. The fight actually started a few metres to the left, near the door to the room. The blood droplets under the desk seem to indicate that the attack started there or near the door, where we have a large drop on the door handle. So we can imagine an anti-clockwise movement from the door, to the desk, to the corner where the main blow was inflicted, where she was pushed to her knees, and then the final act as she was dragged to where she was found.

There were no gasps of horror from her colleagues. Nor even surprise, like the guffaws of admiration when Sherlock Holmes or Poirot reveal their theory. Only questions. Niggling ones, fired over functional reconstituted pine and half-drunk cups of coffee.

'What are those five arches on the inside of the wardrobe wall?' asked fingerprint expert Giunta. He was referring to one of the most outstanding blood marks: five arches of blood about 10 centimetres in length, that looked like a child's finger painting, or a small rainbow painted only in red.

'They look like fingermarks,' replied Stefanoni. 'Her left hand had blood on it, so she could have dragged her fingers across the surface trying to reach out or grab on to something. But more interestingly they could also be spurts of blood, each arch corresponding to a powerful jet of blood spurted out from her freshly cut artery. Falling down in sequence, in height, as she falls to the floor.'

Moving on, Stefanoni began to choreograph Meredith's last moments. The actions and reactions had an air of a martial arts fight rather than of a victim who'd gone quietly.

'She had been struck before,' Stefanoni said, referring to the first subduing blow in the left-hand side of the room. 'You notice the small droplets under the table on the other side of the room. 'That's where the attack started. She defended herself, struggled and got jabbed in the throat. She could have been on her feet or already on her knees.'

'OK, so explain the bloody left hand,' Mignini interrupted.

'She brought the hand to her throat,' Stefanoni said confidently. 'So she must have freed it from her aggressors, who already held her right arm – producing the bruise on her upper right forearm.' Her explanation was succinct and foolproof.

'So where do the bruises to her inner thigh come in?' someone fired.

'Attempted sexual assault,' Stefanoni said without blinking.

She's on her knees, her head pushed up against the wardrobe; they try to rape her, force open her thighs, the knife goes into her neck again to cower her more because she's fighting back. But the irony is that the wound gets larger and larger the more that she wriggles, trying to free herself. Or simply moving in tandem with the shock and pain. The blood spurts out, causing the arched patterns as she goes lower and lower. She coughs up blood on to the wardrobe. When they realize what has happened they move her, turn her over and she's still coughing, so she gets the blood droplets on her chest.

'So when do they cut her bra off?'.

'The whole undressing thing is another staging operation,' Stefanoni concluded. 'They want to stage an attempted rape. They undress her. When the murder happens she's dressed. They slit her bra and the bra clasp falls off because they've bent it so much it no longer hooks into the bra.'

'How do you explain the mixed blood in the bathroom?'

'They've washed the knife. Amanda's hurt from the fight. She's bleeding too,' Stefanoni replied. 'The blob of her blood on the tap shows that she's losing blood. It mixes with Meredith's. She touches the cotton-bud box. Her blood is mixed with Meredith's on her fingers. She switches off the light. At some point they try to clean up, get their feet dirty, leave marks.'

Someone played devil's advocate: 'Sorry, but surely the stuff in the plugholes could have come from either of them having their period?'

'Not the same kind of blood,' Stefanoni rebutted. 'There's a difference, I promise. Looks different, for a start.

'The most interesting thing isn't the nice footprint in the corridor or on the bathmat, it's that confused trace in Filomena's room.' The DNA specialist really came into her own now. 'It's mixed blood, Amanda and Meredith.'

Mignini pressed on: 'How do we know that it's blood from both and not blood and biological material of another source?'

Stefanoni: 'The peaks in DNA are much higher when produced by blood. Both Amanda's and Meredith's peaks are high. Both blood, I can assure you.'

The implication was that this was irrefutable proof that Amanda had taken part in the murder. How else could her blood be in the bathroom and Filomena's room?

'Did they clean up?'

'They might have. There's nothing of Amanda's DNA or blood actually in the victim's room. There's only one fingerprint of hers in the whole house.'

Conclusion: it's too good to be natural to only have one fingerprint of Amanda in her own pad. In addition, she was careful to cover her tracks in Meredith's room where her early clean-up efforts might have been focused. The blood mixing and footprints were a mistake because their cleaning got sloppier later – and, crucially, they were disturbed.

'And what do you make of the knife shape on the mattress cover? Is that compatible with the murder weapon?'

'Well, it doesn't look very much like the murder weapon, I must say, but we could say that it's not incompatible.'

Mignini: 'So, in summary, how would you describe the dynamics of the attack? I need to be 100 per cent on this.'

Stefanoni didn't disappoint. For the grand finale she added breadth and depth to her hypothesis, neatly trying to hang every supposition on a fact. 'The victim is on her knees in front of the wardrobe,' she repeated.

Guede, whose DNA is on the left tracksuit sleeve wrist, holds down her left arm and begins fingering her from the rear, pulling her jeans down while Sollecito holds down her right arm with Amanda pricking her. Meredith frees her right hand. Tries to defend herself. Gets pricked by the knife. She shouts. They push the knife in from the front. She falls and coughs up blood. Falls over. Grabs the wardrobe. Her left hand is released and she brings it to her throat. They turn her over on to her back, and leave her to bleed to death.

Now there were gasps of surprise, especially at how hard she'd gone in on Guede. The assessment was damning and left him no quarter. In Stefanoni's eyes, Guede's story about romancing her and sitting on the toilet wasn't convincing. He was as guilty as the rest of them.

The report hit the Prosecutor's desk as it landed in the defence lawyers' in-boxes. Carlo Torre and Vincenzo Pascali were called in to interpret. Backs had been got up. Eyebrows had been raised. Desks had been thumped. The experts would now have to earn their money. Everything was open to interpretation – well, prove it.

'No way,' responded Carlo Torre of Turin.

That knife wound was inflicted by someone standing behind her, otherwise it wouldn't be so wide. The knife blade they've got is 17 centimetres long and only 3 centimetres wide while the wound is 8 centimetres wide. So either they have the wrong knife or they have the wrong angle of penetration. I think they've got the wrong knife, to be quite honest. It's either the knife or the position that are wrong. What we've got to prove is that the wounds were inflicted by a single attacker.

In the Sollecito camp, Pascali also responded to his employer Luca Maori with equal defiance. No one was rolling over. That was a promise. That's still our position. Maori said:

The bra clasp was contaminated. We need to find the exact moment of contamination. Look at the film of the second visit to the house, when they find the bra clasp. They pass the clasp from hand to hand. Three pairs of hands. That's when it happened.

Look at the black bedside lamp. It's in Meredith's room. But it actually comes from Amanda's room. No doubt bringing Amanda's DNA with it. We can use that as a source of contamination. The bra clasp is the only thing they've got on Raf. And it's not good enough.

Silently the Guede camp realized the threat. If the Knox and Sollecito lawyers could prove that the murder was the work of a single player, then there was a strong chance they could pin it on Guede. Guede was there, they couldn't deny it. He was there but didn't do it. They had to stick to that story, but Guede had already raised several areas of concern where his credibility was under threat. The Adidas shoes were one example. They all knew he was probably wearing Nike Outbreaks, the box of which had been found in his house, and had later thrown them away. His credibility was his only shield. Now it was slipping.

The matter of the mobile phones needed to be sorted once and for all. Arguments raged in police stations, lawyers' offices and in the blogosphere, with all parties vociferously advocating that the records proved their wildly conflicting positions. Postal Police expert Simone Tacconi received the order from the Prosecutor's office to settle the dispute. The instruction was simple: use the best technology you have to identify the whereabouts of each of the four telephones the Perugia police were most interested in over the course of the twenty-four hours between the end of Halloween and the morning of

2 November. Find out who everyone called and when and from which geographical location. That would help establish the movements of the victim, her telephone and those of the suspects.

He had already collected the telephone logs from the service suppliers. Now he had received the read-outs from the three cell towers that covered the murder scene. Each tower had three antennas, each covering a 120-degree span, so that each tower was capable of covering a full 360-degree spectrum. A particular telephone would log on to an individual antenna. To plot the location of that phone required two main calculations. Firstly, Tacconi could determine the general area by finding out which tower the phone connected to. Then he could find out the approximate line direction the phone was calling in at by narrowing it down to which antenna it had connected to. Further fine-tuning, analysing the strength of the signal and observing how a phone on the move switched between the three towers, could often lead to an exact cross-reference.

Everything went swimmingly until Tacconi encountered a big problem – the officers found that 7 Pergola Road was at the precise intersection of the three towers. Frustratingly, different parts of the house were covered by different towers. So, depending on where in the house a person was, he or she could actually switch to one tower or another. After much testing and thinking, the conclusion was unavoidable: it would be extremely difficult to prove that Meredith's telephones were at the house or in Mrs Lana's garden at any particular time.

Tacconi ordered his men to verify where the signal came from in Mrs Lana's garden, just so they could be sure. The technician called his boss. Now a second problem presented itself: there was no signal in Mrs Lana's garden. The patch of land was like a black hole for communications signals. They had raised their own antenna and the metal rod had done little more than bend in the mountain wind.

Once again Mignini presided over a technical meeting. He had begun to feel more like a scientist than a lawyer. However, unlike most people, he couldn't turn off when the maths and the graphs came out. He had to get his head around it. He had to quietly put up with never getting a straight answer in black or white. If the case was going to be solved, he'd have to make do with their probabilities and codicils. He called a meeting with the members of the Postal Police of Umbria and Tacconi's team from Rome. The Umbrian police had analysed the confiscated computers to work out the timings and, together with the Rome team, had worked out the geography of the telephones.

Mignini was surprised when Tacconi's case proved more rigid than he had come to expect. The quietly spoken Tacconi went over the data at his disposal.

'Now this is what the telephone logs say,' Tacconi said.

Knox's telephone receives the 20:18 call from Patrick Lumumba via the dell'Aquila cell which covers the town centre, but then sends a reply to Lumumba at 20:35 using the Ponte del Rio cell which covers Raffaele's flat. At 20:40 Jovana Popovic saw Amanda at Raf's flat, so that works. They are the last calls she makes until 12:07 the next day to Filomena's phone.

Now let's have a look at Meredith's phones. The Wind SIM registers calls made from Pergola 7 at 14:30, 15:30, 15:55 and then nothing until around 22:00. We have a 21:56 made to her mother's phone and a 22:13 made to the Abbey bank. They were all recorded by the same Ponte Rio cell. But, as you can see from the logs, several calls we know were made from the flat also went through the same cell, so we can't know for sure where the phones were when those calls were made. In other words, we can't be sure whether Meredith's calls came from the flat or Mrs Lana's garden in Sperandio Road.

Now, the complication is that Sperandio Road, outside the black hole of Mrs Lana's garden, is also served by the same tower. Luck would have it that each antenna covers 120 degrees and that the actual antenna that captured the call was not the same that covers Sperandio Road outside the black hole where the phones were found. So by deduction it is reasonable to assume the phones were not yet in Mrs Lana's garden when Meredith's phone called the bank and her mum's number. The midnight call/message she received from her father was delivered the next day, when the phones were turned on in the police station.

The conclusion was simple: the calls had been made from Meredith's flat or possibly walking up the street to Sperandio Road.

Mignini smiled. Tacconi ploughed on through his mind-boggling spreadsheet of numbers so long they resembled Swiss bank account statements. His multicoloured graphs looked as if a spider dipped in ink had walked across his laptop.

'Let's have a look at Sollecito's phone,' he said.

Last call made from the area of Garibaldi Street at 20:42. No more calls until 06:02 in the morning, when he picks up the goodnight message from his dad actually made at 23:14 on the 1st November. So he didn't talk to his dad on the night of the murder. So his phone was off from some time after 20:42 to 06:02 in the morning. Or, better, he received and made no telephone calls. Compared with the average regular use of his phone, that's down, and he usually keeps it on until about four in the morning.

On the morning after the murder on 2 November he makes a call at 09:30 from his flat, or from the Garibaldi Street area, and then calls his sister Vanessa at 12:50, then the Carabinieri at 12:51 and again at 12:54.

Another officer butted in, smiling: 'What does he tell the Carabinieri? That there had been a break-in. And guess what? He tells them nothing's been stolen. How did he know nothing had been stolen!' Mignini had received a detailed report from the military force so he knew this already. The officer had made a good point and he acknowledged it with a nod.

'Now, how does that fit in with what we know from the computers?' Mignini asked.

'We've examined Sollecito's computer,' the electronics boffin answered, taking over from the phone guys.

And it shows no interaction after 21:15. Peer-to-peer downloads often don't register interaction, but we know that the film *Amélie* ended before then. He has recently said they watched a cartoon, but even then it can't have lasted more than twenty minutes. He can't prove either. And then how does he explain the fact that it turns on again at five in the morning and his phone is on at six? Amanda's computer's hard drive is damaged, so she can't back it up anyway. None of the others show anything interesting.

Mignini: 'So, Sollecito's alibi stops working at about 21:15 when his computer goes into battery saving?'

Computer expert: 'Correct.'

Mignini: 'And neither he nor Amanda make calls after 20:42 of the 1st until 06:02 of the 2nd, too early for someone who'd smoked his head off the night before to be up and about.'

Computer expert: 'Correct.'

'However,' resumed Tacconi, taking up the baton from his colleague. 'There is another problem.' So far he had delivered the good news. Now it was time for the bad. He'd lay it on Mignini at the end of the meeting, so that he could shoot back to Rome while the others pondered. Tacconi hit him with it: 'The estimated time of death is set between 22:00 and 23:00. So why is Meredith or at least her cell telephoning around 22:00, to her mother and then to her bank?'

34

The Mystery Files

Eventually the police got round to finding the first proper witness. She was one of a number of mystery bystanders who had seen and heard things on the night but had been missed in the opening hours of the investigation, some of whom were reluctant to come forward. Mrs Nara Capezzali was the old lady who, from her bedroom in a flat overlooking 7 Pergola Road, had heard terrifying screams. The pensioner also heard the sound of feet running away, up the iron steps and down the road into the countryside, about a minute later. The good news was that she was credible – Mrs Capezzali had for years taught handicapped kids. The bad news was that she couldn't remember the exact time, saying it could have been 23:00 or 23:30, or maybe even earlier. She had gone to bed around 21:00 and had got up after her 'first slumber'. But still, the police were relieved that at least someone had heard something.

For a while after that, the police struggled to unearth any further eyewitnesses. They did have slightly more success with character witnesses, which was not surprising considering the investigation's obsession with building up a picture of their suspects' seemingly flawed personalities. The line of inquiry was knocked by critics for being a haphazard form of offender profiling.

Detectives picked up a surprise at the ONAOSI hostel for children of members of the medical profession, where Raffaele Sollecito had been lodged until he left for Germany on his Erasmus exchange course. Hostel director Francesco Tavernese told them how he had found particularly violent porn DVDs in Raffaele's possession. He was backed up by Leonardo Fazio, a fellow lodger who had been shocked by the obscene material he had found in Sollecito's room. Up until then police had tended to characterize Raffaele as weak and meek, an Amanda-follower who had been easily influenced. In the minds of the police that view was now beginning to change.

Even though Raffaele's reputation was under severe pressure, he still had an ace up his sleeve. If he decided to detach himself from Amanda in his alibi once again, as he had done at first, and this time keep to his story, the police would have a big problem. The character assassinations would immediately be neutralized. As things stood, by saying that he was with Amanda at his flat that night, his own story appeared shakier, as more evidence emerged that placed Amanda at the scene. By default, he was being dragged back to the scene with her, against his legal will, by remaining hooked up to her in his alibi. In addition, he was doubling his chances of being placed there for good by the cops in the future, because there was the potential to find two lots of evidence there, his own and hers.

Going solo would be a deft and daring move, the kind of legend-making legal dribbling that lawyers marvel at over private dinners, but which goes over most people's heads. Raffaele mulled it over, the option giving him a sense of power over his investigators. They looked on: which way was he going to jump?

The police on the ground soon put paid to his deliberations. They took a statement from his Serbian friend Jovana Popovic, who had knocked at Raf's flat to tell him she no longer needed a lift to the station. She found Amanda there at 20:40. Any hope that Raffaele could detach himself from Amanda was gone for good.

On a roll, the cops mooched around Raffaele's street a little longer, looking for more gemstones. A pearl was soon unearthed in the form of a dry-cleaner who had become suspicious of a request from Raffaele after the murder. Raffaele had asked him to clean a multicoloured shirt, even though the garment looked clean already. He had specified a quick but thorough treatment, and had picked it up two hours later. Had Raffaele cleaned the shirt already and was he making doubly sure that all potential evidence was removed? That was the supposition.

The police also found the rich kid's cleaning lady, Rosa Natalia Guaman Fernandez de Calle, who reported finding two bleach bottles under Raf's kitchen sink and a bucket of water on the morning of 5 November. She always went on Mondays. The only problem was, they had taken their time getting around to her.

However, the witness-finding efforts of the police were about to be eclipsed by the dogged reporters of the local *Umbrian Journal*. Editor Giuseppe Castellini and his team of three reporters, Francesca Bene, Antioco Fois and Luca Fiorucci, sensed that there was a goldmine of mystery witnesses to be found, and set about the task with an industry that would earn them the name 'The Witness Factory'.

The police had stopped talking to the inhabitants around Pergola Road early on. Like all good reporters, Antioco Fois, who lived near Grimana Square, worked his patch like a pro. The students still played basketball there, and he began asking around. The small-town outlook of Perugia, a lack of inquisitiveness that caused many people to switch off from anything that wasn't directly their concern, had led several witnesses to hesitate over coming forward.

The police had asked people living there if they had seen 'anything strange' but until Amanda Knox was arrested they couldn't say what they were looking for. Fois did. He focused his attention on Antonio Curatolo, the gentleman of the road whose sharp blue eyes and ferret-like expression suggest a greater intelligence than his social status might imply.

'Yes, I saw them sitting there, discussing heatedly and going over to the parapet to look into the house down there . . . it was the night after Halloween, I remember. The student buses were leaving for the clubs, so it must have been after eleven . . .' The *Journal* wheeled him out as a star find.

Doing what the police should have done, reporter Fois targeted his resources on the Grimana Square area. His dark complexion and open Sardinian smile had gained him the trust of many of the locals. Grimana Square was an ecosystem all to itself, often impenetrable to outsiders; the hosts saw much but said little. The square's newsstand owner told Fois that a shopkeeper called Marco Quintavalle had remarked to him that he had seen a young woman fitting Amanda's description when he opened his shop at 07:45 a.m. on 2 November. Fois stopped by the shop to hear the story from the man himself.

'Yes, I remember her,' Quintavalle confirmed. 'She went straight over to the back of the shop where I keep detergents. I saw her leave – she turned right, towards Grimana Square, not left towards Garibaldi Street' – the direction of 7 Pergola Road. Increasingly the Prosecutor wondered why he was getting these tip-offs from a small team of reporters and not from his own army of cops.

Another mystery witness then came forward under the paternal guidance of editor Castellini. Antonella Monacchia lived further down Pinturicchio Street, in a flat that gave on to Via Sant'Antonio – further away from Pergola 7 than Nara Capezzali but, because of a twist in the city wall, within better earshot. She told the newspaper she had heard a quarrel in the flat, in Italian, which must have started around 22:30. She couldn't see if Meredith's light was on because her flat is on the other side of the victim's room, but at the end of the quarrel she heard a scream. She remembered the flat and confirmed the acoustics because the year before she had called the police to quieten a noisy student party that was keeping her awake. She was a primary schoolteacher and had to get up early.

The *Journal's* hit rate on premium-quality eyewitnesses with interesting stories to tell was now an embarrassment for the police. Antioco Fois heard that two young teachers had seen something odd. Maria Ilaria Dramis would come forward as a witness. She lived with her sister in Melo Road, near Mrs Capezzali, and confirmed she heard footsteps running away. She brought up another strange detail: a dark-green car that was parked in the driveway of Meredith's house on the morning of 2 November. The mystery of the dark-green car would never be solved.

The Witness Factory system was finely honed. Fois would call Castellini, who was a well-known local personality, and they would go to see the witness together. The witness would be persuaded to go to the police, while Castellini called Mignini to tell him what to expect, on the understanding that he would get the scoop. In return the *Journal* were fed the story back exclusively, with an official quote to back it up and to confirm to readers that the authorities were taking the witness seriously. The cooperative approach helped Castellini build up a rapport with the police and the Prosecutor.

The amicable relationship would be tested to near-destruction, however, when one of the case's most dramatic mysteries would be solved by *Journal* hack Francesca Bene. Rumours that a man had been seen covered in blood in Grimana Square on the morning after the murder had floated around the case from the off, like a cloud. The police had tried to get to the bottom of it, but had quietly dropped their probe when it became a needle-in-a-haystack job.

Francesca Bene was covering a completely unrelated story when she had the wherewithal to spot the solution. In February 2008, nearly four months after the killing, she was interviewing staff at the local hospital's accidents and emergency ward for a 'state of the system' piece.

One of the officials was explaining the thoroughness of their record-keeping. He pointed to an entry for early November. 'This is the man we picked up in Piazza Grimana on the morning of 2 November,' he recounted. 'He was pretty agitated because he's one of our methadone clients and when he can't get a fix he loses it. Our ambulance was coming in and just picked him up. He spent a week here.'

'Piazza Grimana, on the 2nd of November?' Bene repeated. 'What time?'

'About 7:30 in the morning,' the official replied. 'He had blood on his legs and hands and he'd been seen shouting into the telephone, "I'll kill you bitch" – you know. He was out of his mind. It was the same day they found Meredith's body.'

Francesca coughed, partially because she had smoked too much, but also because her throat was beginning to tighten and dry up. 'What did the police say?' she said hesitantly, fingers crossed for the right answer.

'The police never came round to ask,' the official confirmed. Bingo! Music to her ears. Exclusive! A key bloodied-up witness. Astonishingly, one the police had missed. The hospital is the first place the officers should have called. An irrepressible impatience, common to reporters the world over who have just landed a big one, welled up in her like a cramp. One that couldn't be soothed. She had to tell her news desk – now!

Seconds later she was on the phone to Castellini. He told her to get a name and a description of his clothes. He would call her back in two ticks. With a similar unquenchable haste, he got the information from her and then dialled Mignini's number.

Castellini: 'Did you know about a drug addict called Claudio Pellegrini who was found in Grimana Square on the 2nd of November at 7:30 in the morning covered in blood?'

Mignini: 'Er, no. Tell me about it.'

Castellini gave him the nub of the story. Nothing more was said but an arrangement was made to meet for a coffee.

Castellini told Mignini that the bloodied man had been dressed in light-coloured trousers, a dark coat and a white head-warmer. He told the Prosecutor he was about to publish the article. Mignini nodded gravely. He knew that it would severely embarrass the police, casting aspersions over the quality of their investigation. After a street knifing, the first thing beat cops do is ask local A&E staff if anyone's come in wounded. Perugia's elite flying squad hadn't done this, even though a murder had been committed.

Copious amounts of tobacco were inhaled, Mignini on his pipe and Castellini on his Tuscan cigar.

Finally Mignini said 'Publish.' He could have used his weight and his respect to get it pulled. Instead of saving face, he'd take the hit – and use it to give the police a boot up the backside. They'd have to get better.

The next day the *Umbrian Journal* carried the news. Mignini called Profazio in. Profazio called Castellini and asked him to kill the story in the later editions, if he could. Mignini had told him he was handing the investigation of Claudio Pellegrini over to the Carabinieri. 'At least they will be thorough.'

Fortunately little more was heard of Claudio Pellegrini. He turned out be a red herring whose injuries were not connected to the case. He'd had an argument with his girlfriend, stabbed himself by accident in a drug-fuelled rage and then spent the morning shouting abuse at her over the phone in a bid to get her to let him back in the flat. On the surface, the police were grateful he'd been eliminated. The undercurrent was that the affair had exposed serious flaws in their throroughness. All sides could use it as ammunition if they so wished.

Their fortunes did not improve with the emergence of one of the strangest witnesses in the case. Hekuran Kokomani was the Albanian who claimed he had been forced to stop his car near 7 Pergola by what appeared to be two black rubbish bags in the road. However, the bags arose like an apparition – and, surprise, surprise, they were Raffaele and Amanda. Importantly, Amanda, he says, was brandishing a large knife. Raffaele told him not to worry. 'What could a girl possibly do?' Raffaele said with a laugh. Kokomani drove on and bumped into Guede, whom he remembered from the Caporalis' country restaurant where they used to work together – Rudy had the same second name as one of Kokomani's cousins.

'Don't worry, there's a party going on; she's about to cut the cake,' Guede explained to the unnerved motorist why Amanda had a knife. Bizarrely Guede offered Kokomani 100 euros and then a further 250 to borrow the blue Golf. He told the Albanian that he needed to move some furniture. But Kokomani refused, saying he couldn't do it until the next day. Kokomani tried to move off but there was a large van in his way. He saw Raffaele coming at him again and punched him first, causing Raffaele's glasses to fall off. As he tried to manoeuvre away, the last thing he saw was Raffaele running after him as he backed up to the crossroads – the van was still blocking his way forward. In the meantime, if his remarkable story is to be believed, he had had the time to give another driver directions to a town called Cesena. Rain poured on the whole weird sequence.

Almost immediately leaks sprang from Kokomani's statement, when weather reports and other witnesses proved that there was no rain on the night of the murder. In addition, the Albanian wasn't watertight – he had known links to criminals he might be trying to help in order to ingratiate himself as part of a hidden agenda. Critics said that if the police hadn't been so desperate they would have kicked Kokomani's off-the-wall tale into touch as soon as it had left his lips. The opposite was true. Officers were impressed because at worst the 'story' at least proved the trio of suspects knew each other. It had rained on the evening of Halloween on 31 October. Kokomani had got either the dates mixed up or the weather. Mignini reread the statement and puffed on his pipe.

'The odd thing,' he told Profazio, 'is that Kokomani refers to the van that stopped him advancing as containing a couple with a young child. Which is also what other witnesses refer to on the evening of the crime – the breakdown truck with the broken-down car's family sitting inside while the mechanic fixes it. It makes sense.'

One of the other offices nodded in agreement. 'Somehow the wackiness of it made it feel real – there's something there but I don't know what.' Another problem was that Kokomani waited until January 2008 to give his version of events, explaining the delay in coming forward by saying he had been abroad. The final hurdle was that he was arrested in early 2009 for cocaine smuggling, blowing a substantial hole in his credibility. Despite this, the prosecution allowed him to testify in court. The police had faith. Kokomani was to become another of the many mysteries of the case.

Other witnesses slowly came forward. Thankfully, all of the mystery witnesses were found, somehow or other, and made statements before the trials got under way.

Alessandra Formica was walking down the steps in Grimana Square around 23:00 with her friend Lucio Minciotti. A tall black man bumped into them as he rushed up the steps. She also saw the broken-down car with a man calling a pick-up truck; the car was parked in front of the Pizzeria 'Il Contrappunto' and contained the man, his wife and a baby. Alessandra Formica noticed no other car in the area. Soon the pieces came together – the tow-truck driver and family were traced. Giancarlo Lombardi, the driver of the pick-up truck, did notice that there was a car in the driveway to 7 Pergola – just as Guede had. Maybe, the police thought, Guede was telling more of the truth than we supposed. Lombardi remembered because he had to turn his truck around in front of the car park in order to back up to collect the broken-down car. There was no one in the mystery vehicle and the house lights were off. The couple whose car had broken down were also contacted and they noticed neither the car nor any other activity around the house.

When Kokomani placed all three witnesses together, he gave a welcome boost to the police theory of a sex-game motive. Eventually the other witness was found who claimed to have seen them together before the murder. The Pizzeria 'Il Contrappunto' was again mentioned by this other witness. Fabio Gioffredi was coming out of the pizzeria when he saw Rudy, Raffaele, Amanda and Meredith coming out of the driveway of Pergola 7, together.

A final witness came forward just in time. He was a Somali immigrant by the name of Momo who testified to the police that he knew Rudy and that Rudy was a crackhead and cocaine user and was obsessed with white girls. He sold his story to the commercial TV channel Italia 1 before going to the cops.

In November the witness roster had been a virtual blank page. Now it was filling up like a guest-list. The question was, would they pass muster with the judges? As the next round of official hearings loomed, the cops could only wait in hope.

35

Fast Track to the Big House

January 2008–January 2009

Between New Year 2008 and New Year 2009 the Meredith Kercher case reached a plateau. The initial day-to-day, hour-by-hour action of the police investigation petered out into a plodding, more procedural pace. Frantic gave way to considered. Pressure gave way to manageable deadlines. Periodically, the steady flatline of legal wheel-turning was interrupted by big spikes of sensational activity, usually when key reports or hearings went public or when pre-trial witness evidence found its way into the papers. Photographs of the suspects looking like *Big Brother* contestants rather than remand prisoners also drew all eyes back to the case.

For the specialist detectives, frontline intensity was replaced by regular confrontations with defence lawyers over DNA. The arguments kept them on their toes. Other than that, the first major event was when Prosecutor Giuliano Mignini interviewed Amanda Knox again on 17 January 2008, hoping to trip her up on a few of the unexplained loose ends. The same old contradictions were put through the mangle once again until every fresh drop of nuance was squeezed out.

Mignini: 'Miss Knox, how can you explain that you still had a shower when you saw all that blood in the bathroom?'

Amanda: 'Well, I wasn't that concerned. I didn't think somebody had been *murdered*. I mean, it's not the kind of thing I'd expect.'

The sarcastic quips did not go down well. Her breezy, no-big-deal style made her appear abnormal. She told how she had left her towel in her bedroom whilst she had a shower, so used the blue bathmat to 'scoot' down the corridor to get it, bringing the mat back afterwards. She had taken a plastic bag full of clothes to her flat from Raf's.

Mignini listened, doggedly but politely poking her where it hurt. 'After the door was broken down,' he asked, 'how did you know *exactly* how Meredith had died? Who told you about the wound to her *neck*?'

'A police interpreter,' Amanda replied.

'You mean Mr D'Astolto? But he knew nothing about how the crime had been committed that day. Neither you nor Raffaele Sollecito could have seen into the room . . .' Amanda couldn't give him any more.

Mignini also felt unfulfilled by the answers she gave in connection with the mop she had taken to Sollecito's. In addition, Knox had failed to tell Sollecito straightaway about the open door at 7 Pergola, mentioning it to him only after they had shared breakfast later that morning at his flat. The Prosecutor found that strange. Mignini also felt let down by her answers concerning the phone calls to Filomena and the transatlantic calls made her to her mother on the morning of 2 November. The pace of the questioning accelerated.

Mignini: 'Miss Knox, why did you accuse Mr Lumumba of murdering Miss Kercher?'

Amanda: 'I told the police what I thought might have happened.' As she veered into hand-revealing, statement-explaining, motivating-factor territory there were protests from Giancarlo Costa, one of the three lawyers present, who considered it dangerous for her. Though concerned, Carlo Dalla Vedova and Luciano Ghirga remained silent.

Mignini: 'But why Lumumba? No one had mentioned Lumumba.'

Knox: 'They showed me the telephone message . . .'

The image of Lumumba in Grimana Square and then her blocking out Meredith's screams with her hands over her ears were about the only events she claimed to remember.

Mignini: 'But Miss Knox, if you can't remember, then how can you say you were at Raffaele's?'

Knox: 'I was scared, I was confused, I was under stress, they insulted me . . .'

Mignini: 'But why Mr Lumumba, and why the scream?'

Knox's face creased. There was a danger Mignini was exerting the same pressure. Knox was reduced to tears. Mignini played it by the book and broke off the engagement. Sympathetically, he turned to the officer recording and writing up the statement: 'I'd like to make it clear now that Miss Knox is crying,' he said. 'Do her lawyers want this questioning to continue or should we stop?' Predictably, the lawyers opted to bail out.

The hard ground thawed. The light of spring brought warmth to the gloom-laden city. Cobwebs were blown away and windows that hadn't been open for months were creaked into use. New life sprang from the death and misery of winter. The trees and bushes around 7 Pergola Road began to blossom in white and green, almost erasing the memories of a few months earlier. People's perception of the Meredith case had been so heavily influenced by the autumnal backdrop that it didn't look like a crime scene anymore. But one suspect's memories could not be erased that easily.

Surprisingly, Rudy Guede also asked to be interrogated again – twice. He wanted to spring-clean his conscience.

In March he told Giuliano Mignini he had to get something off his chest. Astonishingly, he finally admitted that the nine-ring shoeprints were his. 'No, not Adidas shoes,' he explained, 'but Nike Outbreak.' The police officers couldn't contain their joy. He went on to say he had another clarification to make: 'After the doorbell rang I heard Meredith say, "We've got to talk," and Amanda say, "What's the matter?"' He went on to describe the fight.

'When I got up from the floor where I had fallen,' Guede revealed, 'I looked through the window.'

'Which window?' Mignini queried.

Guede: 'Filomena's window.'

Mignini: 'The room was tidy and the shutters open, you said last time?'

Guede: 'Yes. The room was tidy and the shutters open.'

However, there was one fantastic revelation that he had not included in his first series of interviews.

'I saw the outline of a woman,' Guede told Mignini, referring to a ghostly apparition of a witness he claimed to have seen hanging around outside the house.

Mignini controlled the gulp in his throat. He didn't want to freak the suspect before he asked the next question – the obvious one, which hung upon his dry lips like the first taste of a new season's wine from the vineyards. Mignini asked the crucial question. And he got the answer he was hoping for.

'Yes,' Guede said. 'I can say I identified Amanda Knox's voice and I saw her from behind in the driveway.' The disclosure was hugely decisive – the first time a witness and suspect had put Amanda within the murder scene. Just as important in terms of witness management was the issue of future compliance. If he was naming Amanda now, would Guede go that little bit further with the mystery knifeman and name him as Raffaele, as everyone suspected? The clues that Guede had laid down so far were almost board-game-like in their obviousness – the 'A F' meaning and sounding like Raff, and the cartoon-like description of the knifeman; they were classic signs of a suspect thinly trying to protect an accomplice.

Unfortunately, technically, although Guede's two-fold fact-straightener had been a welcome gift to the prosecution, the confession would not bring him any credit in terms of his own legal position. Too much had happened by then and it was too late for the system to look favourably on him. The final pieces of his statement jigsaw boosted his credibility but, under Italian law, he wouldn't be walking free or having his sentence slashed. Deals were now firmly off the table. Even his appeal to the Supreme Court against the incarceration failed, along with those of the other two accused.

Meanwhile, Sollecito's dad and uncle were very satisfied to hear they had been right all along about the Nike Outbreak. Their offensives were paying off and spurred them on to further amateur paralegalling. However, the next move was not a wise one and backfired badly. The Sollecitos had injudiciously released the full video film made by the CSI squad, showing Meredith's body, to a local TV station in Bari. The hope was to expose irregularities and garner support ahead of a key legal hearing. But the film went out uncensored, sparked outrage, and the TV director was penalized with a six-month suspension. The film went to air the day before the panel of five judges of the Supreme Court was to make its decision. The string-pulling by the Sollecitos, all duly recorded by the police, landed them with an indictment for attempting to pervert the course of justice.

However, their behind-the-scenes lobbying did bag one success. Against the odds they managed to hire one of Italy's top lawyers. Giulia Bongiorno was a heavy hitter, well placed in Italy's legal and political elite. She was president of the parliamentary commission for legal reform and had defended former premier Giulio Andreotti against accusations of having ordered the murder of a left-wing journalist in the 1980s. Her clients made up a list of the great, good and not so good of Italy's cliquey power elite. Raffaele Sollecito was the latest member of that very exclusive club.

Knox's supporters back home tried a little high-level politicking themselves. They persuaded Judge Michael Heavey of the King County Superior Court to send a letter to the disciplinary body of the Italian magistrature, claiming that Amanda could not be fairly tried in Perugia and complaining about the release to the press of her diaries. When Mignini got hold of a copy he stared at the headed notepaper. The seal was certainly impressive, grand almost. He puffed on his pipe. Pressure was the name of the game now.

The ante-upping, the constant feeling of pressure, the dark influences snaking through the corridors of power, were making everyone jumpy. From now on, everything had to be done on the up and up, cleaner than white, holier than thou. Heads were going to roll as a result of this case, and no one wanted it to be theirs. The first to go was the original pathologist, Luca Lalli. He had given a few off-the-cuff remarks to a TV big-wig after an early press conference, which now seemed so long ago that it felt like an age of innocence before the whole thing became vitriolic. A big fuss was made about what was, in reality, a minor indiscretion. Dr Lalli paid the price: he was publicly criticized, removed from the case and not allowed to take part in the second autopsy. If the defence could knock holes in him, by default they could try to undermine his first tranche of evidence. They had asked for a second autopsy and had got one.

Raf's lawyers also requested a new examination of his computer to prove he was on it at the time of the murder. The event is called an *incidente probatorio* or 'proving moment' and is like a mini-trial but is concerned with only one piece of evidence. Raf handed over his passwords and told the cops where to look, but there was no evidence of activity on the computer after 21:00.

The Kerchers had one more ordeal to go through. In a closed court hearing in April the parties were invited to examine the result of the medical examination. The question they needed to answer was whether or not there had been rape. A crucial question that no one had answered convincingly thus far. This second *incidente probatorio* failed to answer the question.

That left two substantial legal issues to negotiate. Firstly, there was the final indictment. This document was essentially Mignini's thoughts on the case – his basis for sending the suspects to trial, and why he thought they were guilty, not that he had all the evidence to draw upon yet. The custom was that the Prosecutor theorized about what he thought had happened, backing his 'vision of events' with his reasoning, and explaining how the evidence fitted it. The second important matter was the pre-trial hearing, which, put simply, was Mignini's indictment brought to life and put to the test. All the witnesses' statements and evidence mentioned in Mignini's document were hauled into court, if necessary, and the defence was allowed to offer alternative explanations that fitted them.

The final indictment was deposited on 18 May 2008. The case for premeditation was derived from the fact that the knife had been brought from Raffaele's flat to Amanda's. Sollecito's propensity for violent sex, as testified to by his fellow guest at the ONAOSI hostel and by his manga collection, supported this thesis.

There weren't many surprises for those who were well acquainted with the case. For instance, on Amanda there was her DNA mixed with Meredith's in five different places in the flat, her footprint on the pillow cover and her blood-soaked bare feet in the corridor. Then there were witnesses who proved that the four knew each other: Kokomani and Gioffredi, of course, and also Antonio Curatolo, who had seen Amanda and Raffaele together that evening, peering suspiciously into Pergola 7, and Marco Quintavalle, who had seen Amanda buy what he thought was bleach on the morning of 2 November.

Mignini stressed premeditation because they had brought the knife with them and because, if Kokomani had seen the three the night before, not on the night of the murder, then it must have been that they were rehearsing their attack on Meredith. Compared to a run-of-the-mill case, there was more there than Mignini needed to prove his position. In summary, he said that Meredith had been murdered after a sex game had gone wrong.

The problem with indictments is that prosecutors are encouraged to come up with a theory and stick to it. They are asked to pin their colours firmly to a particular mast and sail on regardless. Problems arise when new evidence emerges, certain scenarios lose favour or accusations of police bungling are levelled. Then prosecutors can find it difficult to change their theory. Indictments leave them little wriggle room. Prosecutors have often complained they are faced with terrifying dilemmas – of having to cobble a case together into an indictment when starting off with inadequate police investigations and stories filled with holes.

The preliminary trial was set for 18 September, when a new judge, Paolo Micheli, would decide whether Mignini's assessment and the investigators' work underpinning it would stand the scrutiny of a full trial. The world's press gathered. The photographers who were given permission to snap inside the court building weren't disappointed. The three accused were paraded down a corridor in front of the media before they went into the closed-door hearing.

The first surprise sprang from Guede's defence. His lawyers explained to the press outside the court:

> We have opted for a fast-track trial for Rudy Guede for the following reasons: there is an obvious and blatant attempt to pass Rudy off as the sole perpetrator of this crime, whereas he is the only one of the three to have kept to the same story, which we believe is the truth. We don't want his destiny to be tied to the destiny of the other two accused. We also agree to accept the evidence brought to court by the investigators without indulging in our own investigation. We believe that the evidence brought before the court actually proves Rudy's innocence.

In effect, Guede and his team were making a clever move. The fast-track trial is a way of saying: 'We are not disputing anything the police or prosecutors have found at present. We are not saying our man is guilty, just that we are accepting what the police say for now.' Politically, this was smart. Guede was not trying to rile the police. He was distancing himself both from attacks by the police and the justice system and from the Knox and Sollecito camps. In addition, by fast-tracking he would get an automatic right of appeal in a year or so, by which time he hoped they would have unearthed new evidence, or that Knox and Sollecito would have destroyed each other in the trial proper, leaving him to swoop in, untainted, to claim the glory and freedom. Guede's defence team now hoped that Knox and Sollecito would descend into a cut-throat defence – one in which co-defendants turn on each other in court. Guede would watch it from the sidelines and come in to pick up the pieces later.

The coup was effective. Guede would be tried there and then, and not have to undergo the stress of a full trial. In addition he would benefit from any remission the Italian state handed out to compliant defendants.

Mignini was not rattled. He made his case. For the time being, there was no reason to establish who did what, as they were all proven to be there. Who did what was irrelevant. The sexual attack on Meredith Kercher was carried out by all three. He supplied three alternatives for the actual dynamic of the attack, but said he was most inclined to believe that Meredith had been stabbed while on all fours in front of the wardrobe. He used the term 'Satanic' when describing the context of the crime: the night after Halloween; Sollecito's sexual tastes as showed by the comic strips he read. With hindsight, use of the term was unwise. The occult implications undermined the credibility of his case and would haunt him for months afterwards, especially when associated with the Monster of Florence case that still loomed.

Micheli grilled the witnesses, especially DNA expert Patrizia Stefanoni. 'Was there any reason to believe the knife had been contaminated in the box it had been sent to the lab in?' Judge Micheli asked. 'No,' she replied. Vincenzo Pascali, Sollecito's forensics expert, failed to attack her on the weakness of the knife and bra-clasp DNA. On the contrary, he brought to the court's attention that there were three DNA traces on the bra clasp – Amanda's, Raffaele's and Meredith's – so it was highly unreliable. He pointed to the possible sources of contamination, the forty-six days that elapsed between the first crime-scene investigation and the recovery of the bra clasp itself. He indicated all the errors the police had made: not changing shoe covers often enough, not changing gloves, swiping the blood traces on the edge of the basin and the bidet with the same swipe used to collect material in the plughole. He used the film to portray the police as clumsy and incompetent. However, even the Sollecito defence had to admit that the evidence the Postal Police had collected from Raffaele's computer and from the telephones, that there had been no activity on the computer after 21:06, was overwhelming.

Guede's lawyer Valter Biscotti played it cool. He stated to the court that he accepted the findings of the police and had nothing to complain about with regard to the DNA analysis. However, he wanted to hear several witnesses, such as Guede's pal Gabriele Mancini and his mother. (Mrs Mancini was his teacher with whom he had left his money until he was able to get a bank account.) The Mancinis would act as good references. On the other hand, Guede's team wanted to call Kokomani so that they could discredit his eyewitness evidence, and Momo, the Somali who accused Guede of being a drug addict obsessed by white girls.

Judge Micheli duly called them. The picture of Rudy that he received from the Mancinis was that of a good but unlucky black boy with a heart of gold and a tendency to be vague. Biscotti showed the judge the film of Momo asking a journalist for money for his story, thereby discrediting the police witness completely. Kokomani stepped up and told his story too.

The upshot was a sparse but valiant defence – but it didn't help Guede in the short term. The judge sided with Mignini's view of Guede. He was found to be unreliable. He was not helped by inexplicable acts of betrayal, or at least that's how he saw them. His friend Alex Crudo, on whom he was relying to back up his story of how he had gone out after the murder, had stated that he hadn't seen Rudy that night. Crudo said point-blank that they hadn't gone to the House of Delirium pub together. Guede couldn't believe what he was hearing. If Guede could not be believed on this part of his story, how could the Judge be expected to believe that he sat on the toilet, oblivious, while Meredith was being stabbed?

The court heard how the appointment with Meredith was impossible since they hadn't been at the same party together on Halloween. The conclusion was that Guede had told too many lies. But, said Micheli, Guede did not hold the knife. Without thinking twice he sentenced Guede to thirty years in jail. A fast trial really was quick justice. That was his final word on the matter.

The judge was serious and unforgiving. With similar efficiency he sent Amanda and Raffaele for trial, after having established that the break-in was faked and that more than one person had been involved in the murder. No one was spared from the judge's summary decisions. He made a couple of jabs at Mignini too. He ridiculed any connection with Satanism and established that the murder could not have been premeditated: Amanda didn't know that she would have been free that night until Patrick sent her the fateful SMS message.

It had been a tough fight. Only the judge was left standing intact. Everyone else was spinning and reeling. Even the Knox and Sollecito defence teams did not dare attempt to appeal against the confirmation of incarceration. This was the tenth judge to visit the case. They had just lost again. No one wanted to incur more wrath.

36

The Super Detective

Colonel Luciano Garofano of the elite Carabinieri is Italy's top forensic scientist. The authors of this book asked him to investigate the murder of Meredith Kercher separately from the civil police and independently assess the evidence. The aim was to help to try and solve some of the unanswered questions that have dogged the case and offer alternatives, showing how things could have been done differently.

The Colonel's qualifications are exemplary – he set up Italy's first DNA laboratory and led the country's premier hoodlum-busting squad, the Reparti Investigazione Scientifiche. From his grand offices at an ancient French-style Louis XV palace in wealthy Parma, he followed the Meredith case with interest. If Raffaele Sollecito had called the Carabinieri first, and his officers had arrived at the scene before the Postal Police, then he would have been on the case officially. As it was, he could now only offer his wealth of expertise as an outside observer. His black uniform and silver facings symbolize his authority as a leader in the field, recognized by forensics bodies the world over.

'Everyone has a right to justice,' his report began.

In the first place the family of the victim has a right to justice and that is what the Italian state guarantees, allowing them to be civil plaintiffs; however, the right to justice also extends to the defendants, and the Italian legal system provides quite sufficient guarantees towards obtaining justice. More than most.

I would like to show you a few differences between what the Carabinieri do and what the Police does, though. For example, if you look at the scene of the crime video footage, you can see a lot of people walking around. We in the Carabinieri tend to limit the number of people allowed to enter the room. You will also notice they use laboratory filter paper to collect the blood samples and tend to rub them until they disappear. Of course, they have labelled and photographed the place, so there is a record of what was found, but we in the Carabinieri tend to use cotton buds and when we see that the cotton on the buds is coming off the stick, we replace them with polystyrene ones.

However, although there are many differences between the way the Police and the Carabinieri work, I have every confidence in the way my colleagues in the Police have done their job.

Let me also explain one last procedural aspect of the investigation. The Prosecutor has the right to order a completely different unit to carry out the laboratory tests from the one that collected the materials. Also, although the unit that performs the test is called a 'consultant', no money passes hands between government agencies. However, private consultants are paid. The goal is to ensure that there is complete transparency and independence of the Prosecutor with respect to the unit carrying out the task.

Colonel Garofano made it clear from the outset that he believes there is no one single, definitive piece of evidence that proves who killed Meredith Kercher. He said: 'Forensics and especially DNA cannot be given the sole responsibility of condemning a person. I might also add that in this particular case there are many "soft" areas where the behaviour of the suspects constitutes serious evidence, although as far as I can see there is no smoking gun.'

Colonel Garofano also pointed out that although the defence experts should be at the police labs for the whole session while the testing is going on, to ensure fair play, they don't always stay the course.

Now let's get to the DNA. The DNA testing is done using machines. There is nothing to see or understand. The legal experts often don't remain the full time during the period of analysis in the labs because everyone knows the procedures.

I have come across some of them before – Dr Pascali, for example, or Dr Torre. They have often been on the defence team when I was producing analysis for the Prosecutor. Sara Gino works closely with Dr Torre; she's his DNA expert. They must all have been there for at least some of the time when the tests were done, although they do take hours and the costs mount up. We have to assume that all the data presented in the case has been thoroughly scrutinized by the defence.

The procedures are long but the protocols are well established. The DNA is extracted using different standardized procedures, quantified using a first polymerase chain reaction machine, which will take up to two hours, then reproduced (amplified) using a second PCR machine. This PCR tags the DNA so it can be recognized later. They are tagged with a fluorescent primer so that the tops and tails of each short tandem repeat are marked and countable using a laser counter. The number of repeats of each short tandem repeat is specific to each locus in each individual. *But the profile obtained from all sixteen STRs is unique for each individual.* Remember there are two values, reading the electropherogram, because one number of STRs come from the mother and another number of STRs come from the father. So for each locus we have three values: the number of repeats of each locus in each half chromosome and the peak which represents the relative fluorescence units – the number of molecules counted.

He laid out the piles of papers on the table before him.

We lay them out so that we can easily compare the sample electropherograms of Meredith, Amanda, Raffaele and Rudy. The report lists the findings in each individual locus in table form, but the electropherograms tell you much more.

So you want to know about the knife. Let's look at the knife. The knife shows a strong presence of Amanda on the handle and a very small presence of Meredith on the blade. The report doesn't tell us whether a second test was performed or not, so we would need to see the laboratory logs for that. However, I can see from the report that the tetramethylbenzidine test was carried out and found negative. The TMB test is extremely sensitive and if it is negative then this sample is not blood. Remember that the TMB test looks out for haemoglobin in red corpuscles, while the DNA test works on the white, so there is no excuse for carrying out both tests on the same sample – you don't destroy the sample by testing it once with each test. As Dr Tagliabracci said in the trial, the logs are important to establish the procedures used to obtain any single result. If the Real Time PCR machine produces a readout saying 'too low', that doesn't mean there is no DNA, but it does mean the procedure used to find it has to be extra delicate and we need to know what procedures were used. There seems to be no log of what was actually done.

However, Garofano was critical of the police for not removing the blade from the handle. He said: 'Did they open the knife to see if blood had dripped between the metal part of the handle and the plastic? No? Pity. That would have been a sure place to find blood if there was blood. Secondly, they say it was cleaned with bleach. If an object is cleaned with bleach, there is no DNA left. And if any were left there would be the same amount of DNA belonging to Amanda Knox as to Meredith Kercher. Next to nothing.'

In short, Garofano believes that the police analysts have been lucky, very lucky indeed, to find Meredith Kercher's DNA on the blade. He cannot recall a similar case and is at loss to explain the extraordinary luck that produced the results. He said: 'So the fact that there is a lot of Amanda Knox's DNA and a little of Meredith's doesn't sound logical to me.'

Looking at the numbers, Garofano pointed out that the readings are below the level that is considered minimum standard.

Now let's look at the values. The peaks are relatively high but look at the scale. Not one of them reaches above the

value of 50 RFU (relative fluorescence units), and we usually
consider the figure of 100/150 to be the minimum. However,
as you can see, every single locus has two nice peaks that
stand out above what we call background noise. These low
peaks that are all along the graph would be unseen on an
electropherogram that involved peaks in the area of 500 or
600 RFUs but here are like hillocks with regular peaks that
stand out above them at exactly the places where you'd expect
to find the victim's peaks. The laboratory has done an
extremely good job in finding those peaks by concentrating
the sample many times over.

Garofano stressed the risks of contamination when working
with low-value samples. He said: 'The danger in doing that is
that the solution is not always completely void of other molecules that show up on the graph all the same.'

Again identifying the element of luck in the findings,
Garofano said:

By sheer luck the STRs seem to have all shown up clearly.
Pity there was not enough material to do a second run. It is
very lucky because mostly when there are so few molecules of
the original DNA, the molecules in the PCR solution find it
hard to bind with the molecules in the original sample, so
they bind haphazardly. It's a chemical issue. Under a certain
critical mass of the original DNA, the PCR no longer follows
the rails it is designed to follow and the polymers bind with
anything that's there. That's the background noise you get.
However, if you are lucky and extremely careful, you can get
a meaningful result in a number of loci. Extremely hard to
get them all, starting from a trace so small.

Again, it is the defence experts' responsibility to make sure the tests are carried out properly. They are required to be present. We have to assume that the standard protocols were used.

Colonel Garofano then turned his attention to the mixed blood spots in the bathroom next to Meredith's room. Again, he criticized the methods of collecting samples. But, he said, the presence of Amanda Knox's DNA is decisively bad for her defence. 'Now let's have a look at the washbasin,' he began.

I saw on the film the way they collected the sample in the washbasin. The fact that the sample was collected by wiping both the edge and the plughole is dangerous. You're likely to find all sorts of stuff in the plughole. However, here is the electropherogram and you can see that the RFU value is very high, so the sample is undoubtedly blood, which is the body fluid that provides the greatest amount of DNA. In some cases you see higher peaks of Amanda's DNA than Meredith's. Amanda has been bleeding. Nor is it old blood, as the defence might say, because blood decays fast. We have the same result on the cotton-bud box. The light switch was over-scrubbed, but from the film the way the cotton-bud box was handled was definitely good enough. There too we have mixed blood. So that's pretty significant for Amanda. Unfortunately for her, she bled at the same time Meredith was bleeding. That's a lot to explain.

However, the bidet evidence is less powerful.

I would not use the bidet swab as useful evidence because the swab was again taken from the edge of the bowl to the plughole and this is a typical area where menstrual blood collects. However, one has to say that an American would not use the bidet for washing herself. She may wash clothes in it, maybe knickers with menstrual blood on it, or some other item of clothing that was dirty. But the blood trail is a drip, and doesn't appear like a residue from washed clothes, that leads from the edge of the bidet to the plughole. We'd have to ask Amanda to explain that.

Garofano cannot rule out that the mixed blood could have come from a violent confrontation between Knox and Meredith. But he plays devil's advocate to show how Amanda could explain the clues away as totally innocent, unrelated bloodstains.

It's just blood as far as I'm concerned and I can say no more, but the fact that the blood was mixed does indicate that Meredith and Amanda were bleeding at the same time. However, it doesn't necessarily have to be a wound, it might be that Amanda had a bloody nose, or she cut herself on the knife, or she cut her feet on the glass in the other bedroom, or even that she washed something that had her blood on it in the washbasin, squeezed it in the bidet and touched the cotton-bud box. Look at the electropherograms, there's a lot of Amanda's DNA there, and of course there's a blob of Amanda's blood on the tap.

So we have those three key pieces of DNA evidence against Amanda Knox: the tap with her blood on it; the basin with her and Meredith's blood mixed, and the cotton-bud box with her and Meredith's blood on them. Let's try to explain them for Amanda. Menstrual blood? In the bidet the blood could be menstrual blood, or it could be her washing bloodstained knickers in the bidet. She could have washed them in the basin and then rinsed them again in the bidet. She would have touched them and touched the cotton-bud box.

That does not explain why Meredith's blood is there too though. Amanda's own bloodstain on the tap is recent. It is dry, but has not been touched or cleaned. There is no fingerprint in it. It is logical to put that bloodstain in relation with the blood in the bidet and washbasin, but let us assume for a minute that they are unrelated. For example, that the bloodstain on the tap was from a pierced ear and the blood in the bidet and washbasin was from her period. All Amanda's blood in the small bathroom can be explained in one way or the other. How can Meredith's blood be explained? Let's say the assassin used the basin and the bidet to wash the knife: if you look at the electropherograms you'll see that there seems to be more of Amanda's blood than Meredith's. There is a copious blood loss by Amanda. Not from a pierced ear, nor from washed underwear, but from bleeding. A bleeding nose, maybe, a cut, or two cuts because we have to consider the bloodstains in the corridor. Which is a different issue.

37

The Big Clues

Colonel Garofano then focused on some of the key clues, such as the foot- and shoeprints, the bra clasp and the telling blood-stains in Meredith's bedroom that might hold the key to reconstructing her final minutes. His findings are surprising in that he talks down the usefulness of the best print of all – the one on the blue bathmat that police say is Sollecito's. He is also critical of the way police used Luminol to highlight the invisible prints. In short, their technique could be described as sloppy or imprecise. Garofano also explained why he thinks the suspects can be divided into two camps, suggesting that they may have operated and moved separately about the murder scene.

First, Garofano looked at the bloody footprint on the blue bathmat in the small bathroom next to Meredith's.

We have a nice red stain on the blue bathmat, and other bloodstains. The foot is quite clear but we can't tell where the heel is, so the full size of the foot is unknown to us. It does not match Guede's foot, we are told, but it does match Sollecito's in a number of places. But not in all. It is imprinted in Meredith's blood. So whoever left the footprint walked in Meredith's blood. The problem I have with that is that there should be a negative somewhere – a print or outline in a pool of blood somewhere, probably in her room, that is the same shape as the one on the blue bathmat. There should be a footprint where the blood came from somewhere, but I can't see that in the photographs.

The angle of the big toe seems to be different too. This, however, doesn't really mean anything because the stain is incomplete. The most you can get out of this stain is the general size and shape of a foot. However, it may be enough to support a logical hypothesis. It can never be conclusive.

The other problem I have is the way the Luminol was applied. The size of the blobs shows that it was not carefully vaporized, but squirted. That creates two problems. It dilutes the sample and it dilates the print. We have a print attributed to Sollecito, which matches his foot in the size of the big toe, the width of the metatarsus and the width of the heel, but does not present the characteristic details each of our feet present. The print can be said to be compatible, but not 100 per cent.

The Colonel turned to his computer: 'This is what can be achieved if the Luminol is vaporized rather than squirted.' The picture he pointed to was a clear footprint, with the crease lines and scars.

Pity. The print is oriented towards the flat's front door, so its owner was walking away from the crime scene, in the direction of the sitting room, maybe Filomena's room . . .

Now let's have a look at the prints attributed to Amanda Knox. There's one in her bedroom facing the exit to the room, and there are two right feet in the corridor walking in the direction of the victim's room. The same goes here. The method of application of the Luminol is insufficiently subtle to positively identify a foot, but the result can be said to be generally compatible with Amanda Knox's.

But I didn't see who else they compared the prints with. Just Rudy, Amanda and Raffaele? So we only have a choice between those? We don't have the footprint of other women or men, as a comparison? Pity.

But let's see what the prints actually mean. First of all, from their sheer luminosity they are blood. The DNA test showed Meredith's blood in all cases except for two places in which we have a mixed Amanda and Meredith sample. And there's one in Filomena's room, where no footprints are identified.

At this point Garofano talked about some of the most interesting and chilling conclusions that can be drawn from footprint analysis. In short, where people walked and why.

OK, so we have mixed blood from Amanda and Meredith. That falls in line with the findings in the bathroom. Amanda was bleeding while Meredith's blood was travelling about the house. She walked in her own blood, blood that she had also had on her body, while walking around with Meredith's blood on her bare feet.

If they had tried to clean the crime scene we would see the swipe marks of a mop, but there are none. The prints simply would not be there. If you have ever walked in paint, you'll have noticed that the prints you leave get fainter and fainter until they disappear as you walk away from the place you walked in it. But if you looked for the trace with some magic substance, you'd still find it although invisible to the naked eye. The same goes for blood. They couldn't see what they had left behind. They didn't need to clean because they were under the misapprehension that they were safe, that their tracks were already covered.

My question now is: how did Amanda's blood get into Filomena's room? Did she cut herself on the glass? Why aren't there any other prints along the corridor?

Now there's the question of the small shoeprint in the pillow. There is neither the heel nor the toe, so it's hard to say the size of the shoe. You could estimate where they might be, and that estimate has been made in the area of size 37 or 38, which, of course, is Amanda's size. Hard to prove, though. Here we are in the realm of suggestion.

On Guede's footprints he adds:

There is a nice series of footprints that belong to Guede too. The Nike Outbreak 2 shoes are all left prints except for the print on the pillow, which is a right print. Except for the print on the pillow they follow a direction out of the house. The interesting thing about the footprints is that we have bare feet for Amanda and Raffaele, but shoe footprints in the case of Rudy Guede. There are so many things in the flat that separate the three into the Knox/Sollecito group and Guede. Guede goes to the toilet, Guede is dressed, Guede leaves a fingerprint. It's as though Guede is there for longer, but dressed and shod, while Amanda and Raffaele are there more briefly but barefoot. There's no Guede in the small bathroom, for example. All this tells me that they were not acting together at the time of the murder itself. But we'll talk about Guede later.

The Bra Clasp

Now, what do we have against Raffaele? The bra clasp. The bra clasp is tested in two places, and on the metal hook we find the DNA of Meredith and clearly of Raffaele, in much smaller quantities, but still significant amounts. And look, in nine out of sixteen places we have peaks that correspond to Amanda and in some cases we have peaks that correspond to a fourth person. That is strong. I'd say there is a strong likelihood that Amanda touched this bra clasp too. The fourth person is not Guede, it seems. This mystery fourth person hasn't been mentioned much.

Look at the electropherogram and compare with the three. Of course, Meredith's DNA is overwhelmingly present, but look at this. If we go along the graph line, yes, we have a lot of Raffaele too, but in the first locus we have eleven and twelve STRs, which is the same as in Amanda's DNA profile, twenty-nine and thirty (remember, one from the father and one from the mother) in the second, eight and eleven in the third, also the same as Amanda's, nothing in the fourth, maybe a fifteen in the fifth . . . look, ten out of sixteen loci have peaks that correspond to Amanda's DNA profile. The hypothesis is that Amanda also touched the bra clasp.

However, having said that, look at the film. The bra clasp isn't tagged and collected until the 18th of December, forty-six days later than the other exhibits. It is found under the blue carpet. It is now dirty. They must have realized the mistake but couldn't go back for it until all the parties agreed. Now, obviously DNA doesn't fly, and even if the police had been to other rooms they might have touched some of Amanda's stuff, but certainly not Raffaele's. From the film I see that the first thing they do is go to Meredith's room, so it would be unlikely that they transported Amanda's DNA from her room to where the bra clasp is. Yes, admittedly, they do manipulate it a lot. Look how bent the metal bit is. It's been pulled off violently, or maybe it was simply the weight of the body as they pulled it up to snip it off.

My conclusion is that the bra clasp certainly works as a piece of evidence – it is a strong clue against the suspects Amanda and Raffaele. The RFU number is high enough. So the result is perfect. One has to assume the protocols were followed to the letter. If the defence experts were there they would have seen for themselves. If the experts weren't at the lab, they have a problem, because they are under a moral obligation to their clients to be there, as is their right. Some lawyers leave early because it takes so long, but I trust that in such an important case the defence experts here did not. If they can't see they can't criticize. They can criticize the way the bra clasp was collected but not the way it was analysed. In America, the defence doesn't have a right to be present at the DNA testing, but everything in the laboratory at that time is the subject of cross-examination – even personal notes and doodles.

So if we assume that the bra clasp was analysed properly, and that, despite the risk the police took in leaving it in the house for forty-six days, there was no contamination, then it is the only piece of evidence that ties Raffaele Sollecito to the crime scene except for the footprints. It also ties Amanda to the crime scene, although not as decisively.

The colonel's conclusion was stark. Bra clasp = Raffaele Sollecito.

Reconstructing Meredith's Last Moments

What can we say about the dynamics of the crime then? I have watched the film and seen the photos of the crime scene and I can only make comments based on this. I have tried to come to an independent evaluation of the dynamics of the murder. Let me say that I agree that the break-in is staged. The stone is too big, the window's shut and I follow the logic the police used to establish that it is a false break-in.

Take a look at the photographs of Meredith's room. Look at every single photograph and blow it up to maximum size. You can tell a lot from the pictures.

Where did the attack begin? We don't know. The room isn't very big. Let's start where the big bloodstain is, near the middle of the room, in front of the wardrobe. There's a small, cleanish square shape that was protected from the blood, and that might be where the Collins dictionary was at first and that was moved afterwards. What is a pocket dictionary doing on the floor? Where might it have been before? There – look under the desk, the chair's leg is resting on a *Corriere della Sera* newspaper, which has been torn. The dictionary would have been there, under the desk, and kicked towards the wardrobe during the fight.

The indication is that the fight was fast. There aren't many signs of a fight going on. The glass is still standing, the postcards on the chest of drawers are still there. No, there's not much sign of a fight. So the action moves from near the white desk around the room in anti-clockwise fashion to the area in front of the wardrobe.

This anti-clockwise movement was broadly in line with what Stefanoni had said, except that she believed the fight had started even further to the left of the desk, at the door.

Garofano continued: 'The knifing would have happened near the wardrobe. The wound was to her left throat, so the bleeding would have gone all over the floor. There's a lot of blood there, but not enough. The person who stuck the knife in got most of it on his or her clothes. The victim swivelled round and began coughing blood on to the wardrobe. Her head was low, so presumably she was kneeling at that point.'

The Colonel looked at the photograph of the five swipes inside the wardrobe. 'Those look like jets of blood, but also like fingermarks. If we blow up the picture we can see, however, that they are slightly blurred at the edges. Blood jets don't do that. Blood pumped out of an artery leaves neat marks. So let's assume they are fingermarks. But they are too strong to be the fingermarks of someone dying.'

Colonel Garofano then tried to explain this point using paint. The watercolour box came out and a wooden board. He wet his finger in the watercolour. First the left hand. He had difficulty holding the board with the left hand to make those arches. 'Look, her hand would have had to be upside down here. She would have to have been on her knees on the left of the wardrobe, which we know she wasn't because of the blood droplets on the side of the wardrobe that show she was on her back at that point. And a dying person wouldn't have had the strength to make those marks. '

He went to wash his hands. He looked at the photograph again.

So could they be blood spurts from a severed artery? No. Look, the heavy blood is on the inside of the wardrobe. If the artery had spurted into the wardrobe, the mass of blood would have been at the point of impact and then it would have dripped down. But no, you see the mass of blood is inside and the movement is outwards and then there's the scrape mark along the edge of the wardrobe. No, it's a hand. It has to be a right hand. Look at the space between the fingermarks. There's a centimetre marker just above it. They are 2 and a half centimetres apart, even 3. So it's a big right hand.

Out came the board and watercolours again. This time he dipped his right hand in the fake blood. He swiped it against the board. 'Look, the forefinger and thumb trajectories cross over – just like in the photograph. No. This is a man with bloody fingers using the wardrobe as a lever, his right hand pushing against the inside of the wardrobe, maybe as an anchor to some other effort he is making.'

Colonel Garofano's conclusion was interesting because no mention of a man's hand causing the arches had come from the police. The police had suggested that they were sequential spurts of blood.

Moving back to Meredith's body and the blood pattern near it, he said:

Look at the clotted blood. Where there are large blood clots indicates that she was long enough in that position to create a puddle of blood. With that kind of wound it wouldn't have taken long – tens of seconds, not minutes.

Then while she is bleeding, so still alive, she is flipped over and moved to a supine position where her wound continues to bleed into the corner between the wall and the wardrobe. Now this is very interesting. Look at the wardrobe side here. She is still coughing little droplets of blood. The blood pattern analysis done by the police is good. It indicates that highly oxygenated blood droplets coming from her airways are coughed in a nice oval pattern on to the wardrobe door, but she goes on coughing all the time, right up to being supine with her head almost against the wardrobe. She is still alive and gasping for air as the blood oozes into her lungs, coughing it up all the time. The fact that the autopsy says there are droplets on her chest indicates that she was still coughing when supine.

Let's look at some of the details. There's a hot-water bottle beside the wardrobe. Behind her boots. There are three parallel blood marks on the floor just north of the white bag. Those look like shoe stains. Pointing towards the wall. The blood drops on them are full, so the marks were made before the blood drops fell on them, and if we presume the blood drops come from the knife then those marks, maybe shoe marks, could belong to the killer. They are in the right position. Look, you can see the blood drops under the desk, nice big blobs, similar to the ones we've just mentioned. Those shoe stains look like they are coming from the same foot stepping sideways. Then the knife's out and moving around, dropping blood under the desk.

But what's this? A cotton bud! A cotton bud against the wall. What's that doing there? It's a blue one, not like the white ones in the bathroom, so it can't be attributed to Amanda, but it's interesting all the same. No, it's not the same make; it must be from Meredith's own washbag. However it's odd that it's there and I haven't seen it mentioned in the laboratory report. Meredith sounds like a tidy girl. I'm surprised she left a cotton bud in full view like that, or maybe it got pulled out from under the carpet in the scuffle.

Where was the carpet? It is clean, so must have been a long way from the action. Probably beside the bed. What I am looking for here is the big blood spurt from the wound as the knife comes out, and it just isn't there. It must be on the clothes of the person who stabbed her. Thrown away, with the shoe which left its mark on the pillowcase.

Let's look at the crime scene bearing the autopsy in mind. We know where the main wound was. In her left throat. She has bruises on her right upper forearm, left inner thigh, on her lower abdomen and on the back of her head, which could have been when she fell over on her back. And of course cuts to her right hand. The bruises to her thighs might have been made when the attackers were trying to force her legs open, while the bruises to her right forearm mean her attackers were holding it down.

However, nothing in the room indicates that there was a long-drawn-out fight, and yet her parents say she would have fought off an attacker, and that she was a karate expert. Raffaele is a kick-boxer and a knife-collector, although apparently not prone to violence. Imagine you knew how to defend yourself using karate, what would you do if threatened with a knife? You'd use your right hand to push the knife away from your face and punch with the left hand. Not the other way round, because a left-handed action against a right-handed attacker pushes the knife across your face. So the attacker's been punched in the face. Has a bloody nose. But the karate user has also got closer to the attacker by putting his or her leg between the attacker's leg so as to be able to swing them round on to the floor more effectively.

But something goes wrong. Her right arm gets pushed back – by a second attacker maybe – and gets a bruise. A knee goes into the lower abdomen because the two bodies are too close for a full kick. The knife swings back now that the defender's right arm has been pulled away and there it is, it goes into the throat. The second attacker is pushing the defender's head back in the fight.

Look at the wound, there's a cut just below it as though there was a first swipe, then there's the deeper cut on the left side, maybe a second knife, then the fatal wound which is deep. We need to look at those three marks again to see if the attack could have started there.

From then onwards, the police findings work. Rape? Who knows?

'What does the Vaseline tell you?'
'The Vaseline could mean anything. Not only anal sex. Interesting to see the lavatory paper on the table and a roll of it on Amanda's bedside table . . . but I can't see any direct connection.'

Rudy

Let's have a look at Rudy. His is an interesting story. Let's take it at face value and see if it works. OK, it all starts with his appointment with Meredith, which, say the judges, he can't have had because he didn't go to the same Halloween party.

But still, let's assume she opened the door to him, as he said. She becomes furious against Amanda because the money's missing. They settle down to some heavy petting. The fruit juice in his stomach interacts with his gut and he has to go to the bathroom. He hears two and a half tracks of music. Then hears the scream. Two and a half pieces of music are maybe seven to eight minutes.

Within that time, Amanda comes in, the two fight and someone jabs Meredith with a knife. They make for the door, Amanda first. Rudy catches the suspect male in the door-frame and gets a knife wound, falls to the ground, and the other bloke splits too, saying, 'A black man found, a black man condemned', or words to that effect.

So back to basics. Did they find the fruit juice in the fridge?

'Yes, pineapple juice.'

OK, he says they petted on armchairs. Highly unlikely. But can't disprove it. He went to the toilet. Took his time. In fact the toilet has no signs of blood in it and the fact that he didn't flush it indicates that his departure was precipitous. He has wounds on his right hand, which correspond to what he says in his statement. Are there any signs of blood on the floor in the sitting room, apart from the concentric rings?

Yes, between the sofa and the fridge there are two small elongated bloodstains. OK, so it may be him falling over. What kind of works, but not entirely, is Meredith's bedroom. He says the body was more parallel to the chest of drawers, and you can see that she has been moved to a more diagonal position rotating around the head and shoulders. There are swipe marks and the shape of her arm in the blood close to the chest of drawers.

However, he says he wrote 'A F' on the wall while kneeling on his left knee, which is almost impossible, even for a tall man. The towels he used to stem the blood flow are there. I see they didn't test for his DNA because mould had got to them. However, there should be some of his DNA on those towels if he was bleeding and then mould won't have destroyed the whole sample.

What I don't get is the pillow. He says the pillow was on the bed. And I can understand his putting his bloody hand on it inadvertently, but I can't understand his shoeprint. If the pillow was on the bed, the shoeprint shouldn't be on it. That's difficult to explain. He doesn't say he put the pillow under her, and he says the duvet was red. Those three points don't convince me at all. The rest sort of works, so he could be telling the truth or part of the truth.

He said he was wearing a T-shirt with a dollar symbol on it. They found it and tested for blood but found none. Even if he had washed it, Luminol would have shown up blood-stains. If he had been there when all that blood was flying about he would have got some on his clothes. Obviously his shoes would have had blood on the uppers as well as the soles, but he threw those away, didn't he?

What about the chair? He says he fought off the attacker with a chair. Have they found his blood on a chair? No? I suspect they didn't look. Remember the crime scene was closed on November 5th and reopened on the 18th December. They took no chairs away with them on that date.

So, there were Italy's top forensic expert's conclusions laid bare. One piece of forensic evidence, the DNA on the bra clasp, ties Sollecito to the murder scene. Amanda is tied to it by mixed blood samples, but not in Meredith's room, and a trace of her DNA on the bra clasp. And Guede was looking more credible and could not be written off completely as a liar. From now on, only the court case would prove whether his theories were right or not. A trial date was pencilled in for January 2009.

38

Under Pressure

The Trial: Overview to Opening Shots

February–June 2009

'I just imagined what it must have been like,' said Amanda Knox, shaking her head. First, she pushed her hands away in disgust. Then she reinforced her point with a noise of mock horror. An 'urrrgh' sound bounced off the ancient stone recesses, reverberating faintly through the tall, state-of-the-art PA speakers in the corner. Was she showing her age with the histrionics? Or had she been genuinely moved? The judge and jury would have to decide.

The Trial of the Century, as it had been billed, was finally underway. Amanda was explaining to the court, in good Italian, how she had actually *known* or at least *thought she had known* that Meredith had suffered when she had died – a detail that Amanda had specified to police and others in statements after the fact. If Amanda wasn't present during the murder, then surely she couldn't have known whether Meredith had suffered? But she wasn't rattled by the line of questioning. Under the judge's fixed gaze and in front of the hushed galleries her excuse, perfectly perfunctory and plausible, was delivered like a pro. As she had thought about it more in the hours after the murder, it had seemed to her, she claimed, that Meredith's suffering was self-evident. It wasn't a secret. That was the plain reasoning behind her rebuttal.

It was 12 June 2009 and the height of her testimony in her own defence. A blistering cold-sore scab blemished the outline of her lips, as she went on to explain away several other points that had tainted her statements, and her reputation, in the preceding year. Why she had landed Patrick Lumumba in prison. How she had known that Meredith's body had been found with her throat slit *and* near the wardrobe. And why she had shaken like a leaf when put to the test in front of the knife drawer in her own kitchen. Two circular gantries of lights, in the style of a mediaeval chandelier, hung over her head. Above them was a metal lattice ceiling illuminated with fluorescent strips. Drained of colour by the lighting, at times Amanda looked mundane. During the recesses, the background chatter was more appropriate to a town-hall meeting than to a big murder case.

Patrick Lumumba's lawyer Carlo Pacelli had opened the cross-examination. He had asked for Amanda's previously struck-out statement to be re-admitted into evidence. The Supreme Court had earlier ruled the document inadmissible because it was self-accusatory and made without a lawyer being present. Pacelli's new argument was a clever manoeuvre: his team weren't interested in the statement's value as a murder exhibit; it simply constituted an act of slander against their client. The judge agreed with them and, to Amanda's chagrin, the statement was back in effect.

The wheels of justice had turned slowly. It had been more than a year since the prosecution had first deposited the evidence against the three suspects. Amanda Knox was taking the stand in the trial against her for murder and for destroying the reputation of Patrick Lumumba. In Italy, falsely accused suspects are entitled to sue for compensation and, unusually, the civil trials are allowed to run concurrent with the criminal ones. A few seats away, guarded by two uniformed officers, Raffaele Sollecito was also up for murder.

The trial took place in the vaulted hall of the medieval palace of justice. St Francis had been held prisoner in its icy dungeons before becoming a hermit. Like a set from a Mafia film, in a corner stood an ominous cage where dangerous criminals faced trial, literally behind bars. The excitable atmosphere of the first day on 6 February 2009 had led some of the more adventurous journalists to occupy this caged area, in the hope of getting closer to the action. The Carabinieri and police were good-natured enough to wait for the Judge to order them out before executing this simple act of public order. The first part of the trial, the prosecution case, swallowed up the first four months and ended on 2 June 2009.

Contrary to popular belief, Italian trials are businesslike and methodical. There is little of the Perry Mason-style drama and easy banter associated with the American system, or of the wig-and-gown pomp, undercut with ruthless adversarial aggression, that is the trademark of a British court. The relaxed nature of the proceedings in Perugia belied the gravity of the crime. The judge was quietly spoken. The courtroom was an efficient mixture of plain, modern furniture and tasteful historical architecture. A giant whiteboard, linked to a PC on the left side of the court, gave it an air of a modern classroom. The low, pine-topped metal desks contrasted with ancient but neatly restored brick walls. The arches were gently hued with pink light.

More often than not, the people who provided the high

points were the suspects themselves. On 14 February Amanda Knox came to court wearing a T-shirt emblazoned with the words 'All You Need Is Love'. No one in authority seemed to be bothered, but the press were – journalists went hysterical, speculating that it was a coded Valentine's Day message to Raffaele to keep him sweet. In Britain, Amanda might have been found guilty of contempt of court.

The judge sat with an assistant, six permanent members of the jury and four substitutes. Each juror wore a sash. Three sat on either side of the judge to represent balance. They included a middle-aged woman, a young bespectacled female and a man with a fine grey moustache. The Italian judicial system, much reformed in the 1990s, is based on the Napoleonic Code. The judge and jury sit together and decide as one, a discrete body within the process. Every legal objection raised by defence or prosecution is weighed up by the judge and jury together. Every decision the judge and jury make has to be based on the Code and justified in legal terms. There has to be a specific rule or law written down somewhere in the Code to cover the judgement being made.

The system contrasts starkly with US and British justice, which is based on a hodge-podge of codified statutes passed down from Parliament or Senate, and common-law cases that are often open to differing interpretation. In English-speaking countries, precedent, often based on loose legal concepts and ideas, is strong enough to justify a judge's decision. But in Italy everything has to be done by the book, more so in recent years, as though to dispel any doubts that the country has cleaned up its act once and for all.

The judge impressed the media with his keen knowledge of due process. He repeated time and time again the fundamental principle of the Napoleonic Code: the court is sovereign; the court is where truth is established, and the court alone. This was not a place to trick witnesses, he urged, but to encourage them to tell the truth. It was as though the slate had to be washed clean before the suspects and witnesses took the stand. The prosecution and defence had to hammer it out in front of a firm but fair umpire.

Judge Giancarlo Massei was the eleventh judge to have reviewed the paperwork, but now he was the only one with the power to decide whether to let Amanda and Raffaele go free or to give them life sentences. Amanda took the stand in her own defence on 12 June 2009, the climax of the case and a moment the world's media had been waiting for. But much had happened before that day.

When the trial opened on 6 February 2009, Barbie Nadeau of *Newsweek* had headlined one of her articles 'Trial of The Century'. The defence's PR machines had turned it into a trial of the Italian judicial system. Prosecutor Giuliano Mignini had been much maligned on US public television networks by experts drafted in to support the Knox case. Little notice had been taken of the fact that he had asked for – and obtained – the support of a second prosecutor. Manuela Comodi was a good-looking public lawyer with the smile of a tiger. She took over part of Mignini's burden, which had been increased by the investigations into the Monster of Florence case that had been thrust on him. By reinforcing the prosecution, the state hoped to negate criticism that it was flawed.

The trial ran at half speed because the court could sit only on Fridays and Saturdays. This atypical arrangement was due to the prior engagements of Raffaele Sollecito's star lawyer, Giulia Bongiorno. A strong-looking middle-aged career politician, Bongiorno was the chairperson of the parliamentary committee on legal reform in Rome. As a high-flying member of Silvio

Berlusconi's People of Freedom party, she was effectively a card-carrying member of the ruling elite. Her parliamentary duties came before the trial and that was that.

The Sollecitos were banking on her lightning-fast brain to support their firepower – not least because their defence team had lost important members in the run-up. Vincenzo Pascali had left and presented his bill for 50,000 Euros. He had been replaced by Adriano Tagliabracci, a top DNA specialist. In general, the Sollecitos had reined in their tendency to be aggressive in their tactics. They had taken a back seat in the PR campaign against the prosecution since 1 April 2008, when the whole forensic-squad film, body and all, had been broadcast on TV at their behest. They had also been indicted for attempting to interfere with the course of justice by pulling strings with friends in politics to have key investigators moved. Luca Maori had also lost his partner, Marco Brusco. But Maori stayed with the team, now led by the fiery Giulia Bongiorno.

In the Knox camp, Carlo Dalla Vedova had lost the support of Giancarlo Costa, his good friend and experienced criminal barrister, who had suggested a different approach. Luciano Ghirga, the elder lawyer of the Perugia courts, with his shock of white hair, remained to keep an eye on what his younger and less experienced colleague was doing.

The prosecution, too, had had to make a few changes since the preliminary hearing, but these concerned the motive for murder on which they would rest their case, rather than personalities. In an awkward change of emphasis, all mention of Halloween, the occult and Sollecito's love of Satanic comic strips had been removed. The sex-game-gone-wrong theme was still the front runner but now it had been adapted. The previous judge, Paolo Micheli, who had tried Rudy Guede, had established that the murder could not have been premeditated. This was based on the simple premise that Amanda could not have known that she would be off work that night or that she would see Meredith. The prosecution had been successfully chastised into dropping several of its core beliefs. From now on, they would have to bring the case to trial with forensic evidence and witnesses only – no prepared hypotheses.

When the Knox defence team failed to have Amanda's handwritten statement thrown out, it was clear that the strongest point against the American would remain her alleged lies. The feeling that her alleged dishonesty would weigh as much as the forensic evidence was underlined when the judge and jury also decided that Amanda's statement to Mignini was admissible in the slander trial.

Giulia Bongiorno went for gold when she asked the judge to release Raffaele immediately. The request was as much about Bongiorno's attitude – her power and fearlessness – as it was about legal niceties. She argued that the document by which Mignini had ordered Raffaele to be kept in isolation for the first forty-eight hours couldn't be found in evidence. It was a simple 'point of admin' that lesser lawyers might not have had the confidence to wage war with. Careful not to rebuff her without good reason, the judge calmly threw out her objection, saying that it was self-evident that due process had been followed because in the meantime Sollecito had been seen by ten judges and formally remanded to trial by the preliminary hearing judge. It was a taste of what was to come.

39

The Big Push

The Prosecution Attack
and Civil Plaintiffs

February–June 2009

The core of the trial was plain to see – the quality of the forensics. How the forensic evidence had been collected and processed would be crucial to the success or failure of the case against the two suspects. The prosecution witnesses included the key players in the crime-scene investigation. The scientific police film showed filter paper being used to collect long drops of blood leading from the edge of the basin and bidet to the plughole. The jury heard about the dangers of the procedure. But the resulting electropherogram proved that luck had been on their side on this occasion. There was no major contamination. However, the films did show police, the pathologist and the prosecutor moving freely about the house, clearly increasing the risk of mingling the evidence. Not everything had been done in accordance with best practice. But crucially, the prosecution argued, not enough had been done wrong to undermine the results.

The telephone cops were called in and showed the thoroughness of their investigations – even proving that Mrs Lana's garden was, telephonically speaking, a black hole. No, the computers were off, they reaffirmed, and the telephones made and received no calls until 06.02 on the morning of 2 November. Their frustratingly complex data pushed the limits of what could be understood in a general court of law.

The first pathologist, Dr Lalli, and the other experts were called in to establish whether there had been a rape or not. Once again, he was inconclusive. An important point for the prosecution hung in the balance – to shore up the motive of a sexual attack, there had to be signs of rape. But worse was to come: there was even some doubt as to the origin of the bruises on Meredith's inner thigh. Questions were raised about whether they had indeed been caused by violence.

By March the trial had settled into a rhythm. Every day, the teams of prosecutors would make their way up into the old town on the escalators that have been dug into the rock foundations underneath the city, to transport people up inside the mountain. The series of narrow moving stairs is an astonishing feat of engineering. The atmosphere is singular, a blend of smells: hot rubber, wet plaster and damp rock. The young female lawyers, casually dressed in jeans and puffer jackets, politely refused help in carrying their big boxes of legal documents. The trademark independence of the new Italian feminism. Crowds of young American student girls, just like Amanda Knox, gazed in wonder at the ancient Roman ruins that had been excavated and uplit with gold floodlights. The 1970s posters and stone dove sculptures gave the vast caverns a haunting retro feel.

Agatino Giunta and Dr Lorenzo Rinaldi, the footprint identifiers, said many specimens matched Raffaele's and Amanda's. The prints revealed by Luminol, however, were largely discounted for not being precise enough. Crucially, the unflappable

Patrizia Stefanoni landed the first decisive hit on Amanda Knox. She said that the five mixed-blood locations undoubtedly pinned Amanda to the time and place of Meredith's murder. Amanda's lies and DNA seemed to paint an ugly picture that would be difficult to shift from the minds of the jury.

In comparison, the defence teams rebutted recklessly, asking the same question over and over again. How could Patrizia Stefanoni get such a clear picture of Meredith Kercher's DNA from such a small sample on the knife? It was a valid question but they didn't have the bottle or the data to stitch up Stefanoni completely. Stefanoni stuck to her guns, explaining the better-than-expected outcomes in the same way as she had at the preliminary hearing. Even with a lot of 'background noise' on an electropherogram, sixteen loci were identified. She gave an effective slide-show, winning the court over with a concise Power Point demonstration that proved that hideously complex data could be successfully introduced into a criminal trial. She left the hearing with her head held high.

Other witnesses proved more problematic. The nosy tramp Antonio Curatolo was uncertain about the time he had seen the heated discussions between Raffaele Sollecito and Amanda Knox in Grimana Square. Firstly, he was vague about the time – anything between 9:30 p.m. to around 11:30 p.m. Then he changed the date altogether, from Halloween to the night after. Convenience-store owner Marco Quintavalle, on the other hand, gave a good account of himself. He was relentless in displaying his accuracy to the court: he remembered perfectly that it was on the morning of the 2nd that he saw a woman who matched Amanda's description in his shop. Even so, he couldn't remember exactly what she had bought. He recalled distinctly that she had turned right towards Grimana Square instead of left towards Raffaele's flat. Mrs Nara Capezzali, too, couldn't remember the precise time she had heard the scream, and she also moved the clock back to later than 11 p.m. Meredith's English friends confirmed what they had heard and seen. Despite the shaky brushstrokes, the picture was steadily building.

It was easy to get bogged down in the immense amount of detail. Sometimes potentially explosive evidence seemed to be obscured by the matter-of-fact, understated tone of the proceedings. One such revelation concerned Meredith's missing money. Little had been made of the fact that 300 Euros had been lost or stolen from Meredith's room, even though Amanda had been formally charged with the theft. On the evening before her two Italian flatmates left for their long weekend, Meredith had told Filomena Romanelli that she had withdrawn the money for the next month's rent. They paid 300 Euros each but Meredith was careful to point out that she had withdrawn only 200 Euros from a cash machine. Filomena assumed she had the extra 100 Euros knocking around. Filomena confirmed the conversation, among many other important lines, when she took the stand. The mystery was that the police had never found the money after the murder, either in Meredith's room or on her person. In his evidence, Rudy Guede had asserted that the money had gone missing even before his arrival and that Meredith had been fuming over it.

The new revelation was astonishing in that it cast doubt on the sexual-attack motive. Could the murder have been some kind of botched robbery? Some observers took it further and speculated that a seething tension had grown between Amanda and Meredith. Filomena had confirmed as much in her evidence. The feud had started over silly student things such as the division of housework, irritations that often occur in shared accommodation. This escalated into a row over money. That night the girls had clashed, fuelled by hangovers and frayed tempers. The furious Amanda urged Raffaele, who was desperate to impress his new beau, to stick up for her, and he did. The speculators claimed that Raffaele, the insecure passive-aggressive, exploded and went too far.

Another theory was based on the fact that Amanda and Raffaele were using a lot of drugs and were desperate for money. They learned of Meredith's 300 Euros and 'cardmarked' Rudy to steal it for them, promising him a share of the loot. Yet another theory, popular with Raffaele and Amanda's supporters, claimed that local drug dealers had robbed Meredith acting on their own. They pointed to the mystery car and the various Mafia links that dogged the case. No matter who was responsible, bloggers accused the police of downplaying the robbery-gone-wrong theory because it ruined the sex-game motive in which they had invested so much.

Under the rational scrutiny of the court, however, the theory did not stand up. Even the cash-machine records weren't straightforward. The withdrawal should have been the last transaction on Meredith's bank card. Firstly, Sollecito's private investigators found the bank read-out. There had indeed been several withdrawals, but they occurred later than 1 November. The bank manager was summoned to court to explain. Frustratingly, he said there was no way of telling if the debits referred to transactions carried out before or after the date: they were simply registered after the date. He wasn't even able to establish which ATM machine had been used. Like the ballistics expert, the bank manager was a flop. Consequently, the robbery motive was never given the time or credit it probably deserved.

Untested motives were disappointing, but it was worse when evidence was missed altogether. The prosecution did not mention the fact that the towels that had been used by Guede to mop up Meredith's blood had gone mouldy whilst in police storage. Further tests, which might have proved relevant to Amanda and Raffaele, were now rendered difficult. Colonel Luciano Garofano could not believe that this had been allowed to happen, and that the police had not at least tried to test the towels again. In addition, the police did not secure the mop that Amanda had removed from 7 Pergola and taken to Raffaele's to clean up his leaking sink before returning it to the scene of the crime. Any evidence that could have been hiding in its tangled strands was not investigated. Nor did they drain the sump of the washing machine – which, suspiciously, had been running when the police arrived – to check for blood.

Following the defence, the case moved on quickly to the next phase: dealing with the victim's rights. Quietly and with dignity that was lost on few journalists, the Kerchers took the witness stand shortly before Amanda. It was 6 June 2009. That week the family drew the press corps's attention to the pop video in which Meredith had made a ghostly appearance (see Chapter 29), which was set in a church not dissimilar to the one where her funeral would be celebrated. The family were Francesco Maresca's star witnesses. Their expert geneticist Francesca Torricelli, of the Institute of Florence University, was only too happy to back up Stefanoni's prosecution line that the DNA of a single cell could be used to identify a person.

Next came Patrick Lumumba, who described his ordeal. Even the defence counsels avoided crossing swords with the other innocent victim of the case. Last among the civil plaintiffs was the owner of 7 Pergola, who was suing the state for more than 20,000 Euros in lost rent and increased security. Alda Tatanelli wanted the crime-scene tape to be officially cut so she could have her house back. By now, the detritus of mourning and the vigil that had remained outside the gate for nearly eighteen months had given the house a cold and gloomy air. Hundreds of respect-payers had left symbols of their sympathy. A red monster key ring. A Tasmanian devil furry toy, soaked and shabby now. A burnt-out plastic candle with a ragged picture of the Pope on it. A green electric light, battery long drained, with a prayer for a bearded saint on the side. Two bunches of wizened yellow flowers with poems for Meredith. A mouldy Perugian chocolate, with bits of insect stuck to it, that had been one of her favourites that she enjoyed at the chocolate festival. A plant in a plastic holder, stuck to the gate with insulation tape. Ragged red ribbons, last messages . . .

Curiously, the deserted flat had been raided twice during the trial. In one instance, the knives that had remained in the drawers had been found on the floor pointing east. The spectacle was seized upon as a Mafia-style secret sign of *omertá* to the Albanian and Italian criminals who some believed were the real culprits, or at least knew a lot more than had come out. It was claimed that there was an underlying threat: don't tell the police anything else. But now that the appetite for the occult and offbeat was waning, the event didn't even make it to court. In another drama, the mattress with the knife outlines on it was stolen from Meredith's room. The strangeness added to the mystery, the unease, the sensation that not everything about the case had yet been uncovered. However, it did not interfere with business either at the court or at the local estate agents. The house owner's wishes were eventually granted and in October 2009 Meredith's room was re-let to an African student – astonishingly, for a higher rent of 370 Euros. The new tenant said he did not believe in ghosts.

40

Last Chance: The Trial Defence

12 June–29 September 2009

The summer of 2009 was the last throw of the dice for Amanda and Raffaele. Their defence in court would be the last stand – a final chance to stop themselves going to jail, possibly for the rest of their lives. The big question was: would they put up a fight appropriate to the gravity of the situation?

The answer depended on three factors. Firstly, could they keep their arguments simple and strong? Secondly, could their legal teams overcome egos and internal politics to unite in attack? Thirdly, would they have the courage to come out of their comfort zones and really have a go at the police? All of the variables were dependent, in part, on the flexibility of the Italian justice system. Many foreign observers were left wondering if such a plodding trial procedure would allow a vociferous and thrusting defence to shine. To break through the bureaucracy and reach out to the jury was the objective – but could Bongiorno and the Ghirga–Vedova double act pull it off?

The first major hurdle was the scheduling. In a very Italian way, the judge announced that there would be a six-week break for summer, right in the middle of the defence. Surely that would affect the momentum of their attack? For the American contingent, who had rolled their eyes in amazement at the two-day week, this was a frustration alien to their work ethic.

However, when the defence kicked off, there were times when Knox's and Sollecito's supporters must have wished that the whole thing would stop altogether. The manoeuvres of their highly paid legal teams – Edda Mellas had re-mortgaged her house to the hilt to pay bills that some estimates put at $1 million – often seemed confused and uncoordinated. Victories seemed to be stumbled across rather than won systematically. Frequently, golden opportunities turned into near misses. A lack of focus seemed to be the main problem. For instance, lawyers repeatedly failed to keep the police witnesses in their cross-hairs, as when the matter of Patrizia Stefanoni's too-good-to-be-true DNA results came up again.

It was 18 July and the trial was winding down for the summer. Little more than a month after Amanda had told her tale, another bombshell fell. Stefanoni was becoming increasingly irate with people who kept saying that there was simply too little DNA on the knife to give a meaningful result. She wrote her feelings down and passed a note to the joint prosecutor Manuela Comodi, probably to reassure her and to spur her on to defend the police findings more aggressively. 'How can you say the quantity of DNA on the bra clasp is low' Stefanoni wrote indignantly, 'when we know there were 1.4 nanograms of substance?' Comodi studied the note carefully and nodded an acknowledgement to her incensed colleague.

The key phrase was '1.4 nanograms'. Sollecito's forensics consultant Adriano Tagliabracci jumped on the point as soon as he got wind of the message. He had already been slamming the police for leaving the bra clasp untested for forty-seven days and having too many officers handle it and move it around. Now he had the ammunition to go in for the kill.

'Sorry,' rebutted Tagliabracci, 'how do we know how much DNA is on the bra clasp? There are no records of what the PCR read-out was.' In effect, Tagliabracci was saying that he had never seen the actual results. Neither had many of the other lawyers, despite the weeks of attention paid to the DNA evidence during the prosecution phase. Perhaps some of them had been too embarrassed to admit it. After all, they had been invited to watch the process for themselves in Rome, but several had not taken up the invitation. Tagliabracci, however, had an excuse that other experts did not: he hadn't been on the case at the time so couldn't have seen the process even if he had wanted to.

Sollecito's hatchet-woman Giulia Bongiorno immediately sprang to her feet to second her comrade.

'Are you telling me,' she blasted, 'there are records that have not been presented to the court?' Tagliabracci cut to the quick. 'It is vital for us to understand,' he said, 'how the DNA findings were reached in order for us to ascertain the how reliable they are . . .'

If there was ever a chance to discredit Stefanoni, now was the moment. Get the DNA thrown out, and the defendants would have a 'get out of jail free' card – or at least that was the theory. They could, also in theory, have accused Stefanoni of all kinds of skulduggery – anything from corruption to incompetence. The objective was to throw as much mud at her as possible, in the hope that enough would stick and her findings would be fatally impaired.

After a heated discussion the judge ordered the prosecution, and by extension Patrizia Stefanoni, to provide *all* the documentation that the laboratory had produced: the paperwork that supported the conclusions she had so brilliantly outlined just a few weeks earlier. For the defence, first base had been reached. The golden girl's sheen was rapidly becoming tarnished. The data included the read-out from the Real Time PCR which established the actual quantity of DNA extracted from the sample. The teams waited breathlessly for the police to warm up their photocopiers. Hundreds of pages would have to be bundled and sent out.

The tussle was a turning-point in the trial. Up until now, the defence witnesses had not dented the prosecution case. In vain, even Amanda and Raffaele had tried in person. On half a dozen occasions they had stood up to make 'spontaneous declarations' on points of contention. The tactic was deployed in the hope of circumventing the life-draining protocol of the law, in order to present a more human face, and perhaps thereby weaken the effect of the prosecution's arguments. Amanda explained why she had kept a vibrator in her sponge bag. It was a toy 'Rabbit', she said, a joke gift that had been given to her before she left for Italy. She said this to save face – to prove that she wasn't a slut, and to counter the 'soft' evidence that the police were stirring up. Judge Massei tolerated these interruptions benignly. But neither Amanda nor Raffaele managed to give an impression of complete transparency. In the big picture, their pleas were next to worthless – but if making them made them feel better, fine.

The defence teams had done their own research, but some of it looked clumsy. Independent state coroner Francesco Introna, who was called in support of Sollecito, did the defendant proud – at least at first. On 20 June he undermined his own colleagues by stating that the knife used was only half the size of what Mignini thought. He blasted Mignini's multiple-attacker theory out of the water by saying that only one person could have stabbed Meredith. His claims supported Sollecito's and Amanda's 'lone wolf' theory and therefore piled the blame on

Guede, if not by name then at least by implication. However, after a promising start for the defence, the coroner strayed off the script, claiming there had been rape, when both teams had decided it would be better to assume there hadn't been. In any case, it couldn't be proved either way. Finally, Introna undermined his own credibility by admitting that he had never been to the murder scene – so he couldn't state with any credibility whether one or several attackers could have fitted into the room.

Other defence witnesses were caught out for not doing their homework. The Sollecitos brought in an ex-colonel of the Carabinieri to disprove the staged break-in, a cornerstone of the prosecution case that seemed almost too solid to challenge. At first he did well, appearing to demonstrate that the stone found in Filomena's room could indeed have been thrown by a burglar from the driveway. However, under pressure, he was unable to answer basic questions, such as what kind of throw it had been, and whether it was underhand or overhand. Simple points – but his lack of grasp didn't impress a judge and jury obsessed with detail. The prosecution case might not have been perfect but its structure was firmly based upon four key pillars of evidence: witness, behavioural, forensic and circumstantial. It seemed strong enough to withstand any attempt to chip away at it with small, highly specific attacks.

The A-list witnesses, Amanda Knox and her mother Edda Mellas, were not expected to make the same mistakes. In Italy, the accused is not required to take an oath, so the court quickly got down to business. Lumumba's advocate Carlo Pacelli convinced the judge that he should be the first to quiz Amanda as the slander proceedings were separate from the murder trials. His questions were terse and simple.

'Were you afraid of Patrick Lumumba?' he barked.

'No,' replied Amanda.

'Why did you say you were terrified of him?' (Protests – the statement had been judged inadmissible. Counter-protests: this was a separate charge. The judge agreed with Lumumba's lawyer.)

'Why did you accuse Patrick Lumumba of having murdered Meredith Kercher?' Pacelli pressed on.

'I told the police what I thought they wanted to hear. They insulted me, they told me I was a liar, they hit me on the head, they were telling me I was protecting someone, but I wasn't . . .' Amanda said that a dark-haired female officer had struck her. The prosecutor and police thought about suing her for slander. In Britain, people giving evidence in court can virtually say what they like: they are protected, by an ancient law of privilege, from being sued for damaging another's reputation. Foreign observers, including Knox's father, were unhappy at the short-comings of the Italian system. On the one hand, it seemed that Amanda couldn't speak her mind; for instance, she couldn't accuse the police of brutality without fear of reprisals. On the other, the system seemed rigid because of the Napoleonic code.

'Miss Knox, did you ever think of offering Patrick compensation?' Lumumba's lawyer continued.

Amanda laughed nervously. 'Me? No!'

Amanda did not endear herself to the court. She described the death as 'yucky'. But she did provide helpful details. Asked why she had said to Lumumba, 'See you later', she answered that it was an American way of saying, 'See you tomorrow.' And she came across as self-assured, particularly for a young woman just a few weeks short of her twenty-second birthday. She spoke confidently in Italian with a strong American accent, and put on the toughest show she could. On the second day she endured five hours of testimony but stayed calm and assertive during repeated clashes. Arguments broke out when her defence lawyers kept raising objections about the Prosecutor's hardline questions.

Mignini described the interruptions as 'impossible'. As always, the *Umbrian Journal* got it right when they described Amanda as having 'an angel face and the character of a warrior'. Her father thought she had done just fine and he was proud of her.

Then Edda Mellas stepped up to the plate. She described their home life and Amanda's upbringing. She was at pains to explain Amanda's strange behaviour. The picture she painted was of a girl from a city halfway round the world who simply enjoyed a different culture: sex was freer, people practised yoga and stretching in the street, they used American slang words that couldn't be translated using the *Cambridge Italian–English Dictionary*.

Edda did an excellent job of rationalizing Amanda's oddest moments. Of course she had had to buy underwear from the lingerie shop in the aftermath of the murder: she had been shut out of her flat; the crime scene was locked down. It was nothing to do with an expression of her libido. Of course she did exercises and stretching at the police station: she was under stress. Yoga was a coping strategy. For Seattleites, it was normal behaviour. For a lot of people it clicked – *yes, that sounds right*, they thought. *My God, the police have put a terrible spin on seemingly mundane stuff.* That was a common reaction from observers who had watched Edda give evidence, whether they were pro-Amanda or not. If the police could make so much out of a simple thing like buying underwear, what other games might they have played to stitch up this vulnerable young woman?

Edda wasn't cold-calling with her wares in court; there was nothing random about her performance. For months she had been talking to the press with the same explanations in a series of big set-piece interviews. In the UK alone, she had been featured in the *Sunday Times* and *Guardian* magazines. The Gogerty, Stark & Marriott troops had regained a lot of PR ground since the demonization of their charge in the early days.

Then Edda dropped a clanger. She couldn't understand why Amanda had never mentioned to the police a key telephone call that she had made to her mother. Amanda had called Edda at home in the States at 12:47 Italian time – several minutes before Meredith's door had been broken down. There was much speculation about the content of this call. Edda never mentioned it again. In addition, the prosecution said Amanda had admitted that Lumumba wasn't involved in the murder in taped conversations she'd had with Edda at Capanne prison. This wasn't good, the prosecution implied.

Character witnesses David Johnsrud and Madison Paxton praised Amanda for being virtuous and even said she got on well with her flatmates, contrary to what Filomena had said. However, the Knox PR team scored an own goal when they wheeled out Amanda's little-known fourteen-year-old stepsister Ashley for photographs in front of 7 Pergola Road. The other sister, Deanna, was censured for being scantily clad in the pictures. Perhaps the attacks were too harsh – the critics had not taken into account that Deanna was only twenty years old and that the Italian summer was very hot.

The DNA clashes turned nasty when the Scientific Police finally handed over their notes to the court. The defence jumped on the words 'too low' written in English on read-outs from the Real Time PCR. However, it wasn't as cut and dried as it first seemed. Outside the court Colonel Garofano explained to journalists that in reality 'too low' meant nothing.

The Real Time PCR spits out a tape with a figure on it. If the figure is zero, it may mean that there is a chemical agent inhibiting the DNA, which could be anything from heat to dyes from clothes. Remove the inhibiting agent and re-concentrate, and you may still get a DNA read-out. Spin the sample through the system and you may still get a meaningful electropherogram. Who wrote the words 'too low'? And why? Unless the defence can pinpoint the exact place where a mistake was made, unless they explain how the chemistry works, they simply can't make a case against the results.

In frustration, Sollecito's DNA consultant Adriano Tagliabracci hit out ferociously, accusing Stefanoni of botching the cat's-blood samples from the downstairs flat. Prosecutor Manuela Comodi handled this cleverly, pretending to be hurt, making out that he had gone too far and accused them of being liars – a breach of court convention. Tagliabracci back-pedalled. 'Not "lies",' he said sheepishly. 'I never said "lies".' It seemed that to save face and a ticking-off from the judge, he stopped short of going in for the kill. Comodi was embarrassed, but knew she had won.

Knox's expert Sara Gino was also chastened. She was shot down because she had not been present in Rome when the knife was analyzed. As Stefanoni had reminded those there at the time: speak now or for ever hold your peace.

Sollecito's computer expert Antonio d'Ambrosio fared better. Astonishingly, he identified computer activity where none had previously been found: four seconds, late in the night of 1 November (00:58), which could prove that their boy was at home and his alibi impregnable. More activity was detected late at night on 5 November, when Raffaele and Amanda were at the police station. Who was on the computer? Conspiracy theorists said it was unauthorized police officers altering the electronic evidence to fit him up.

Meanwhile, outside court, Rudy Guede and his team were busy preparing for his automatic right of appeal. First, his lawyers Valter Biscotti and Nicodemo Gentile rebutted every negative media story that the Knox and Sollecito camps had been spinning against him. The next step was slowly but surely to build up his credibility by independently proving various parts of his story. Soon they struck gold.

They had heard rumours that some of Guede's friends had betrayed him in his hour of need, either lying to police or not coming forward because they pretended not to have seen him on the night of the murder; they didn't want to get themselves dragged into the mess. The lawyers decided to trap the witnesses in an undercover sting. Perugia is a small town and a relative of one of the lawyers knew some of the students Rudy had said he had gone out with after the murder. The young relative tracked one of them down on Facebook and called him up. They began reminiscing about the fun they had had so long ago when they were students. 'Pity about Guede. He was there that night, wasn't he?' the amateur sleuth asked, following the lawyer's script.

'Yes,' replied Guede's former friend. 'I was sorry I couldn't back him up. But none of us wanted to be involved.' Bingo! The telephone conversation was being taped. Guede's reluctant alibi-giver had well and truly been turned over. Now the Biscotti–Gentile team could pull those witnesses in. If they could prove that Guede was telling the truth about going dancing after the murder, that would help with the other shaky bits of his story.

The next piece of the jigsaw involved tests that controversially had been missed. The two lawyers asked for the mouldy towels to be checked for Guede's blood, and for the Luminol analysis to be carried out on Meredith's clothes. They hoped to debunk many of the myths surrounding their client, in much the same way that several of the spooky coincidences that had mired the case had been explained.

41

Shock and Awe

Closing Speeches

November 2009

'The answer to this riddle lies in Filomena Romanelli's room,' Mignini pronounced. 'If the break-in is staged, then logic has it that the murder was committed by someone who had free access to the house.'

The whole point of a closing speech is to make a Winston Churchill-style oration that will rally the jury. Mignini did not fail. It was his finest hour – or rather seven, as it turned out.

First, he attacked the thriller-writers, part-time detectives, bloggers and bar-room lawyers who had rounded on him and the Italian judicial system. Then he kept his arguments simple, by refusing to get bogged down in DNA waffle.

'Where is the logic, I ask the court, in the defendants attacking Rudy Guede as the only perpetrator of the crime, if they imply they were not there? If they spent the night comfortably in Raffaele's apartment, why worry about Guede? Methinks they protest too much. How could they possibly think that there is just one murderer? As Dr Introna and Dr Vinci said: "How do they know he was there if they weren't there too?"'

Mignini waded into Amanda head-on. Why did she forget to tell the police that Lumumba had nothing to do with the murder, when she had told her mother so during one of their first encounters in Capanne prison? Logic was simply not on her side, Mignini argued. On the morning of the discovery, why did she tell Filomena that she was going back to Raffaele's when he was either standing next to her or she could have called him on her mobile phone?

Finally, Mignini unveiled his secret new weapon – to gasps of genuine surprise from the court. *He moved the official time of the murder back an hour or so to around 23:30.* Many of the different times given by various witnesses now dropped into place. As if Mignini had waved a magic wand, all the pieces of the jigsaw fitted neatly together. The down-to-earth Prosecutor used every trick in the book. He branded the defence as snobbish for discounting witnesses because of their social standing. Yes, Antonio Curatolo was homeless tramp, but he could tell the time because he had a watch, and because a large digital clock overhung the street. And he could say with authority that he saw Amanda and Raffaele in the square until just before 23:30 on 1 November 2007.

Mignini then recovered Hekuran Kokomani from the witness scrapheap to prove that Meredith and her killers all knew each other. No, Kokomani wasn't lying. Yes, there had been problems with his testimony. But that was because he was a macho Albanian who didn't want a woman interpreter. Then, with another wave of his wand, though still credibly, Mignini moved Kokomani's evidence from the night of the murder back twenty-four hours to the previous night. He had seen Raffaele, Amanda and Rudy on 31 October – when indeed Meredith and Filomena had put on loud music while Meredith was getting dressed for her Halloween evening. Mignini brought Fabio

Gioffredi into play to back up Kokomani: the four knew each other definitely, of that there was no doubt.

From then on, the murder timeline ran like a trans-Alpine train – bang on schedule. Amanda and Raffaele had found themselves in a position to carry out the murder on that particular night because they had unexpectedly become free of commitments. At 20:18 Amanda knew that she wasn't wanted at the bar. She had picked up Lumumba's telephone call while walking in town, but had not responded by text until 20:38, when she got to Sollecito's flat. At 20:40 Raff became free after his pal Jovana Popovic said she didn't need a lift to the station. Both phones now go off.

By 21:00 Meredith was at home writing an essay for next day's class. She ate a mushroom and read lecture notes on her bed. Yes, she did make a telephone call at 22:15 to her bank, albeit a quick one. *She was still alive.* This was a true surprise to judge and jury. Observers noted that she may have been worried about her bank balance after money had gone missing.

Then Curatolo picked up the story again. Amanda and Raffaele were in Grimana Square from 21:30 to around 23:30. Mignini described the scene of the broken-down vehicle in the carpark and the pick-up truck arriving. None of the witnesses noticed anything strange – of course they didn't, because now the murder had been pushed back to a later time. Pick-up driver Lombardi ended operations at 23:15 – a full fifteen minutes before Meredith was attacked. Yes, there was a dark car parked in the driveway, but it was now irrelevant because the murder happened later. Mrs Nara Capezzali now came into the picture. Around 23:30 she heard the spine-chilling scream, which was also vouched for by other witnesses.

At about 23:30 Amanda, Raffaele and Rudy let themselves into the house. Amanda and Raffaele went into Meredith's bedroom while Guede went to the toilet. Amanda was irate. The fight, Mignini now said, could have started for any number of reasons: Amanda and Mez no longer got along, missing money, petty jealousies. Gone was the hypothesis of occult activity. Gone was the sex-games-gone-wrong motive as the only reason. That was the beauty of the Italian justice system. The judges were there to iron out the faults in the investigation. The prosecutor was here to iron out mistakes made by the police. And now they had finally arrived at an account they were happy with.

Under Italian law, the prosecutor (in this case Mignini) is allowed to change his arguments, such as the motive and time the murder, as and when he likes, as long as the judge doesn't object. It's the jury's job to weigh up whether that looks sloppy, or simply honest. In the Italian system, the prosecutor may start off the trial with a certain set of theories. But during the course of the trial he can refine and sculpture those beliefs in line with new evidence and with guidance on what the judge thinks best. So by the end of the case he can be left with a remodelled argument that has been whittled down, bit by bit, by the trial, until he is left with a fresh set of facts which he believes fit the evidence best. Mignini was playing this flexibility to his full advantage. The British system is more rigid. In British trials, the prosecution often starts off with a single motive or time and then has to stick to that scenario. The basic details have often been agreed at pre-trial hearings. The prosecution can only change the case by bringing a separate trial, such as re-trial or an appeal.

He then surprised the world with a new twist. Yes, Rudy was in the bathroom when the fight started, but when he came back to see what was going on the violence was in full swing. Amanda was throttling Mez with a clawing action while Raffaele was banging her head against the wall. The fight started in the corner between the wardrobe and the window and Meredith was standing up. Then along came Rudy, who wanted to show Amanda what he could do, and the rape began in earnest. Mez was forced to her knees and a second blade – Sollecito's flick-knife or something similar – came out. Using her martial arts Mez struggled in the corner, until the big kitchen knife, which Amanda had brought from Raffaele's, was plunged into her throat. By Amanda.

Mignini still believed in the rape. Mauro Marchionni, the only gynaecologist on the team, had confirmed as much, telling the court that 'the kinds of bruises found on Meredith's labia were typical not of poor lubrication, but of violence . . .' Even the Sollecito expert said Mez had been raped, Mignini pronounced.

Maybe Rudy was looking for a phone to call the police when he put his hand into Mez's handbag, he went on. Guede had left the scene last because he had at least tried to stem the flow of Meredith's blood, leaving the fingermark on the wall. Moments earlier, Raffaele and Amanda had dashed up the iron staircase leading to the Sant'Antonio carpark. A few minutes later Rudy got the same idea and legged it down Bulangaio Road and eventually round into Sperandio Lane – possibly with Meredith's phones.

Rudy had panicked but Amanda didn't. Raff turned on his computer at 05:30 the next morning together with the telephone, receiving his father's text at 06:02. At 07:45 Amanda was in front of Marco Quintavalle's shop to buy cleansing fluid. They went back to the house and began a clean-up, when Amanda hurt herself and left mixed blood traces. This was the barefoot moment. And another piece of evidence that had been awkwardly passed over now clicked seamlessly into place – the mysterious black lamp.

Way back on the day of discovery, police had found an incongruous black table lamp in Meredith's room. The lamp was Amanda's – or at least had come from her room, where it was part of the furniture inventory. What was it doing in the murder scene? No one had ever come up with a satisfactory answer. In fact, Amanda's defence had shamelessly used it to their advantage, he claimed, blaming the lampstand for contaminating the crime area with Amanda's DNA, implying that it had rubbed up against the bra clasp. Today Mignini solved the riddle. In the minutes after the murder, the devilish duo had taken the lamp from Amanda's room themselves – because they needed an extra light source to see what they were doing. To illuminate their handiwork. To take care of details. To make the rape look real. It was a beautifully simple explanation. Unpretentious prosecuting at its best.

'But–' began his final argument in the seventh hour of the conclusion. Mignini further stripped the case to its bones. 'The worst enemies of Amanda and Raffaele were their lies . . .' He raised his voice in a crescendo of emotion to hammer home the point and bring his argument full circle. That was that. End of story.

Mignini's deputy Manuela Comodi was left to sum up the trickier evidence. Whereas Mignini had been rhetorical and heated, Comodi was cold and ironic.

'Ladies and gentlemen of the jury, what do *you* think?' She lampooned the defence's attempt to dupe the jury with sample contamination. 'There are four Luminol-highlighted footprints in the corridor and Amanda's bedroom. So Sollecito and Knox walked in fruit juice or grass before walking around the house? Do you really think so?' Sweet and virtually spot-on, most observers agreed.

She dismissed the mystery activity on Raffaele's computer with equal contempt. The session lasting four seconds was an automatic connection to the Apple site, she said. On another occasion the screen saver came to life on a default programme. None of it was human activity. The defence was being disingenuous in suggesting that cops had logged on, while Raff was being questioned on 5 November, in order to fit him up.

Comodi then rounded on what she saw as the most dangerous members of the Sollecito team, the two consultants who might have fatally damaged the prosecution. Francesco Vinci had tried to pass the footprints off as Guede's, not Sollecito's. Adriano Tagliabracci had come closest to harming the prosecution with his 'too low' rants against the knife and bra-clasp DNA. Vinci was easy to dispose of. Comodi laughed off his theory that Guede had walked around with one shoe off and the other on. She hopped on one foot comically, and again asked the jury: 'What do you think?'

With Tagliabracci she stated the obvious. Her tone was humble and serious. 'This is a trial for murder. Do you really think that when *Dottoressa* Stefanoni examined the DNA on the bra clasp and the knife, she would have given up simply because the first read-out was too low? She was looking for a result, of course she was, and she found it because she is a professional . . .' She compared the Scientific Police to a family doctor: there to cure, not to philosophise.

That would have been enough. But to ram it home, the prosecutors then played a blinder. They had made a twenty-minute computer-animated video of the fight to kill Meredith. The colourful reconstruction even showed Amanda and Raffaele going back to the crime scene to clean up afterwards. In a gesture of compassion that betrayed her, Amanda covered the body with the beige duvet. It graphically and credibly established a dynamic that the jury could remember.

On the back of his success, the defendants' guilt presumed, Mignini immediately turned to the issue of sentencing. He began suitably with a Latin quote from an ancient champion of human rights, the Roman jurist Ulpian. 'Justice is the constant and perpetual will to render to every man his due. To live honourably, to harm no one, to give to each his own.' Knox was easily angered by people who said no, Mignini continued. Raffaele was cold but soft, a weaker character who would do anything rather than say no to Amanda. Together they had left Meredith's family with nothing but a tombstone to remember her by. Mignini demanded the maximum sentence from the court – life for both. Plus a bonus hardship for good measure: nine months' daytime solitary confinement for Amanda and two months of the same for Raffaele.

Amanda burst into tears. 'This is an absurd situation,' she cried. 'Meredith was my friend, she was good to me. This is pure fantasy.'

42

End Game

Closing Remarks
to the Verdict

November–December 2009

The portents did not look good for Amanda and Raffaele. Two days before the closing remarks began, Rudy Guede's separate appeal hearing popped up, as if from nowhere – just as he'd unexpectedly appeared on Skype exactly two years ago to the day. The timing could not have been worse for his co-defendants. Gone was the flaky drifter. Battle-hardened by jail, Guede was focused and aggressive. Immediately he hardened his stance against Knox and Sollecito, saying he definitely saw a woman who looked like the fair-haired American at the scene and even heard her arguing with Meredith. Significantly, he threw his weight behind the stolen-money motive.

However, because the two separate trials couldn't mix, and the prosecutors were different teams, serious and inexplicable contradictions suddenly came into view. Guede's prosecutor, Pietro Maria Catalani, launched a stinging assault on the appellant, describing Meredith's body as having been struck thirty times by a knife; whereas in the main trial, a few days later,

Mignini said that Rudy had not been involved in the attack until after he came back from the bathroom. Catalani implied that Guede was a merciless killer. Mignini disagreed, saying that he stayed to stop Meredith's bleeding, painting a picture of a young man infatuated by Amanda but also capable of pity. One of the unanswered questions was: what did the state really think about Guede's role? The authorities couldn't have it both ways. But before a storm could be whipped up, and to the relief of all sides except Guede, the appeal was suddenly postponed until after the main verdict.

Meanwhile, back in the central arena, it was the civil plaintiffs' time to sum up against Knox and Sollecito. The pair were on the ropes after Mignini's knockout speech, but the Kercher lawyers chose to show restraint instead of issuing the *coup de grace*. Dapper and well-prepared, the Kerchers' advocate Francesco Maresca simply put into words the supreme dignity of the family he had the honour of representing. In comparison, an emotional Carlo Pacelli, for Lumumba, seemed to go off the scale in an oratory the Spanish Inquisition might have been proud of. By describing Knox as '*Luciferina*' (little she-devil) he alienated many women (there were four on the jury including a judge) and even the press corps, who had grown weary of the demonization of Amanda because she was a young female. Why was it bad for Amanda to keep condoms, her lawyers asked, when Health Ministry campaigns promoted their use? Was a vibrator really evidence of evil?

Next came the top-of-the-bill act – the defence closing speeches. Whereas Mignini's team had painstakingly used page numbers to help the jury refer to evidence, the theme of Sollecito's Giulia Bongiorno was simplicity mixed with measured emotion.

'Raffaele is accused of conspiracy, ladies and gentlemen of the jury,' she began. 'Conspiracy between people who did not know each other?' Her tone was ironic and mirrored the sarcasm assistant prosecutor Manuela Comodi had used to effect. 'What murderer would call the Carabinieri to the crime scene? Ah! So you say the police were already there? But look at the CCTV timings again . . .' She repeated an earlier assertion that the camera's clock was ten minutes ahead, thereby showing that Sollecito had sounded the alarm before Inspector Battistelli's arrival. 'Why would the devilish duo ask the police into the house if they were the murderers? Wouldn't they have tried to keep them out? The police were looking for Filomena Romanelli, not for Meredith Kercher.'

Then she turned to Amanda. A juncture had been reached. The stress on Amanda's face was visible. Bongiorno had three options: to cut Amanda free, to turn on her, or to include her. 'Although I am defending Raffaele,' Bongiorno began, 'he has been portrayed in this case as an appendix to you, Amanda. So now I will say a few words in defence of you both.' Amanda looked relieved – they were sticking together. As one until the end. Their fate entwined. She capitalized on the backlash from Pacelli's characterization, saying she was no 'Amanda the Ripper'.

Bongiorno attacked the police for not giving Amanda her proper rights under questioning, then returned to her own charge. She said that ten judges had been misled into thinking that Rudy Guede's Nike Outbreak 2 trainers were Raffaele's Nike Air Force Ones. 'Now that we know, from Rudy Guede's own mouth, that the shoeprints were his,' Bongiorno reasoned, 'and that the ten judges in good faith were in error, should we still give the findings of previous courts the weight the prosecution seems to give them?'

After spotlighting systematic errors, Bongiorno tried subtly to ignore the basic premise of the trial: that this was the place for the truth, not for tricks. The diminutive star of the law courts urged the jury to doubt. 'You should not be sure. You should be anxious. If you are anxious, if you doubt, you seek the truth.' She was evoking the concept of reasonable doubt.

The closing speeches for Knox concentrated on human rights and male chauvinism. Maria Del Grosso, her defence team's assistant, counted the partners Amanda had brought home, not including Raffaele, in the month she had been in the flat – one: Giacomo Silenzi's cousin. The string of lovers, supposedly demonstrating Amanda's promiscuity, could not be shown to exist. Where did that leave Mignini's thesis that the fight had started because Meredith didn't like Amanda bringing men home? Nowhere, said Amanda's defence. Amanda Knox was no more immoral than any other young woman of her age. To add insult to injury a double standard was being applied, raged the defence. The night Knox had brought home her solitary one-night stand was the same night Silenzi had spent the night with Meredith. The investigators were hypocritical, the defence team said, when looking into the sexual histories of the young American and the young Briton.

Amanda Knox was now the key to the strategies of both defendants. But despite valiant efforts, none of the lawyers was able to find a thread that could be tugged on to unravel the prosecution's case. The flimsy evidence – the weak DNA results and the lack of a clear motive – remained unassailed by the closing speeches. In a last stand, both teams committed their reserves to the battle. Raffaele and Amanda made speeches in person.

In fluent but trembling Italian, Amanda said: 'I could be pulling out my hair, taking apart my cell, but I just take breath and try to be positive at important moments like this.' She even thanked the prosecution. The philosophy that she was studying in prison had steeled her with the Aristotelian virtues of magnanimity and stoicism. However, she ended by replacing reason with flowery rhetoric: 'I am afraid of the mask of the assassin that is being forced on to my face,' she said. The rich prose didn't do her any good. According to profilers, it was classic guilt-ridden language. At no point did she utter the words 'I did not kill Meredith'.

She had swapped her Beatles hoodie for a green woollen jacket. Though smart, up close it was suitcase-creased, giving her an air of prison austerity. The fitted coat and braided hair, untidy and greasy, made her look vulnerable. Prison life was wearing her down. Sollecito, his wealthy sheen long faded under a lank wedge of brown hair, said he was not a 'dog on lead' dominated by Knox. He wore a cream, fur-lined hoodie that made him look older and barrel-chested. Worry and a high-calorie penal diet had piled on the pounds. 'If Amanda had asked me to do something I didn't agree with, I would have said no.' He was trying to counter the theory that he was an explosive passive-aggressive who'd flown into a knife-wielding rage to defend and impress the girl he had been extremely lucky to bed. 'Let alone if she had asked me to do something like killing a girl.' Sollecito hadn't spoken much at the trial; his taciturnity lent more impact to his final words. He softly told the court that he was living through an 'absurd affair about which I know nothing'.

'I would like to understand today, because it is not at all clear, why I should have participated in a murder,' he continued, pointing out the lack of motive. 'I had only known her [Knox] for a few days. I certainly cared for her, but they were the very first days [of the relationship] and there was no dependent relationship there.'

No philosophy or baroque language here – the meaning was enough. 'Why would I commit something as horrible as murder? You are deciding my life. I am not living a nightmare any more, but something far more dramatic.' Workaday prose, such as one might expect from a computer science student. He ended his defence by saying, 'I did not kill Meredith. I was not in that house that night. I hope the real murderer comes forward and confesses. I still have faith in justice. For me it represents everything. Thank you for listening to me.'

The following day, Friday 4 December, the jury retired at 10:30 a.m. Lunch and dinner were ordered but no beds, suggesting they would deliver their verdict that evening, in line with arcane Italian tradition. The moon had waned by a sliver; the full phase had passed two days earlier and the disc above Perugia was silver and discreet against a blood-black sky. The rain had stopped. The fog had gone. For Amanda the sign was good: the full phase meant ripening and completeness. But it was also the time when the moon's energy was strongest – full of magic power, soothsayers warned.

The hard-nosed TV news producers weren't interested in the enigmas of nature. The only illumination they saw was the powerful arc lights of their outside broadcast units. The press pack homed in on the ancient hill city. The Christmas lights were up. A nightmarish funfair atmosphere unsettled the gravity of the moment: incongruously, a merry-go-round had been set up just outside the court, tucked in among the TV vans, spinning hypnotically, its playful music eerie. The esplanade in front of the choicest hotel in town, the Brufani, hosted a Ferris wheel. There were a few cranks and ghouls rubbernecking the grisliest trial in years, but mostly tourists and Christmas shoppers mingling with jumpy scoop-chasers.

The major networks were there too, ABC, CBS and NBC, preparing for the big night. A ping-pong game of information and disinformation kept the journos on their toes and almost hysterical. Had the networks paid for a homeward-bound ticket for Amanda? Were they really sure she would get off? It was a race for ratings. An exclusive interview would get more eye-balls, so more ad revenue. Simple as that. And Amanda, as ever, was the story. One US programme distinguished itself from the mass trawling for the exclusive: NBC's *Dateline*. Among the journalists, Andrea Vogt for the *Independent* and Barbie Nadeau for *Newsweek* had made names for themselves as pundits; they knew the case inside out and were the ones to be interviewed when the networks could not fathom the details. Both of them went against US public opinion and were able, honestly and transparently, to affirm that Amanda and Raffaele had had a fair trial in a country whose judicial system was among the most advanced in the world.

However, no journalist knew what was going on inside the closed jury chamber just a few metres away. Almost twelve hours earlier, as soon as they had retired, the jurors had made up their minds instantly. Knox and Sollecito were guilty. There was no debate. The two judges and six jurors agreed unanimously, straightaway, that the evidence had not been undermined. The only subject of discussion was the severity of the penalty.

Each charge was considered separately. In turn, each sub-clause was analyzed and referred to the Penal Code, which offered a mathematical formula to work out the sentences.

Premeditated Murder
Verdict: both guilty to murder but knowing each other couldn't be proved, so no premeditation. Sentence: 22 years each.

Premeditated Sexual Assault
Verdict: this was made concurrent with the murder charge, so no added sentence.

Theft of the 300 Euros and Credit Cards
Verdict: not guilty. Sentence: none.

Theft of Telephones
Verdict: both guilty. Sentence: one year each.

Staging the Crime Scene
Verdict: both guilty. Sentence: one year each.

Carrying a Concealed Weapon
Verdict: both guilty. Sentence: one year each.

Aggravating Circumstance of Futile Motives (jealousy)
Verdict: both guilty. Sentence: none.

The extra years that could have been handed down were cancelled out by time in jail deducted for mitigating circumstances for all of their criminal actions committed on 1 November 2007: namely, that Amanda and Raffaele were young and had no previous convictions.

Slander (applied only to Amanda for falsely accusing Patrick Lumumba of murder)
Verdict: guilty. Sentence: one year.

Result
Amanda received 22 + 4 = 26 years.
Raffaele received 22 + 3 = 25 years.

At around midnight Judge Giancarlo Massei announced the verdict to the world in his quiet voice. Two women jurors wept and Amanda sobbed out loud. Sollecito's stepmother shouted, 'Be strong, Raffaele.' Amanda embraced her lawyer Luciano Ghirga. Sollecito turned round and realized that Giulia Bongiorno was no longer there for him; she was outside, as though to say that the appeal began right now, there and then. Certainly there were grounds for a fight back. Confusion reigned. If they were not guilty of stealing the 300 Euros, how could Mignini rely on the theft for his motive and Guede on it for his appeal?

All over Europe and the US, the news stations interrupted their schedules. The big story had been the build-up to the Copenhagen summit to save the world from global warming, but it was blown away by the verdict from Perugia. Sky and BBC News 24 showed an almost riot-like scene outside the court as hundreds of media representatives jostled for position. Under the fairy lights, onlookers on Perugia's streets shouted at the Knox family, '*Assassini!*' – 'Killers!'.

Inconsistencies swirled around the decision like the Etruscan ghosts that reputedly roamed the alleyways behind the court. How could Guede get thirty years after opting for a fast-track trial? Why did Amanda and Raffaele receive less after pretending to be innocent for a costly eleven-month case? Hadn't Guede risked a fast-track decision in order to get a discount on his sentence? 'He has not had the advantage of the extenuating circumstances being applied,' said Valter Biscotti and Nicodemo Gentile, his lawyers. He was referring to the credit Amanda and Raffaele had received because they were young. Not because they were white.

Giuliano Mignini was satisfied. He hadn't won what he had aimed for, life sentences with solitary confinement, but he conceded: 'It's a balanced verdict and we're not going to appeal against it. These are two young lives, after all, and justice has been done. That's what counts.' Some had thought they saw his eyes go moist while the sentence was being read. He had children around the same age. As he stepped out into the chill, he now faced the biggest trial of his own life – proving his innocence in the Monster of Florence case, with all its booby-traps.

The murder-squad officers present didn't gloat. They shook hands to acknowledge their professional skill – and their luck, for it was an act of God that had started the whole affair in the first place. If Meredith's mobile phones had not been found by an old lady, the murder might never have come to light. What if the killers had had time to hide the body and cover their tracks? Would Meredith have been listed as a missing person? Or as the victim of a mystery assailant? The 'what if's would be the subject of much canteen speculation over the coming months. Meanwhile, on the night of the verdict, the lights of Mrs Elisabetta Lana's house glowed bright on the hillside.

The backlash began immediately. Washington State Senator Maria Cantwell contacted the Italian Embassy in the American capital and the State Department, expressing her fear that anti-Americanism had played a role in the verdict. Hillary Clinton said she would talk to anyone who had a concern, but clearly the US Embassy in Rome had no intention of stepping in, other than to verify the general wellbeing of the prisoner.

The last word in public went to the Kerchers. 'This is not a celebration. Not a moment of triumph. We arrived at this point because our sister was brutally murdered,' said her brother John Kercher Jr. 'Two very young people have been put behind bars for the brutal murder of Mez.' Meredith's sister Stephanie had always looked for something positive to say, but she added that there would be a void in their lives. They thanked the prosecutor and the police for all their work but refused to comment on whether they were fully satisfied that justice had been done. 'We have to go by the evidence,' said Meredith's mother Arline.

The Sollecitos and Knoxes retired to lick their wounds.

Francesco Sollecito complained that the jury had not done its duty, and announced battle. The Knoxes slipped out by a side entrance, shrouded in ignominy and loneliness. At first they went almost unnoticed, but when they were recognized they ran a gauntlet of paparazzi as they walked stoically back to their hotel. They had brought the whole family over, including the children of Curt's second marriage. Protectively, Curt pushed a cameraman who threatened to invade their space.

As a lawman, the independent forensics expert Luciano Garofano should have been satisfied that justice had been done. Having retired from the Carabinieri as a Major-General a fortnight earlier, he shoud have been relaxing. But niggling doubts disturbed his peace of mind. Had the police been duplicitous at the start by treating the 'unofficial' suspects, Amanda and Raffaele, as plain witnesses? Had they bypassed the law in order to elicit a false confession? Had the seasoned detectives thrown them enough rope, knowing that they would hang themselves – especially without a lawyer being present? Sollecito was questioned as a witness but his knife and shoes were taken away as though he was a suspect. Both were kept in solitary confinement without proper documentation. The Supreme Court had quashed convictions for much less.

But Garofano's misgivings about procedure were less significant than his doubts about evidence that seemed to be flawed. There had never been a full explanation of how such a small quantity of Meredith's DNA on the knife could produce such a clear electropherogram. The blade's outline on the bed was different from that of the alleged murder weapon. The forty-seven-day delay in recovering the bra clasp was sloppy. The inability to test the towels for Guede's DNA, to prove that he had shed blood in his own defence, was shocking. While Mignini's reconstruction of events was closer to Guede's story and to Garofano's findings, there was no guarantee that a judge on appeal would take the same line.

The hierarchy of doubt was building. The apex represented the sharpest criticism: the motive was simply illogical. Knox and Sollecito had known each other for little more than a week. Profilers and experts, Garofano included, found it hard to imagine them attempting to rape a woman of the same age, at knifepoint, aided by a man they barely knew. Despite a last-minute change, the prosecution's motive had always seemed to dodge the obvious reasons why people kill each other, such as robbery. No one had ever fully explained the role, if any, of the drug addicts who used Meredith's garden as a stash and her path as carparking space. Or of the desperate dealers she had complained about a few days earlier.

Though the jury had been unanimous, two of the jurors didn't believe that Knox and Sollecito were evil, or that they were 'cold-blooded killers'. The left-leaning *La Repubblica*, which had always taken a pro-Knox position, said the verdict was 'eminently changeable on appeal'. If Amanda's and Raffaele's rights guaranteed by the Italian constitution had not been respected, then there was a good case for letting them go free.

In the early hours the lights went out. From a distance, Perugia, the grand stage of this drama, flickered like the embers of a dying fire. At Capanne prison the wings were silent and Amanda Knox, huddled under her prison-issue blankets, cried herself to sleep. Raffaele lay awake, thinking about the next twenty-five Christmases he would spend behind bars. In Coulsdon, Surrey, Meredith's bedroom was frozen in time, kept just as she had left it on her last visit, with her CDs, photos and clothes around – a daily reminder for Arline of her loss.

But the biggest question of all hung over the verdict like the rainstorm gathering over the Appenines – Amanda's behaviour.

Had the police been distracted by irrelevances such as her sexuality? Had Amanda, as Luciano Ghirga said in his summing up, attracted the morbid attention of a handful of policewomen?

A Roman emperor who ruled Perugia nearly two thousand years before had encountered such a problem. Marcus Aurelius, the only emperor to have been a philosopher, and arguably the most successful of the ancient rulers of Italy, could have been talking about this case when he wrote in Book 11 of his *Meditations*: 'Justice is the source of all other virtues. How can we do what justice requires if we are distracted by things that don't matter? Justice cannot be preserved if we are naïve or gullible, rash or inconstant.'

Acknowledgements

The authors wish to thank the publishing professionals who hepled create this project: Kerri Sharp, Senior Commissioning Editor at Simon and Schuster – her nose for a good story, her straightforward approach and her clinical organisational skills were essential. Her tight brief and editorial suggestions helped significantly.

The agents and staff at Peters Fraser Dunlop. Annabel Merullo, Senior Agent in the Books Division, for her professionalism and speed at bringing the team together, ploughing through the paperwork and steering a cross-border venture along. Her advice and experience were much appreciated. Associate agent, Tom Williams.

Copy editor Tony Russell and project editor Katherine Stanton at Simon and Schuster. The legal team for their close eye.

A number of people contributed to this book. One journalist in particular, Andrea Vogt. Her accurate reporting was an inspiration. Together with Barbie Nadeau, she provided advice, perspective and humour at times when the intricacies and troubles of the case seemed insurmountable. Barbie and Andrea are the living memory of this extraordinary case. Andrea Vogt writes for the Seattle PI and the *Independent*, Barbie for *Newsweek* and *The Daily Beast*.

Another journalist, Giuseppe Castellini, editor of the

Umbrian Journal and his reporters, Antioco Fois and Francesca Bene, eagerly supplied local background and insight non-Perugians would never have had access to otherwise. Their ability to sniff out key pieces of information was remarkable and they willingly put their work at the disposal of the authors of this book. Nick Pisa, for his prolific and accurate court reporting.

The authors also owe an enormous debt to three barristers: Francesco Maresca, representing the Kerchers, and Valter Biscotti and Nicodemo Gentile, representing Rudy Guede. They provided insight, material help of every kind and supported the book with documents and information. Their untiring search for the truth has been impressive.

The authors also wish to thank Dr Giuliano Mignini for his friendly and open discussions with the authors, within the bounds set by confidentiality laws. The authors have admired his calm and thoroughness, although do not necessarily agree with the whole case as brought to court.

Index

(The following initials are used in the index. **MK** = Meredith Kercher; **GS** = Giacomo Silenzi; **AK** = Amanda Knox; **RS** = Raffaele Sollecito; **PL** = Patrick Lumumba; **RG** = Rudy Guede)